Lesbian Family Life, Like the Fingers of a Hand

Under-Discussed and Controversial Topics

Edited by Valory Mitchell

 Routledge
Taylor & Francis Group

LONDON AND NEW YORK

First published 2010 by Routledge
2 Park Square, Milton Park, Abingdon, Oxon, OX14 4RN

Simultaneously published in the USA and Canada
by Routledge
270 Madison Avenue, New York, NY 10016

Routledge is an imprint of the Taylor & Francis Group, an informa business

© 2010 Taylor & Francis

Typeset in Times by Value Chain, India
Printed and bound in Great Britain by CPI Antony Rowe, Chippenham, Wiltshire

British Library Cataloguing in Publication Data
A catalogue record for this book is available from the British Library

ISBN10: 1-56023-770-8 (h/b)
ISBN10: 1-56023-771-6 (p/b)
ISBN13: 978-1-56023-770-9 (h/b)
ISBN13: 978-1-56023-771-6 (p/b)

Barbara Collier, the cover artist, has done over 200 pen-and-ink drawings of hands. In addition
to her art, Barbara teaches death and dying, and is director of the Martin de Porres Foundation,
which maintains hospice care, a house of hospitality, and a soup kitchen serving over 200
free meals each day in San Francisco. Pictured here is the hand of her daughter, Camilla.

CONTENTS

FOREWORD

Lesbian Family Life, Like the Fingers of a Hand: Under-Discussed and Controversial Topics

Valory Mitchell

Lesbian identity does not follow the well-worn ruts in the conventional road that lead from sex to gender to gender-role to gender-of-partner. In the same way, our families cannot be neatly mapped according to a conventional family tree, where connections are established by law (as in marriage) or by genetic connections. Invisible through those lenses, our families have thrived nonetheless. And they are very visible now; same-sex marriage, the "lesbian baby boom," and lesbian/gay "families of choice" are front-page news for some, old news for others, and have become "just how it has always been" for the generation of young lesbian women in their 20s. There was a time, not so long ago, when no one spoke aloud that another woman was a lesbian. "She's family," they'd say. It was closet-code, intended to keep us safely invisible to the straight community, yet identifiable to others like ourselves. An interesting choice for a code word. Why "family"? Perhaps it not only designated something we shared, but also hinted at a loyalty, an understanding, an inner circle.

Much has changed in a short time. Just over a decade ago, Laird and Green (1996) edited *Lesbians and Gays in Couples and Families;* they documented the important news that lesbians had families! The papers in that volume showed that many of us were closely connected to parents and siblings, had enduring marriage-like couple relationships, children (even grown children), extended family, in-laws, grandchildren—and, as well, the special families that we made—our families of choice. Today, the existence and richness of lesbian family life is no longer controversial; we, and the scholars who write about our lives, have established our presence.

One thing, however, has not changed: because most laws and institutions continue to penalize, exclude or ignore lesbian, gay, bisexual, and transgender (LGBT) people, we have the challenge and the opportunities that come from living outside them. We can, and must, decide for ourselves what we mean when we say "family" (Green and Mitchell, 2002).

Of course, just as we are a diverse lot, so our families will reflect our many cultures and contexts. There can no more be "THE lesbian family" than there could be one person who represents "THE lesbian." Still, the relationships that make up our families are like the fingers on a hand. Each hand is unique; each finger has a separate name and does a particular set of things; yet they are naturally connected, need each other, and often work together to do things that none could do alone.

WHAT IS CONTROVERSIAL IN LESBIAN FAMILY LIFE?

When I announced the call for papers on under-discussed and controversial topics in lesbian family life, it occurred to me that the submissions could be imagined as data in a social psychology experiment. Taken together, this rich collection—of first-person accounts, theoretical and clinical papers, qualitative and quantitative research—becomes the "evidence" that helps us articulate and define our ideas about lesbian family. Let us consider what is controversial (and why), what we do not (or rarely) talk about (and why), what we have stopped talking about because we take it for granted.

Feminist research methods (Stewart and Gold-Steinberg, 1990) and hermeneutic deconstruction techniques (Cushman, 2000) have taught us to look at silences, at those who rarely have a voice. By considering what is "marginal" as well as what is "in the text" about our families, we can see what has become an accepted part of lesbian family life, and glimpse those issues and themes that challenge us or make us uneasy. And we can confront the tasks ahead. *All in the family? Or are some left out?* Many lesbians feel marginal in our "community," and have responded by creating special families for themselves. Several articles in this book contend that, as a group, we prefer to look away and not talk about our patterns of exclusion. Like the larger culture in which we are embedded, the lesbian community (including the lesbian academic and scholarly community) has played its part in maintaining class, color, creed, disability, and age barriers. Working-class lesbians and lesbians of color (Fisher, 2007), older lesbians (Ariel, this book), and religious lesbians (Hunyady, this book) feel marginalized, rendered exotic or even unwelcome. As voices from these silenced sisters emerge, they describe examples of extraordinary relational creativity.

Age differences and aging. Age differences and aging recur among our under-discussed topics, perhaps because we live in such an ageist culture. Voices of middle-aged (Cayleff, this book) or older lesbians (Cruikshank, 2002), of young women in age-different couples (Bruns, this book) or adult daughters of lesbians (Davies, this book) are rarely heard. As women expand beyond the procreative and paid-work focus that tends to dominate the first half of our adult lives (Helson, Mitchell and Moane, 1984), they become available for profound relational endeavors; as we lift our ageist (and perhaps patriarchal?) blinders, there is much about family building to see here.

Masculinity/femininity in lesbian couples and parents. Lesbians' relationships to gender roles are among the under-discussed topics in lesbian family life. Perhaps homophobia has made us experience lesbian masculinity and lesbian femininity as too dangerous to address. Yet the emergence, in our communities, of people who choose a permanent transgender identity, one that is not on-the-way to one side of the gender binary, demands that we consider anew our confusion of sex with gender. Lev (this book) has suggested that part of our silence about lesbian masculinity and femininity is in response to a mis-reading of the androgynous ideals of second wave feminism. And, in something of a paradox, at the same time that our community embraces gender fluidity, although it has been established that our sons grow up psychologically healthy and comfortable in their lives (Drexler, 2006), the relevance of masculinity for sons has been a conscious concern for many lesbian parents and others (Weston, this book). Here, again, we are not so different from the larger community in our discomfort and inconsistency.

Families in danger: Betrayal and loss. When family is not defined by procreative relationships, we define it by what it brings us—trust, solidarity, continuity. We prefer not to think about relationships where the connection is ruptured—families that are "in trouble" or have lost their sense of safety—particularly when the dangers emerge from ourselves or our partners. Several under-discussed topics concern families in danger— from intimate partner violence (Turrell & Herrmann, this book), from the emotional and psychological violence that is the aftermath of infidelity (Burch, this book), or through the death of a partner (Broderick, Birbilis, and Steger, this book).

These painful experiences are rendered more harsh and isolating by the failure of our community to acknowledge them, or to provide support (Hardesty, Oswald, Khaw, Fonseca, and Chung, this book). Again, we resemble the larger culture in wanting to look away, in being unwilling to integrate death with life, in wanting to pretend that families don't hurt each other. These illusions join with other illusions that are uniquely our own— of a lesbian utopia where we won't get hurt, of women as incapable of aggression—to make us unwilling (as a community) to hear these voices.

Children: Blending "blood" and "choice." In 1991, when the anthropologist Kath Weston published her book *Families We Choose: Gays, Lesbians, Kinship*, she considered the juxtaposition of "blood" and "chosen" family. Was one modeled after the other? Was one a replacement or substitute for the other? Her research led to a clear "No!" on both counts. And the articles in this collection confirm those conclusions.

Because, in lesbian couples, only one partner has genetic ties with the children (unless a member of the other partner's family is a sperm donor), our families of procreation epitomize the blending of "blood" and "choice." Lesbians (and gay men) choose children (no "accidents" here!), and we have chosen them in great numbers. A recent survey of lesbian and gay youth (Savin-Williams, cited in Rothblum, 2007), found that the majority expect to marry their (gay/lesbian) partner and raise children. To do so, we are unique in that all of us require the help of others, birth parents of adopted children or donors and surrogates. Which of these people is and is not family? As our fears of custody loss fade with years of established precedent, we may now become able to look more deeply at this question, in ways that make many of us uneasy (Ehrensaft, this book).

THE BAD NEWS . . . AND THE GOOD NEWS

The bad news is that we bear a striking resemblance to the heterosexual community (and to the heterosexual academic community) in what makes us uneasy, what we avoid talking about, what we consider controversial.

Like the straight community, we avoid facing our patterns of exclusion—our class, creed, color, age, even our gender biases. Like them, we would prefer to think that violence, infidelity, death do not visit our doors—even if that means turning away from sisters in pain. While we acknowledge donors' and surrogates' contribution, like the straight community we are reluctant to think deeply about the meaning—for us and our children—of the role they have played in helping us build family.

Some of this similarity results from all of us being citizens not only of LGBT communities, but of the larger culture—with its biases and blindness—as well. Some is a legacy of the danger felt by LGBT people. Many still believe that it is essential, for survival and acceptance, to hide our problems, lest they be seized on by homophobic hate mongers and used against us, individually or as a group. To explain our vulnerability to these prejudices and illusions is not, however, to condone it. For the sake of us all, we must listen.

The good news is that we have come so far, as a community. We (and the straight community) are now able take for granted many of our strengths; they are well known, well documented, not news. Here are some aspects of lesbian family life that are no longer among the controversial: (1) We make families, independent of legal and blood ties, that are satisfying and enduring; (2) we are parenting couples whose children and community accept, enjoy and legitimate the two-mom family; (3) children raised in our families do as well (or sometimes better) than children of heterosexual parents; (4) lesbian couples, compared to other couple types, experience high satisfaction, high closeness, and high autonomy; (5) lesbian families emphasize equality, and live it out in the distribution of tasks and responsibilities; (6) lesbians blend members of their families of origin, families of procreation, and families of choice to create a fabric of family life across generations and of lifespan duration.

As we celebrate that the existence of our viable and satisfying families is no longer a surprise, a carefully guarded secret, we can recognize that, in a backhanded way, it is an accomplishment that we are now free to grapple with the same sorts of problems as those in the dominant culture.

KINSHIP

In Weston's anthropological study, she described the creation of families of choice as a "foray into uncharted territory" (1991: 110). At that time, everything about lesbian family life was under-discussed and controversial.

And yet the 200 participants in her study listed many characteristics—none of them definitive, yet all descriptive—of their "family" relationships: trust, regular contact over time, mutual assistance, who comes early to decorate for the birthday party, shared history, ability to work through conflict and differences, persistence, continuity, solidarity. We know what we want from family, even while each family relationship truly is a choice, a "customized individual creation" (Weston, 1991: 136). The academic lesbian community has worked hard and long to establish the existence, viability, and validity of our family lives. Perhaps that allows us, now, to take perspective on our families—what they mean to us and why, who is "chosen" in a "family of choice" and why (Mitchell, this book)—and to take up the work of making more conscious choices about inclusion, lifting our blinders and exchanging our illusions for a robust and rewarding reality.

The cover artist, Barbara Collier, has done pen-and-ink interpretations of several hundred hands, including the hand of her daughter, pictured here. Perhaps we know the boundaries and experience of kinship like we know the boundaries and experience of our hands. Like a hand, family is a natural part of each of us—it belongs to us, stays with us, is not separate from who we are. Often, although not always, we can guide its actions—and today we are called on to reach out. It changes, too, with time and experience, and yet is always here, across our lifetimes.

REFERENCES

Cruikshank, M. *Learning to be Old: Gender, Culture and Aging.* Lanham, MD: Rowan & Littlefield, 2002.

Cushman, P. *Constructing the Self, Constructing America: A Cultural History of Psychotherapy.* Reading, MA: Addison-Wesley, 2000.

Drexler, P. *Raising Boys Without Men.* Emmaus, PA: Rodale, 2006.

Fisher, A. *The Identity Formation Process of African-American Working Class Lesbians: A Study of Triple Jeopardy.* Unpublished Doctoral dissertation, California School of Professional Psychology at Alliant University, San Francisco, CA, 2007.

Green, R.-J. and V. Mitchell. "Gay and Lesbian Couples in Therapy: Homophobia, Relational Ambiguity, and Social Support." In A. S. Gurman and N. S. Jacobson, eds. *Clinical Handbook of Couple Therapy, 3rd Edition.* New York: The Guilford Press, 2002: 548–588.

Helson, R., V. Mitchell, and G. Moane. "Personality and Patterns of Adherence and Non-Adherence to the Social Clock." *Journal of Personality and Social Psychology,* 46 (5), 1984:1079–96.

Laird, J. and R.-J. Green, eds. *Lesbians and Gays in Couples and Families: A Handbook for Therapists.* San Francisco: Jossey-Bass,1996.

Rothblum, E. *Comparison of Same-Sex Marriages and Domestic Partnerships.* Presented at the Rockway Institute colloquium, California School of Professional Psychology, San Francisco, March 2007.

Stewart, A. and S. Gold-Steinberg. "Midlife Women's Political Consciousness: Case Studies of Psychosocial Development and Political Commitment." *Psychology of Women Quarterly,* 14, 1990: 543–66.

Weston, K. *Families We Choose: Lesbians, Gays, Kinship.* New York: Columbia University Press, 1991.

More than Surface Tension:
Femmes in Families

Arlene Istar Lev

SUMMARY. This article raises questions about the lack of scholarly focus on butch/femme couples and their absence in studies of lesbian couples and family-building. In an era of lesbian marriage and lesbian parenting, femme and butch coupling and family-building remain unspoken topics within family studies, including lesbian, gay, bisexual, transgender (LGBT)–specific research. Moving beyond a focus on eroticism within the femme/butch couple, questions about how gender expression impacts other relationships dynamics, including the maintenance of long-term relationships, power and intimacy, domestic chores and child-rearing, are raised. The femme role in "homemaking," that is, building and maintaining families, especially needs further exploration.

Arlene Istar Lev, LCSW, CASAC, is the founder of Choices Counseling and Consulting (www.choicesconsulting.com) in Albany, New York, offering family therapy for lesbian, gay, bisexual, and transgender people. She is on the adjunct faculties of S.U.N.Y. Albany School of Social Welfare and Vermont College of the Union Institute and University. She is the author of *The Complete Lesbian and Gay Parenting Guide* (Penguin Press, 2004) and *Transgender Emergence: Therapeutic Guidelines for Working with Gender-Variant People and their Families* (Haworth Press, 2004).

If memory serves, it was 1980 or 1981. I was a young dyke living in the San Francisco Bay Area coming out in the glorious era of lesbian-feminism. I went out with friends to see a new slide show that had recently been put together by The San Francisco Lesbian and Gay History Project called She Even Chewed Tobacco: A Pictorial Narrative of Passing Women. *Our movement was younger then and images of ourselves were hard to find. It was a fun and raucous event and the mostly lesbian audience hooted in joy at the butch dykes dressed in suits and ties and smoking cigars—not that many of us young dykes wore suits and ties or smoked cigars, but we could certainly appreciate that women "like us" had.*

I found myself staring at the old photos, mesmerized by these handsome butches, but I was also aware—acutely aware—of the women standing next to them. One photo stands out in my memory all these years later, of a group of couples, butches in tuxes and their femme partners dressed to the nines for a night of dancing. The femmes looked like any other image of women from the 1940s, women who looked strangely like my mother did in pictures from the same era—in her early 20s—same hairdo, tight low cut dress, wide smile with bright lipstick. Yet, these women in the picture were clearly lesbian, obviously partnered with those handsome butches; they were, I suspected, nothing like my mother at all.

I shyly raised my 21-year-old hand. "What do we know about the other women?" I remember asking. "Their, uh, partners," I said, knowing that although the word butch was a strong, Amazonian, lesbian-friendly term, the word femme would not be so easily accepted. I knew it would bring undo attention to my long hippie skirt, dangling earrings, and extremely long hair that had already put my lesbian reputation into question. My question fell flat in the room, the presenters had little to say, someone shrugged, and we moved on to the next picture.

Decades later, I still find myself contemplating that question: "What do we know about the other women?" I am still surprised at the silence regarding femme identity in the alphabet soup of the now lesbian, gay, bisexual, transgender (LGBT)-queer community, and how that is mirrored in Gender Studies departments.

Themes of gender and sexuality abound, and are the focus of research in diverse fields from critical theory to child development, from family therapy to transgender medicine. Femme and butch identities are a theme in lesbian humor as well as erotica. Nonetheless, femme and butch coupling and family-building remain absent from discussions within family studies, including LGBT-specific research.

Feminists have examined gender bias in mental health and diagnosis (Ballou and Brown, 2002), and family therapists have raised critical questions about the role of gender in heterosexual partnerships (McGoldrick, Anderson, and Walsh, 1991). Lesbian and gay coupling has become a scholarly pursuit in family lifecycle development (Laird and Green, 1996; Savin-Williams and Cohen, 1996), and, in recent years, lesbian and (to a lesser extent) gay parenting has become an important site of research (Gartrell, Deck, Rodas, Peyser. and Banks, 2005; Golumbok et. al., 2003; Patterson, 2001; Patterson and Chan, 1996). Gender has been the focus of sociological analysis, psychoanalytic exegesis, and textual deconstruction (Butler, 1990; Dimen and Goldner, 2002).

However, there is a lack of scholarly research or clinical examination of butch and femme gender identities within lesbian couples and families. Lesbian identity is multifaceted, and lesbians have complex relationships to their gender and gender expression. Gender is a compelling and influential organizer of all human relationships, and masculine and feminine gender roles inhabit, motivate, and inspire many aspects of lesbian love. Butch and femme identities, for all their familiarity within lesbian communities, are under-explored and rarely analyzed as a significant factor in the development of intimacy, commitment, parental and domestic roles, and child rearing in lesbian butch/femme identified couples.

THE HISTORICAL CONTEXT: BUTCH/FEMME RELATIONSHIPS AND LESBIAN-FEMINIST CULTURE

Western culture has long linked lesbian sexuality with cross-gender behavior. Nineteenth-century sexological studies of "inversion" linked what we would now call homosexuality and transgenderism (Hekma, 1994; Trumbach, 1994; Vicinus, 1993). Simply put, lesbians were assumed to be females who dressed like men, acted like men, probably wanted to be men, and were attracted to women, or more to the point, were *therefore* attracted to women. Because lesbians were assumed to be more man-like than woman-like, their desire would "naturally" be heterosexual, that is, attracted to their opposite. Lesbian women with same-sex desire who were not masculine in their dress or manner were invisible; women who appeared to be just like other women, regardless of their sexual interests, were simply not considered lesbians. Lesbianism that did not involve cross-gender behavior was unimaginable, but gender inversion that was not lesbian was equally impossible (Cromwell, 1999), leaving femme lesbians to be a cultural impossibility.

Despite limited anthropological and historical research, gender role expression in lesbian relationships has been discovered in diverse cultural contexts (Blackwood, 1999; Faderman, 1992; Murray and Roscoe, 1998; Nestle, 1992; Smith, 2002; Vicinus, 1993). Butch and femme identities have an especially long history within lesbian cultures in the United States and Europe, particularly within urban working-class communities and communities of color in the 1940s, 1950s, and 1960s (Kennedy and Davis, 1993; Nestle, 1992). Fictional accounts that reflect their own histories and experiences, reveal butch/femme culture as a vibrant part of American culture in the twentieth century (Feinberg, 1993; Lynch, 1986). Indeed, perhaps butch/femme culture was so ubiquitous throughout lesbian communities that it may have been the only way to actively engage in a lesbian culture at that time. However, the history of butch/femme communities has more thoroughly documented the butch narrative (see Nestle, 1992; Smith, 2002), once more obscuring femme identity and meaning.

The rise of lesbian-feminist politics in the 1970s effectively drove butch-femme identities, communities, and expression underground, silencing, and therefore historically distorting, discussions of gender expression in lesbian relationships. Lesbian-feminism challenged cultural assumptions about gender, sexism, and patriarchal power, and raised important issues regarding women's oppression and compulsory heterosexuality (Rich, 1973). However, the *either* masculine *or* feminine role expression of butch/femme dyads became fodder for the early lesbian-feminist critique, which charged butch/femme couples with mimicking heterosexual patriarchal roles (Harris and Crocker, 1997). Feminist theory asserted that the oppression of women was maintained by the social construction of traditional male/female roles (Jeffreys, 1989). Masculinity, in early feminist theory, became a synonym for patriarchal domination.

At the same time, in a twist of logic, lesbians celebrated sisterhood by taking pride in doing traditionally male tasks and asserting and co-opting manners, stance, and behaviors that conveyed male privilege and power. Traditional female clothing was rejected and a watered-down masculine dress code was embraced—wearing male attire was experienced as liberating. In this paradox, lesbian-feminists celebrated much of what was masculine—although this was referred to as androgynous—and aspired to be "like" men, all the while despising male power.

Lesbian-feminist culture and theory, despite its elevation of the mystical concept of "woman," also denigrated what had been traditionally perceived as feminine. The misogyny of the wider culture, which had been played out in various ways within butch/femme bar culture, continued, unabated and unexamined, into feminist politics. Women who enjoyed feminine attire, who expressed their sexuality and identity through use of makeup, nail polish, and wearing high heels, were seen as un-liberated dupes of male oppression. Admitting one was attracted to a feminine woman was as intolerable as wanting to express oneself in a feminine manner. Gender expression itself became seen as a tool of the patriarchy.

Lesbians were critiqued for engaging in role-playing because feminist belief insisted that "all role-playing replicates the very (hetero)sexual structure from which lesbians are supposedly free" (Goodloe, 1999: 2, paragraph 1). It was never explicit what a life outside of "role-playing" might look like, and the dress code of lesbian-feminist culture was itself critiqued by the generation that followed for enforcing an androgynous look (Faderman, 1992).

Assuming that butch/femme couples are replicating heterosexual roles assumes butches wield a male power they may not have access to; it also assumes that femmes are subservient to their butches, the way heterosexual women were traditionally expected to be. Newton (1984) suggests that butch/femme dynamics deconstruct hetero-patriarchal roles, challenging them rather than imitating them. From this alternative perspective, butches could be viewed as brave, visible lesbians who are/were rejecting the limits of what has been possible for women. Butch/femme relationships and desire can be viewed, not as feeble replications of patriarchy, but as women acting from their own agency and desire (Case, 1988–1989). As Rubin (1992: 177) has said, "Butch and femme were brilliantly adapted for building a minority sexual culture out of the tools, materials, and debris of a dominant sexual system".

A lesbian-feminist critique of butch/femme culture was necessary to open up a middle ground for ways to express being female that were not limited by traditional masculine or feminine expressions. It allowed for androgynous dress and social freedoms that mirrored the greater feminist movement's liberation of women. Expressions of lesbianism that are not particularly gendered reveal that butch/femme desire and sexuality may actually be a minority experience within the wider experience of lesbian sexuality.

QUEER CONSCIOUSNESS AND GENDER EXPLORATION

Pair bonding and the development of intimate relationships have been grounded in assumptions about human sexual and gender identities.

Western civilization describes sex and gender as dichotomous. Males and females are considered opposites, and gender identity is assumed to flow from biological sex. Considered immutable and unchanging, masculine and feminine expression is expected to follow the biological assumptions about sex and gender identity (i.e., biological females are socialized and culturally ascribed as women who are comfortable expressing feminine behavior). Sexual orientation is assumed to "naturally" flow from this paradigm, creating a hetero-normative model where opposites (i.e., males *or* females, men *or* women, masculine *or* feminine) literally attract, like the poles of a magnet.

This model virtually disappears from the human family large groups of people who do not fit into this bipolar diagram, including those who are intersex and transsexual. Postmodern and social construction theory, influenced by feminism, initiated a deconstruction of the definitions and boundaries of sex and gender, the meaning of masculinity and femininity, and the assumptions of hetero-normativity. Contemporary understandings of human sexuality have decoupled masculinity and femininity (i.e., gender roles) from exclusively male and female sexed bodies. Additionally, the distinctions between sexual orientation and gender identity, so confusing for the sexologists of the nineteenth century, have become increasingly developed, producing identity constructs for same-sex desire between people with similar gender identities and expressions. In the early years of the twenty-first century, new narratives of sex and gender identities are emerging, that reveal new possibilities for intimate relationships beyond the old binary system (Boyd, 2007; Kane-Demaios and Bullough, 2005; Nestle, Wilchins and Howell, 2002).

The very concepts of heterosexuality and homosexuality highlight the perceived differences in male and female bodies; homosexual relationships are often referred to as "same-sex," signifying the importance of biology, and in particular the identical-sexed genitalia of the partners. Currah (2001: 182) states that the term sexual orientation "remains intelligible only if sex and gender remain relatively stable categories," and butch/femme coupling confounds the simple stability of sex/gender categories. Lesbian couples who identify as butch/femme are (generally) in a same-sex relationship (i.e., they have both been assigned as females), and yet are not a same gender relationship (one partner has a more masculine gender expression and the other a feminine gender expression).

Lesbian-feminist theory presumed that ". . . the seemingly unequal power dynamic of butch/femme relationships [were] a mirror of hetero-sexual oppression" (Gusnoski, 2000, paragraph 2). Feminist theory, with the goal of liberating women, conflated masculine and feminine gender expression with women's oppression, assuming that if people could somehow become gender-free then the power dialectic would be effectively dismantled. This assumes that lesbian relationships that are not constructed within the dialectic of gender opposites could somehow avoid power struggles. Power is, of course, multi-sited, and like race and age oppression, one cannot simply eradicate the constructs in which our lives are embedded—as if gender could simply be eliminated from women's lives.

Butch and femme can only be considered role-playing if all gender expression is role-playing. Butler (1990: 33) has taught that,"there is no gender identity behind the expressions of gender; identity is performatively constituted by the very "expressions" that are said to be its result." Both butch and femme have the subversive potential to bring attention to the masquerade of all gender roles. Gender has surely played an enormous role in maintaining subjugation in the lives of both women and men, and the task of postmodernism and queer theory has been to examine the limits of not just gender itself, but the ways the concept of gender is defined, constrained, mandated, and reified within the cultural discourse. And also the ways it can be reclaimed and resignified.

Pratt says that what "looks like power and domination from the outside . . . that's not what it is from the inside . . . everything looks different from the inside" (1995: 99). Indeed, a movement that began with the concept "the personal is political," had politically analyzed the meaning of gender in lesbian relationships without listening carefully to personal, subjective narratives of the very people for whom these ideas were a vivid reality. As Epstein (2002: 43) says, "Butch/femme roles take place in the context of and are enabled by the hegemonic categories of heterosexuality, but their significance is the internally dissonant and complex way they refigure these categories."

One of the greatest shortcomings of the lesbian-feminist critique of butch/femme dynamics was downplaying the importance of eroticism in the building of intimate relationships. Nestle has said that butch and femme are "complex erotic and social statements, not phony heterosexual replicas" (1992: 138). Butch and femme are, at their root, gendered erotic identities. Butches, assigned and identified as females, experience their sexuality as mediated through masculinity. Femmes, by reclaiming a social scorned femininity, broadcast their sexuality—a lesbian-specific sexuality—by publicizing their attraction to masculine females. Pratt (1995: 117–118) comments on this sexual dance:

You are a woman who has been accused of betraying womanhood. In my groans of pleasure. . . perhaps some would say I have betrayed womanhood with you, that we are traitors to our sex. Your refusing to allow the gestures of what is called masculinity to be preempted by men. Me refusing to relinquish the ecstasies of surrender to women who can only call it subservience. Traitors to our sex, or spies and explorers across the boundaries of what is man, what is woman?

Butch/femme sexuality is "motivated by desire, with romantic and sexual relations constructed around the sexual tensions created by gender difference" (Levitt and Hiestand, 2005: 40). Surely butch/femme couples in previous generations were motivated by the same sexual desires, but placing these identities and desires into a larger postmodern political movement that includes feminist, queer, and trans understandings of sex and gender, allows for the building of communities and families outside of small subcultural context of butch/femme bar culture (Lev 2006). It is within this milieu that butch/femme relationships, desire, intimacy, and family-building must be re-examined.

LESBIAN GENDER

In the late 1980s, I was living in a small city in up-state New York. I was a young social worker, far from the rhythms of San Francisco and big city culture, and also far from the bucolic enclaves of rural (mostly) separatist dyke communities where I had spent my early 20s. It was a warm Saturday night, and I could feel the sexual heat of mid-summer bearing down on me. Although not a drinker or a dancer, I went out to a local "women's dance," hoping for some company, or maybe more. I found myself standing on the side-lines, feeling more out of place than I had since my last high school dance. I looked around at the room of androgynous lesbians—sweet women, laughing and enjoying themselves, comfortable in their bodies and the celebration of sexuality that dancing with your own can bring—and with the suddenness of an electric shock, I realized there was not one woman in the room who I could imagine dating. My community, a home in my heart, left me sexually cold, aloof. I walked home alone, wondering— after nearly two decades of living as an out lesbian—if I was actually still a lesbian.

Although I had always known myself to be femme, for the first time I understood how salient this butch/femme business really is for me, and how pertinent it is to my desire. The word "lesbian," although not incorrect, did not go far enough in describing my sexual orientation, my sexual preference, and my identity.

Laird says that butch and femme are "metaphors of lesbian language and culture" (1999: 61), and even those who do not identify with the terminology, or feel it describes their identity, are familiar with the constructs. Even lesbians who deny any personal identification with butch/femme identities are culturally fluent in the language and recognizing the gendered signifiers in themselves and one another (Loulan, 1990; Levitt and Horne, 2002).

Butch/femme sexuality is, of course, only one specific erotic dance between lesbians. There are many of other ways to explore and experience sexuality between those born female, including (but not limited to) femme/femme sexuality, butch/butch sexuality, and many various forms of androgyny. Gender is not a salient aspect of lesbian intimacy for all women who are sexual with women. It also is worth mentioning that terms like butch and femme are used outside of the lesbian community, and will have a different resonance within gay male culture, or even straight culture; these words will certainly have different meanings in other countries, cultures, and subcultures, across age, race, and class lines. Some females are masculine, or tomboys, but not lesbians (Boyd, 2007; Devor, 1989) some lesbians are feminine, "straight-acting," but not femme-identified, most notable those labeled lipstick lesbians (Maltry and Tucker, 2002).

There have been many attempts to define and explain the terms butch (Bergman, 2006; Burana, Roxxie and Due, 1994) and femme (Harris and Crocker, 1997; Newman, 1995, Levitt and Horne, 2003), and all fall prey to stereotypes about clothing, mannerisms, and cultural signifiers. Gender identity and expression, although certainly performative and culturally embedded, also evokes a core sense of self, an experience of actualization (Levitt and Hiestand, 2005). Wearing male clothing for butches may be rife with cultural meaning, although it may appear to be simply an outward choice of appearance and a "facile presentation of our surfaces" (Borich, 2000: 122, 129); however, more than simple aesthetics urges butches and femmes to wear the clothes they do. It seems that when making "choices" about clothing "more than surfaces is at stake" (ibid.), and that freely made choices are sometimes "choices we are compelled to make." (ibid.).

Female masculinities (Halberstam, 1998) represent a broad spectrum of expression, behavior and identity. Butch is "a category of lesbian gender . . . for women who are more comfortable with masculine gender codes, styles, or identities" (Rubin, 1992: 167). The butch role has been a reclaiming of masculinity, and at the same time an important symbol of rebellion against male power, sexism, and patriarchy; it has represented a lesbian archetype of women's power, and is therefore a profoundly feminist position.

In recent years, many formerly butch-identified females have claimed a male identity, emerged as female-to-male transsexuals (transmen). Creating "border wars" of identity (Halberstam, 1998; Hale, 1998), masculinity in female bodies has become a contested area of embodiment and political alliance. The transgender liberation movement has created a larger space for those born female to explore the meaning of their masculinity and actualization as men. For some crossing over the binary from female to male has resolved the dysphoria of living as a masculine female. However, for others, transitioning can not resolve that dilemma, and can even increase the sense of displacement (Bergman, 2006; Feinberg, 2006); living outside of the binaries of male and female can sometimes leave one homeless. Butch is used here as an inclusive term, including many who also identify as transgender (Lev, 1998), but stops at the place where masculinity is experienced as male. Unlike transsexuals who defy social expectations about gender *identity,* butches experience a cross-gender *role,* that is, they are women who are masculine, not men with female bodies.

Femme identity has been harder to define and classify, precisely because it does not obviously defy societal expectations for what a woman should be. Femme identity is not straight and it is not exclusive to female-born bodies. It is not a passive identity, nor is it necessarily a sexualized or objectified identity, despite the misogynistic stereotypes. Femme is a conscious appropriation of what is traditionally thought of as feminine (although the word feminine itself is often rejected by femmes). Femmes identified that "the label evoked a strong, positive image of feminine sexuality" (Levitt, Gerrish, Hiestand, 2003: 103). Femme lesbian identity represents a comfort with having a female-sexed body and celebrates the pleasure inherent in feminine gendered sexuality. Femme (within the butch/femme dance) celebrates the masculinity of butch lesbians, and in that act heals some of the disembodiment butches can experience.

Femmes have a socially normative biology, gender identity, and gender role, but challenge the social conventions by actively choosing females as sexual partners. By "orienting their sexuality toward a butch woman instead of a man, the femme women made lesbian desire public" (Levitt, Gerrish, Hiestand, 2003: 99); this was historically an enormously radical act, and remains one today. Within the butch/femme dyad, femmes are often perceived as more passionate, more powerful and in charge—traits one might assume to be masculine. Despite their public invisibility as lesbians, femmes are often out and outspoken within the lesbian community, commanding positions of leadership and power. Femme can be strong, willful, empowered, and embodied.

Nonetheless, femmes have been denigrated within the lesbian community (Harris and Crocker, 1997) and even their authenticity as lesbians has been continually questioned. The femme can become "reduced to unrecognized status" (Gusnoski, 2000, paragraph 11), and this invisibility strips her "not only of her identity, but of any understanding of her identity as subversive" (Maltry and Tucker, 2002: 94). It is this subversive element of femme identity that needs further explication, particularly in examining how butch/femme couples form long-term, stable relationships and families.

FEMME INVISIBILITY AND THE MAKING OF A HOME

In 1943 Althea was a welder
very dark
very butch
and very proud
loved to cook, sew, and drive a car
and did not care who knew she kept company with a woman
who met her every day after work
in a tight dress and high heel shoes
light-skinned and high cheekbones
who loved to shoot, fish, play poker
and did not give a damn who knew her "man" was a woman.

(Cheryl Clarke, 1992)

If we start from the acknowledged assumption that butch/femme relationships have historical presence and contemporary existence, and that lesbian intimacy is often formed within gendered parameters, we are left with some questions about the lack of visibility of butch/femme coupling within the research on lesbian relationships and family-building.

The clinical research on lesbian couples has continued to expand in the past thirty years, although it still remains a relatively small body of literature. The focus has primarily been on relationship satisfaction and intimacy, resilience of couple partnerships, the division of domestic chores, and more recently, a growing body of literature on parenting and family-building (Chan, Brooks, Patterson and Raboy, 1998; Goldberg and Sayer, 2006; Gottman et al., 2003; Kurdek, 1993; Mackey, 2000; Peplau, Veniegas and Campbell, 1996). The study of gender dynamics within same-sex relationships has overwhelming shown that lesbians have intimate relationships based on equality of roles and commitment to shared chores and parenting, and that traditional gender role dynamics do not operate in lesbian and gay relationships.

Although butch/femme couples are absent in scholarly documents, lesbian literature is seductive with stories of butch/femme sexuality, and it is undeniable that "femme-butch dyads offer . . . a highly charged sexual and gender specific way of caring for each other as lovers" (Harris, 2002: 75). But after the hot honeymoon, how do butch/femme couples make their way together as couples and partners and how to do they build gendered lesbian lives within the modern day lesbian culture?

Some butch/femme couples, according to emerging reports, enact family roles in sexualized and erotic ways (Harris, 2002; Maltz, 2002), meaning that roles of Mommy, Daddy, Son, and Daughter, are enacted—sexually and romantically—within the intimate narratives of the couple. For those that have lived outside of the confines of family life, this resignification may underscore the primal need for family, actualized through a re-creation of familial roles.

The focus, however, on butch/femme eroticism, as compelling as it may be, might obscure other equally subversive acts. I would like to suggest that one of the most subversive acts that femmes have accomplished is the establishment of a safe haven for their families in often hostile environments, through the creation of homes and through the process of homemaking. Gorman-Murray (2006) suggests that the development of a home plays a unique role in gay and lesbian partnerships, and that the sharing of domestic space helps to establish and consolidate same-sex partnerships.

Homemaking, which has traditionally exemplified the worst aspects of women's oppression and forced domesticity, became a powerful site for reclaiming space, and creating environments where intimacy can develop and flourish. I suggest that femmes have played a unique role in the cultivating of their homes and the nurturing of families, a role that might appear to mirror the traditional role of heterosexual housewives on the outside, but to borrow from Pratt, it "looks different from the inside." An alternative to bars and community spaces, having and maintaining a home creates a foundation in which long-term relationships can mature and move through time.

Homemaking is a private act that takes place outside of the public eye, and has therefore garnered little attention in mainstream society, which has also served to protect butch/femme couples from too much public scrutiny. However, it also isolated couples and hid their home lives from historical and sociological inquiry. In a world that has been hostile toward masculine females and queers in general, femmes—the guardians of more traditionally feminine cultural artifacts—have fostered home environments for themselves and their butches where their identities and relationships could thrive. The act of making a home, a lesbian home, where female couples could build a life together as if they simply had the right, is a subversive act indeed.

In the contemporary world where gay and lesbians couples can build homes and have children, especially in large urban settings, we may fail to see how subversive it is to believe one has the right to exist as a family, and to become, in Borich's words "each other's plot of land" (2000: 118). The subversive act of cultivating a way of life in a hostile world has gone unnoticed precisely because things that belong to women's sphere and domesticity have mostly been deemed irrelevant and unimportant. Sadly, this is as true for lesbian-feminist theorists and gay historians as it was within mainstream culture. Women's domestic work—the work of cooking, cleaning, mending, and kissing "owies"—work that I suspect originated from and was sustained by the hands of femmes in femme/butch relationships, has mostly gone unnoticed or judged irrelevant or apolitical. Butch/femme couples have existed, creating homes in each other hearts, and becoming "each other's plot of land," yet remain hidden from the academic study of "lesbian couples."

The conspicuous absence of discussion about butch/femme relational dynamics in scholarly research makes me wonder if butch/femme couples are simply not taking part in these studies, or if researchers are not asking the kinds of questions that would explore the way gender is experienced within lesbian dyads. Examining domestic chores and parenting styles, or even power dynamics and communication styles, may not accurately measure the way that gender operates within same-sex couples, and for butch/femme couples it may actually mask the way that gender roles are understood and interpreted within the relationship. If research about gender roles assumes a power differential attached to the gender expression, the "equality" within the lesbian couple may hide important aspects of how gender functions in the relationship that is neither traditional (i.e., based in hetero-normativity) nor hierarchal.

In one study on femme identity, Levitt, Gerrish, Hiestand, (2003) discovered that femmes felt housekeeping duties were not divided along gender lines, and that their romantic relationships were based in equality, mirroring the general body of research on lesbian couples. Does this mean that gender is not a salient issue in the domestic lives of butch/femme couples? Are butch and femme only erotic identities, and once past the dating and seduction part of early relationships, gender is no longer important to the organization of their home lives? Or rather does it prove that equality and respect can exist in homes where couples express divergent gender expressions? Can it be that oppressive power-over dynamics are not simply woven into the fabric of gender role expression?

It has been suggested that it may be easier for femmes to find higher paid employment than butches, who may struggle with job discrimination because of their unconventional gender presentation (Faderman, 1992; Levitt, Gerrish,Hiestand, 2003). Does this make for more egalitarian relationships, because the femme is an equal partner in finances; how does being the "breadwinner" impact her identity as a femme? Can researchers find ways to explore how class, education, sexism, gender oppression, and finances function in lesbian couples without falling back on simplistic gendered explanations?

What is the role of gender expression, gender identity, and gender attributes in the daily lives of butch/femme couples? As more lesbian couples are choosing to have children, how do butch/femme couples negotiate decisions about pregnancy, breast-feeding, stay-at-home parenting, and childcare arrangements? How similar is this process to lesbians who do not identify as butch/femme? How can researchers study how gender functions within same-sex couples, and not assume it is "like" heterosexual couples or "like" other lesbian (and gay) couples, but respect that it has it's own unique manifestation?

Butch/femme coupling confounds normative assumptions about gender, sex, and role expression. Just as the erotic dance between butches and femmes utilizes gendered images reminiscent of familiar heterosexual stereotypes (i.e., male and female clothing), yet is functionally a very unique lesbian sexual expression, so to is the domestic lives of butch/femme couples. If researchers assume that there are no gender dynamics happening because both females share household chores and parenting, they are perhaps not asking the right questions about gender and roles within butch/femme families.

Cheryl Clarke's poem outlines how strongly butch/femme identified couples experience gender in complex ways that defy simple stereotypes of masculinity and femininity. Althea (the butch) is a welder who wears suits and ties but also cooks and sews, and Flaxie (her femme partner, unnamed in the excerpt above) wears high heel shoes and tight dresses, loves to shoot and plays poker. They may be stepping out of societal assumptions about gendered behavior, but perhaps they are perfectly embodying how lesbian gender is enacted within butch/femme relationships? Clarke recognizes the masculine/feminine polarity of their lesbian pair-bonding, yet she also poignantly acknowledges that Althea and Flaxie defied both the gendered expectations of heterosexual coupling and the traditional assumptions of gender within butch/femme relationships.

Despite premature statements that femme/butch relationships are an extinct social form, same-sex/opposite-gender relationships have historical existence and contemporary continuity. Focus on the erotic lives of butches and femmes, though titillating, does not do justice to the complexity of long-term lesbian relationships built on gendered identities. Researchers of lesbian families need to develop ways to examine the unique issues of gender within lesbian couples.

REFERENCES

Ballou, M. and L. S. Brown, eds. *Rethinking Mental Health and Disorder: Feminist Perspectives.* New York: Guilford Press, 2002.

Bergman, S. B. *Butch is a Noun.* San Francisco, CA: Suspect Thoughts Press, 2006.

Blackwood, E. "Tombois in West Sumatra: Constructing Masculinity and Erotic Desire." In E. Blackwood and S. E. Weiring, eds. *Same-Sex Relations and Female Desires: Transgender Practices Across Cultures.* New York: Columbia University Press, 1999: 181–205.

Borich, B. J. *My Lesbian Husband.* St. Paul, MN: Graywolf Press, 2000.

Boyd, H. *She's Not the Man I Married: My Life With a Transgender Husband.* Emeryville, CA: Seal Press, 2007.

Burana, L., Roxxie and L. Due, eds. *Dagger: On Butch Women.* San Francisco: Cleis Press, 1994.

Butler, J. *Gender Trouble: Feminism and the Subversion of Gender.* New York: Routledge, 1990.

Case, S-E. "Toward a Butch-Femme Aesthetic." *Discourse,* 8, (Fall–Winter), 1988–1989: 55–73.

Chan, R. W., R. C. Brooks, C. J. Patterson, and B. Raboy. "Division of Labor Among Lesbian and Heterosexual Parents: Associations with Children's Adjustment." *Journal of Family Psychology,* 12, 1998: 402–419.

Clarke, C. "Of Althea and Flaxie." In J. Nestle, ed. *The Persistent Desire: A Femme-Butch Reader.* LA: Alyson, 1992.

Cromwell, J. *Transmen and Ftms: Identities, Bodies, Genders, and Sexualities.* Champaign, IL: University of Illinois, 1999.

Currah, P. "Queer Theory, Lesbian and Gay Rights, and Transsexual Marriages." In M. Biasius, ed. *Sexual Identities—Queer Politics*. Princeton, NJ: Princeton University Press, 2001: 178–197.

Devor, H. *Gender Blending: Confronting the Limits of Duality*. Bloomington: Indiana University Press, 1989.

Dimen, M. and V. Goldner. *Gender in Psychoanalytic Space: Between Clinic and Culture*. New York: Other Press, LLC, 2002.

Epstein, R. "Butches with Babies: Reconfiguring Gender and Motherhood." *Journal of Lesbian Studies*, 6, 2002: 41–56.

Faderman, L. *Odd Girls and Twilight Lovers: A History of Lesbian Life in Twentieth-Century America*. New York: Penguin Press, 1992.

Feinberg, L. *Stone Butch Blues*. Ithaca, NY: Firebrand Books, 1993.

Feinberg, L. *Drag King Dreams*. New York: Carroll & Graf, 2006.

Gartrell, N., A. Deck, C. Rodas, H. Peyser, and A. Banks. "The National Lesbian Family Study: 4. Interviews with the 10-Year-Old Children." *American Journal of Orthopsychiatry*, 75(4), 2005: 518–524.

Goldberg, A. E. and A. Sayer. "Lesbian Couples' Relationship Quality Across the Transition to Parenthood." *Journal of Marriage and Family* 68(1), 2006: 87–100.

Golombok, S., B. Perry, A. Burston, C. Murray, J. Mooney-Somers, M. Stevens, and J. Golding. "Children with Lesbian Parents: A Community Study." *Developmental Psychology*, 39, 2003: 20–33.

Goodloe, A. "Lesbian Identity and the Politics of Butch-Femme Roles." (1999). Retrieved from the Internet April 17, 2007: http://www.lesbian.org/amy/essays/bf-paper.html.

Gorman-Murray, A. "Gay and Lesbian Couples at Home: Identity Work in Domestic Space." *Home Cultures*, 3(2), 2006: 145–167.

Gottman, J. M., R. W. Levenson, J. Gross, B. L. Fredrickson, K. McCoy, L. Rosenthal, A. Reuf, D. Yoshimoto. "Correlates of Gay and Lesbian Couples' Relationship Satisfaction and Relationship Dissolution." *Journal of Homosexuality*, 45(1), 2003: 23–43.

Gusnoski, E. "A Powerful Place to Live: Butch-Femme Relationships and the Politics of Gender."(2000).Retrieved from the Internet April 17, 2007: http://www.exploredesire.com/gusnoski.html

Halberstam, J. *Female Masculinity*. Durham, NC: Duke Press, 1998.

Hale, C. J. "Consuming the Living, Dis(re)membering the Dead in the Butch/Ftm Borderlands." *GLQ* 4(2), 1998: 311–348.

Harris, L. A. "Femme/Butch Family Romances: A Queer Dyke Spin on Compulsory Heterosexuality." In M. Gibson and D. T. Meem, eds. *Femme/Butch: New Considerations of the Way We Want to Go*. New York: Harrington Park Press, 2002: 73–84.

Harris, L. and E. Crocker. *Femme: Feminists Lesbians and Bad Girls*. New York: Routledge, 1997.

Hekma, G. "'A Female Soul in a Male Body': Sexual Inversion as Gender Inversion in Nineteenth-Century Sexology." In G. Herdt, ed. *Third Sex Third Gender: Beyond Sexual Dimorphism in Culture and History*. New York: Zone Books, 1994: 213–239.

Jeffreys, S. "Butch and Femme: Now and Then." In Lesbian History Group, eds. *Not a Passing Phase: Reclaiming Lesbians in History 1840–1985*. London: Women's Press, 1989: 58–187.

Kane-Demaios, J. A. and V. L. Bullough, eds. *Crossing Sexual Boundaries: Transgender Journeys, Uncharted Paths.* Amherst, NY: Prometheus, 2005.

Kennedy, E. L. and M. D. Davis. *Boots of Leather, Slippers of Gold: The History of a Lesbian Community.* New York: Penguin Press, 1993.

Kurdek, L. A. "The Allocation of Household Labor in Gay, Lesbian, and Heterosexual Married Couples." *Journal of Social Issues,* 49(3), 1993: 127–140.

Laird, J. "Gender and Sexuality in Lesbian Relationship." In J. Laird, ed. *Lesbians and Lesbian Families: Reflections on Theory and Practice.*New York: Columbia, 1999: 47–90.

Laird, J. and R-J. Green, eds. *Lesbians and Gays in Couples and Families: A Handbook for Therapists.* San Francisco: Jossey-Bass, 1996.

Lev, A. I. "Invisible Gender." *In the Family* (October), 1998: 8–11.

Lev, A. I. "Transgender Communities: Developing Identity Through Connection." In K. Bieschke, R. Perez, and K. DeBord, eds. *Handbook of Counseling and Psychotherapy with Lesbian, Gay, and Bisexual Clients (2nd Edition).* American Psychological Association, Washington, DC, 2006: 147–175.

Levitt, H. M., E. A. Gerrish, and K. R. Hiestand. "The Misunderstood Gender: A Model of Modern Femme Identity." *Sex Roles,* 48(3/4), 2003: 99–113.

Levitt, H. M. and K. R. Hiestand. "Gender Within Lesbian Sexuality: Butch and Femme Perspectives." *Journal of Constructivist Psychology,* 18, 2005: 39–51.

Levitt, H. M. and S. Horne. "Explorations of Lesbian-Queer Genders: Butch, Femme, Androgynous or 'Other.'" In M. Gibson and D. T. Meem, eds. *Femme/Butch: New Considerations of the Way We Want to Go.*New York: Harrington Park Press, 2002: 25–39.

Loulan, J. *The Lesbian Erotic Dance: Butch, Femme, Androgyny and Other Rhythms.* San Francisco: Spinsters, Inc, 1990.

Lynch, L. *Home in Your Hands.* Johnsonville, NY: Bold Strokes, 1986.

Mackey, R. A. "Psychological Intimacy in the Lasting Relationships of Heterosexual and Same-Gender Couples." *Sex Roles: A Journal of Research,* 43, 2000: 201–227.

Maltry, M. and K. Tucker. "Female Fem(me)ininities: New Articulations in Queer Gende Identities and Subversion." In M. Gibson and D. T. Meem, eds. *Femme/Butch: New Considerations of the Way We Want to Go.* New York: Harrington Park Press, 2002: 89–102.

Maltz, R. "Genesis of a Femme and Her Desire: Finding Mommy and Daddy in Butch/Femme." In M. Gibson and D. T. Meem, eds. *Femme/Butch: New Considerations of the Way We Want to Go.* New York: Harrington Park Press, 2002: 61–71.

McGoldrick, M., C. M. Anderson, and F. Walsh, eds. *Women in Families: A Framework for Family Therapy.* New York: W.W. Norton, 1991.

Murray, S. O. and W. Roscoe, eds. *Boy-Wives and Female Husbands: Studies of African Homosexualities.* New York: St. Martin's, 1998.

Nestle, J., ed. *The Persistent Desire: A Femme-Butch Reader.* Los Angeles: Alyson, 1992.

Nestle, J., R. Wilchins, and C. Howell. *Genderqueer: Voices From Beyond the Sexual Binary.* Los Angeles: Alyson Publications, 2002.

Newman, L. *The Femme Mystique.* Los Angeles: Alyson, 1995.

Newton, E. "The Mythic Mannish Lesbian: Radclyffe Hall and the New Woman." *Signs*, 9(4), 1984: 557–75.

Patterson, C. J. "Families of the Lesbian Baby Boom: Maternal Mental Health and Child Adjustment." *Journal of Gay and Lesbian Psychotherapy*, 4, 2001: 91–107.

Patterson, C. J. and R. W. Chan. "Gay Fathers and Their Children." In R. P. Cabaj and T. Stein, eds. *Textbook of Homosexuality and Mental Health*. Washington, DC: American Psychiatric Press, Inc, 1996: 371–393.

Peplau, L. A., R. C. Veniegas, and S. M. Campbell. "Gay and Lesbian Relationships." In R. Savin-Wllliams and K. M. Cohen, eds.*The Lives of Lesbians, Gays, and Bisexuals: Children to Adults*. Fort Worth, TX: Harcourt Brace, 1996: 250–273.

Pratt, M. B. *S/HE*. Ithaca, New York: Firebrand Books, 1995.

Rich, A. "Compulsory Heterosexuality and Lesbian Existence." *Signs*, 5(4), 1973: 631–660.

Rubin, G. "Of Catamites and Kings: Reflections on Butch Gender and Boundaries." In J. Nestle, ed. *The Persistent Desire: A Femme-Butch Reader.* Los Angeles: Alyson, 1992: 166–182.

Savin-Williams, R. C. and K. M. Cohen, eds. *The Lives of Lesbians Gays and Bisexuals: Children to Adults*. Fort Worth, TX: Harcourt Brace, 1996.

Smith, L. "Listening to the 'Wives' of the 'Female Husbands': A Project of Femme Historiography in Eighteenth-Century Britain." In M. Gibson and D. T. Meem, eds. *Femme/Butch: New Considerations of the Way we Want to Go.* New York: Harrington Park Press, 2002: 105–120.

Trumbach, R. "London's Sapphists: From Three Sexes to Four Genders in the Making of Modern Culture." In G. Herdt, ed. *Third Sex Third Gender: Beyond Sexual Dimorphism in Culture and History*. New York: Zone Books, 1994: 111–136.

Vicinus, M. "'They Wonder to Which Sex I Belong': The Historical Roots of the Modern Lesbian Identity." In H. Abelove, M. A. Barale, and D. M. Halperin, eds. *The Lesbian and Gay Studies Reader*. New York: Routledge, 1993: 432–452.

Infidelity: Outlaws and In-Laws
and Lesbian Relationships

Beverly Burch

SUMMARY. How does one define infidelity in lesbian relationships? Because lesbians cannot marry, they exist outside of the law. Do lesbians, like other "outlaws," create their own code of ethics? All relationships evolve structures in response to social constraints; we must beware of transferring normative assumptions to relationships that develop within their own culture. The boundaries of lesbian relationships are not as fixed as those of heterosexual ones, partly for lack of this legal recognition and partly because they have evolved somewhat in opposition to traditional marriage. Variations on traditional relationships and the different meanings they may hold for the women who create them are explored.

Can lesbians commit adultery? I started thinking about this question when I was asked to write a chapter on lesbian relationships for a book on infidelity. Immediately the complexity of that word, infidelity, troubled me. Because lesbians cannot marry, often cannot receive the legal

Beverly Burch, Ph.D., has a psychotherapy practice in Berkeley, California and serves as a clinical consultant with The Sanville Institute in Berkeley. She has published two books on psychodynamic theory, *On Intimate Terms* (1992) and *Other Women* (1997), exploring issues of gender and sexuality. Her first book of poetry, *Sweet to Burn*, won the Gival Poetry Prize and a Lambda Literary Award.

benefits of marriage, and in many cases cannot even receive the simple benefit of being viewed as a legitimate relationship, how exactly do we define infidelity for lesbian couples? If lesbian relationships are outside of the law, do lesbians, like other "outlaws," create another code(s) of ethics—our own laws, in effect? Then what is infidelity in lesbian culture?

If the word means betrayal rather than non-monogamy—and I think it does—then we can never assume the answer to be obvious. The institution of marriage has evolved—from arranged marriages, child marriages, polygamy, and implicitly sanctioned non-monogamy for some (mostly men)—to the current norm of heterosexual monogamy. Does this norm simply transfer to lesbians, who have no traditional ceremony in which to promise to "cleave only unto one another?" In this postmodern era, we know social context is everything.

What's defined as fidelity and infidelity profoundly shapes one's emotional response to it. Does a woman in a polygamous marriage call her husband unfaithful when he sleeps with another wife? If husbands are tacitly allowed to sleep with other women, do wives feel the same as those whose culture explicitly condemns it? Feelings of jealousy do not necessarily equal betrayal: betrayal is cognitively determined as well as emotionally laden.

Infidelity is a serious transgression in most heterosexual marriages; it violates ethical beliefs, it is socially censured, it can be grounds for divorce. The word is hardly morally neutral. For couples who are simply dating, infidelity may also be a transgression, but without the same weight. "My boyfriend cheated on me" is not quite the same as "My husband cheated on me." The socio-legal limbo of lesbian couples leaves us with a lack of definition. Are we perpetually dating? If we live together, is it the same arrangement as that of a straight couple who chooses not to get married? There are not given rules, and there's no social contract to accept or reject. Common belief says gay relationships, especially male ones, are less concerned with monogamy, less judgmental about infidelity. Between women, monogamy is often an ideal, but the possibility of an affair still has to be settled, not assumed.

These differences are real, but we need to resist the urge to simplify the complex. Many gay male couples are monogamous and some lesbians prefer open relationships. All relationships evolve structures in response to social constraints. As with any cultural difference, we must beware of transferring normative assumptions to relationships that develop their own culture.

OPEN RELATIONSHIPS

In *American Couples* (Blumstein and Schwartz, 1983), the only large study of heterosexual, lesbian, and gay relationships found that a great majority of lesbians prefer monogamy. Twenty-five years later, I believe there's an even higher value placed on monogamy now, as lesbian couples find more acceptance in mainstream culture. Non-monogamy tends to be less appealing with age as well, because younger couples make more tentative commitments or want to experiment with relationships. And, again, it's hard to draw lines between dating, commitment, and formal commitment or marriage when we are comparing lesbian and straight relationships.

But some couples do choose an open relationship. The sense of sexual liberation in lesbian and feminist communities at least nominally allows this choice. To some, monogamy is a regressive notion. For others, it simply does not match their desires. Couples who are highly committed to each other may agree to non-monogamy in general, or decide the occasional affair is not a problem. They may establish rules to make affairs less threatening. Then infidelity means breaking *those* rules, not the usual one of monogamy.

Tolerance can turn out to be in theory only, however. Actual affairs sometimes cause one partner to decide non-monogamy no longer works. Everyone, gay and straight, is steeped in the romance of a "one and only" that permeates our culture. Non-monogamy may be common to the human species, but it seems viable only within a community thoroughly acculturated to it. For women it tends to be especially difficult, gay or straight (Blumstein and Schwartz, 1983).

Being Outlaws

The experience of Suzanne and Brigit, who came to couples therapy over this issue, captures some of the dilemma. For four years they maintained an open relationship. Brigit traveled frequently in her work and they had many imposed separations. Both felt these times apart kept their erotic life lively—missing each other worked like an aphrodisiac. Neither wanted to slip into a "companionate marriage" that relied on common interests rather than passion as a bond, something they viewed as an easy trap for lesbian relationships.

From the beginning they had an understanding: each could be with someone new when Brigit was away. No ongoing affairs; if either felt an affair posed a threat to their relationship, she would stop seeing the other person. Suzanne especially enjoyed feeling like a single woman when Brigit was away. Before Brigit, she had had a number of lovers. She saw herself as fundamentally non-monogamous and thought maybe she would never be in a long-term relationship. The arrangement with Brigit seemed perfect, the best of both worlds. It worked, although there were urgent phone calls and many midnight conversations. But it was exciting and therefore worth it.

Brigit was more dubious. She agreed to the arrangement because it intrigued her. She loved how passionate they were when she returned from her travels. She indulged with an occasional new lover on the road, something she had never considered in her former relationship. These out-of-town adventures felt safe enough, but Suzanne's in-town affairs worried her. So far they had worked things out, but when they came to therapy she was feeling a strain, and her confidence in this arrangement was fading. She said she had grown a bit weary of it.

Another difficulty was that Bridget wanted to change her job. Did their relationship require that she have a job involving travel? She wanted more companionship with Suzanne, even at the price of less passion. She felt she could not tolerate Suzanne having even a one-night stand while she was in town.

Suzanne did not want to change anything. Instead she felt betrayed; they had an understanding and it seemed unfair to change the rules. But she was deeply attached to Brigit now and hoped the relationship could last, even though their conflict seemed impossibly daunting.

When Non-Monogamy Fails

Non-monogamy keeps posing challenges for lesbian couples. Because more women are inclined toward or feel more secure in monogamous relationships, there's often a disparity in their desire for different rules. Sometimes one woman persuades the other that their sexual relationship will thrive this way; sometimes one simply insists that non-monogamy is the only way she will go—it's a "my way or the highway" agreement. Rarely, both women prefer non-monogamy. Again, there's no good data to inform us whether these relationships endure, as they do in many cases for gay men, or whether they are especially vulnerable relationships. But there are usually rules of some kind, even if not explicitly agreed on. Breaking the rules, whatever they may be, is a form of infidelity. And if one's partner falls in love with another woman, doesn't that always *feel* like infidelity?

Even when a couple has not agreed on non-monogamy, lesbians tend to be more open about affairs than married couples do. Blumstein and Schwartz write:

> The interesting thing here is that marriage itself makes couples more deceptive. Couples who marry have traditionally sworn to "forsake all others," and it is rare that couples change the agreement, even if they do not always live up to it. Because most non-monogamous husbands and wives have broken their contract rather than revised it, they are forced into dishonesty. (270)

Revising the contract would be difficult of course, often grounds for divorce. But revising it the other way, back to monogamy, is equally challenging. Brigit and Suzanne's dilemma is a common endpoint of non-monogamy. An open relationship is hard to sustain over time and difficult to change into a monogamous one. It may seem strange that Suzanne would be the one to feel betrayed, but again, betrayal is defined by context, not by absolutes.

More frequently now, lesbian and gay couples do marry—if not legally, at least making a personal and/or spiritual commitment. They hire a hall, a florist, a caterer, musicians, and photographers. They invite friends and family, employ a minister, and exchange rings and vows. Vows are of their own creation, like many heterosexual couples' vows. No way to know whether these vows typically involve promises of fidelity because they are private and unstudied. Perhaps faithfulness is simply assumed, as it is for heterosexuality.

The possibility of legal marriage dangles on the horizon. As the definition of marriage continues to evolve to include gay relationships, its bond of monogamy will likely add weight to most lesbians' wish for that mutual commitment. I expect, however, that the gay community, hardly a homogenous or unified entity, will still tolerate open relationships more than most heterosexuals do. At the same time such a hard-won legal right will be taken very seriously by many and may move the communal ethic further toward monogamy.

For a couple like Brigit and Suzanne, bridging different needs is especially challenging. Relationships resist changing. Over time they may succeed, but there's usually opposition or reluctance, then a sense of betrayal, resentment, anger, that is, the usual aftermath of infidelity. Heterosexual couples go through these stages as they try to re-negotiate gender roles, but at least there's some cultural support in this direction. Deeply held patterns and beliefs do not budge easily. Brigit and Suzanne finally separated, with a great deal of unhappiness and mutual blame. Suzanne seemed certain monogamy would not work for her and continued to resent Brigit's lack of faith in their original understanding. Brigit felt she had tried, but an open relationship held no real future for her. She, the monogamously inclined partner, agreed she was the "unfaithful" one.

ALTERNATIVE FAMILY STRUCTURES

Lesbian couples with children often hold independent, even idiosyncratic, ideas of family and relationships. They have already broken the mold on traditional family life and many feel a necessity to construct a different model. They may live in a matrix of relationships that supports them and gives their alternative family meaning. There may be donors or biological fathers in the family network. One woman may have close ties to an ex-lover. A friend may take some parenting responsibilities. There may be another legal parent—a biological, or non-biological but legal, parent. Aside from single parents, in lesbian families at least one parent is not a biological parent.

Parenting is understood as a psychological relationship as much as a biological one. In *Reinventing the Family* (1994: 145) Benkov writes:

> Families don't exist as independent units within which intimacy unfolds unto itself. Instead, life in every family is shaped as surely by surrounding cultural discourse and institutions as it is by idiosyncrasies of each family member. A question like "Who is the mommy?" reflects the meeting of the world outside and the world within. The ideas that prevail in society profoundly influence how we each construct and feel about our families and our roles within them.

For lesbians the "society around them" is multilayered: the dominant culture, their families of origin, and lesbian and gay culture. Many families develop nontraditional structures. These situations complicate the question of fidelity without ever transgressing sexual boundaries.

A Culture Clash

Jennifer and Zoe met at a professional seminar. They were immediately attracted and friendship led to a love affair. Eventually Zoe left her ten-year marriage and moved with her two daughters into the home of Jennifer and her son, Max. Jennifer's ex, Marsha, is also Max's mother and considers herself, Jennifer, and Max a family even though they separated when Max was two. Jennifer juggles these two families. She's loyal to ties between her, Max, and Marsha. Max is used to this arrangement, including joint vacations and holiday celebrations. Jennifer and Marsha's finances are still entwined. Marsha drops by for dinner sometimes, and Max moves between the nearby houses of his two mothers on an ever-changing schedule.

Zoe can make no sense of this. She and her husband Jeffrey had a traumatic divorce. He remains hurt and angry. It's not easy for them to cooperate as parents to their two girls, who spend half the week with him and half with her. She cannot imagine continuing the kind of family life that Jennifer and Marsha have. She presses Jennifer to make some rules with Marsha, not to give her such free access to their home, and to end vacations with each other.

Jennifer resents and resists Zoe's demands. She's loyal to Marsha—they have helped and protected each other through single motherhood. Marsha dates occasionally but she has not found anyone else. Jennifer feels it would be a betrayal of Marsha and wrenching for Max if she changed the rules. She can handle two families if Zoe can get past her jealousy. She would love for them all to be an extended family, doing things together.

Zoe says she's the betrayed one. She did not realize how involved Marsha was in Jennifer's life until she moved in. Then she assumed their relationship would change. She does not worry that Zoe and Marsha have lingering romantic or sexual feelings, but their continuing relationship seems like a kind of infidelity.

Being In-Laws

In *Unbroken Ties: Lesbian Ex-lovers* Becker (1988: 211) documents the enduring bonds that characterize many lesbian relationships after a breakup:

> To varying degrees, lesbian ex-lovers retain their ties to one another after their breakup and use these bonds to rebuild their lives. An ex-lover remains an important part of a woman's evolving identity: as a woman, as a lesbian, and as a participant in intimate relationships.

Social and family support for lesbians is not guaranteed after a breakup. Support is not always there when a marriage ends either, but the larger social view of what divorce means is at least secure. No one treats the marriage as if it did not exist or did not mean something important. For a lesbian, a breakup might meet with relief from her family of origin. Where is she to turn except to her own community, even to her ex? "Despite the irresolvable differences that resulted in their breakup, lesbian ex-lovers remained connected by an overriding common cause— that of combating negative stereotypes of themselves, their relationship and their lifestyle" (Becker, 1988: 213).

Kath Weston's (1991: 11) study of gay relationships echoes this reality:

> Former lovers' . . . inclusion in families we choose was far from automatic, but most people hoped to stay connected to ex-lovers as friends and family . . . This emphasis on making a transition from lover to friend while remaining within the bounds of gay families contrasted with heterosexual partners . . . for whom separation or divorce often meant permanent rupture of a kinship tie.

Jennifer and Zoe have a "cross-cultural" relationship, Jennifer coming from a lesbian culture that tolerates different boundaries, Zoe coming from a heterosexual one that finds these odd and threatening. Even if she and Jeffrey were friendly, Zoe cannot imagine taking a vacation together. She would not expect Jennifer to accept such closeness. Are she and Jennifer essentially married or not, she asks?

If Zoe had previously been in a lesbian relationship, she might still dislike having Marsha around so much, maybe intensely dislike it. Ex-lovers are not necessarily welcomed into the picture any more than in-laws are. But they *are* like in-laws for many lesbians; they are the people you inherit when you enter a relationship. These ties are not incomprehensible. Are they equivalent to being unfaithful? Many times new lovers do gradually accommodate their partner's ex. As one woman new to lesbian relationships said to me, in an interview for an earlier book (Burch, 1993: 94) on lesbian relationships:

> I'm not like other lesbians, for example, because I don't have ex-lovers. They're all male. That's a really big thing . . . You know there's this stuff about lesbians having extended families, and when we're old we'll all be sitting on the porch rocking with our ex-lovers . . . This weekend we were with some friends who've been lesbian for at least fifteen years, and one of them said to me, "My God, you don't have ex-lovers!" It was like I was missing my right arm.

Once, when divorce was uncommon, we could not imagine that blended families were viable, yet now they are a routine part of the family landscape. Stepfamilies can be immensely challenging, but we understand that each one has to find its own way, has to figure out what arrangements work for them. Because we know the potential harm to children when divorced parents stay embattled, we can believe that close ties between ex-es may be good for children.

With extended lesbian families, one has to side-step normative assumptions. Listening to Zoe's sense of betrayal, I feel empathy. Listening to Jennifer's fears of altering her relationship with Marsha, I also feel empathy. Zoe insists that Jennifer's relationship with Marsha reflects a lack of faithfulness to her. I ask, "How? Are there specific problems?" Then we try to work from there.

Human-Made Boundaries

By holding each woman's subjective experience in the therapy office, I implicitly say that both views are respectable ones. Somewhere in the course of therapy, I let them know that complicated family systems can work, with effort and commitment. Lesbian couples need mirroring and validation by therapists even more than heterosexual ones do, because they do not find it in the broader culture. It's for them to decide if this arrangement must change or if it's ultimately untenable.

Rigid notions of the proper boundaries around a relationship—a favorite concept of therapists and lesbians alike—are not helpful. Boundaries are human-made things, not givens, and not permanently fixed. What's allowed inside and what must be kept outside can change as life changes. The notion of infidelity is fundamentally tied to that of boundaries and, as I keep asserting here, is defined by both personal and social contexts. It involves breaking faith. The question of faith to what, lies at the heart. Which brings us to the question of what an affair is, in the emotional sense.

EMOTIONAL "AFFAIRS"

An Intimate Friendship

Some women have friendships of great emotional depth outside of their primary relationship. A woman may have a friend who's so close that her partner feels threatened or jealous. It does not matter that the friendship is non-sexual, the knowledge that one's lover is really close to someone else—possibly including feelings of attraction, admitted or not—can feel like infidelity. Yet lesbian culture has generated an acceptance of friendships like these.

Women's history, from centuries back, has included "romantic friendships." Smith-Rosenberg's (1975) now-classic study of letters between women, *The Female World of Love and Ritual: Relations Between Women in the Nineteenth Century*, reveals astonishing confessions of love, passion, and intimacy between women who were surely never lovers—in fact most of them were married. Yet these friendships involved long visits with each other, sometimes displacing husbands even from the marriage bed. This tradition of intimacy and strong emotion in friendship reflects women's acculturation. It may also reflect something innate in women or a consequence of our family structures. For whatever reasons, both heterosexual and lesbian women have friendships that occupy a place of prominence in their lives, friendships that in some ways seem to come first or at least affect their availability to partners at times.

Husbands may find these friendships perplexing, relieving (fewer emotional demands on them!), or threatening. But the threat is rarely sexual; it's not equivalent to the threat of a lover. In a lesbian relationship the line is not so clear. Although there may be no sexual transgressing, the possibility cannot be ruled out. Even without that, partners feel justified in being jealous. It *feels* like an affair, an emotional affair.

An Example of Intimate Friendship

When Ruth and Lucie came to therapy they had been together twenty-four years, long evidence of their commitment to each other. They had raised a daughter, now a sophomore in college, owned two homes, and shared each other's good and bad times with parents and siblings. Ruth is a nurse on an intensive neo-natal unit where infants do not always survive. Her work is demanding and sometimes traumatic. She's very close to Roxy, another neo-natal nurse who shares the emotional stress of that work. Roxy is also a lesbian. Ruth and Roxy get together frequently for a drink or a meal. They spend time on the phone with each other. They go skiing and cycling together.

Lucie is in the third year of developing her own business. She works long hours when clients need her, but there are also lulls when she's not busy. She's grown to dislike Ruth's friendship with Roxy more and more. Sometimes Lucie has to schedule her time with Ruth around Roxy's plans.

It's clear to her that Ruth and Roxy share interests she and Ruth do not
have. What's hardest is that Ruth never argues with Roxy the way she does
with her.

Ruth thinks Lucie is unnecessarily jealous of Roxy. She and Roxy do not
find it easy to make social plans, because both of their partners keep raising
objections. Lucie does not love long intimate talks; Roxy does. Lucie does
not like sports; Roxy does. Ruth no longer presses Lucie to do those things
with her because Roxy will do them. Shouldn't Lucie be relieved? She
insists there's nothing sexual between her and Roxy and never will be. She
wants Lucie to trust her and to be more generous about her time with Roxy.

The blurred lines between lovers and friends may be confusing. Weston
writes:

> When I asked interview participants if they were currently involved
> in a relationship, a few were uncertain how to answer. Of those who
> hesitated, the women wondered whether they should count primary
> emotional bonds as relationships in the absence of sexual involve-
> ment, while the men wondered whether to include routinized sexual
> relationships that lacked emotional depth and commitment. (1991:
> 140)

Lucie may trust Ruth, may believe Ruth will not sleep with Roxy, but the
friendship occupies the same place an affair might, and it stirs up similar
feelings. She senses competition between herself and Roxy. In *After the
Affair*, Spring (1996: 56) writes:

> [W]omen have affairs to experience an emotional connection they feel
> is lacking in their primary relationship. They stray in search of a soul-
> mate, someone who pays attention to their feelings and encourages
> meaningful conversation. . . . Women who stray often develop a close
> friendship with their lovers before they become sexually involved.

Intimate friendships do sometimes turn into affairs. The threat can never
be completely dismissed. On the other hand, sometimes lesbian couples
value intimate friendships as a stabilizing force rather than a threatening
one because friendships keep the primary relationship balanced. Many
writers observe an internal pull in lesbian relationships: they can be so
relationship-centered that a sense of fusion develops between the women.
At first fusion is welcomed, but eventually it becomes it's own problem,

stifling individuality and eroticism (cf. Burch, 1997). Relationships that do not tolerate outside friendships may then be suspect.

A friendship can do both at the same time, of course, balancing the primary relationship even while it competes with it. Is that infidelity? Lucie does not feel legitimate protesting a friendship. It makes her look possessive, even to herself. But she senses a risk that cannot be fully denied. Even if Ruth and Roxy are never more than friends, Lucie knows there is some kind of intimacy between them that she and Ruth do not share. That alone is very, very painful. Her jealousy is understandable.

Even without sex, the friendship is compelling for Ruth. It also highlights what's lacking with Lucie. In that sense, is it as symptomatic of problems as an affair would be? Or is it just a natural outcome of a woman's tendency to seek closeness and intensity in friendships? Or perhaps a consequence of the inevitable limits of primary relationships?

Every couple holds its own tacit or explicit understanding of what their relationship should be. Will they be a tightly knit, best friends, intimate-in-all-ways couple? Do they tolerate, even prefer, a degree of independence or emotional distance? How do they value romance, passion, and sexuality? Might they be good companions but perhaps not so passionate? Will they be career-bound, putting the relationship second to work? Do they tolerate conflict, keep important outside friendships, hold close relations with extended family, or not? Do they want children? Are children their primary bond? The work of a relationship requires sorting out these unnamed concerns.

FOREVER ALTERED

Breaking Faith

Having advocated for a loose understanding of infidelity in lesbian relationships, I also want to recognize what is the same in all relationships. Infidelity means breaking faith. However it's defined, breaking faith in a relationship causes intense pain, ongoing distrust, and anger. Healing is possible, under the right circumstances and with the right effort, but even with healing, the relationship is forever altered. That's the bad news and the good news. Usually something needed to change. Not by means of an affair of course—it's one of the worst ways to make change. But couples who survive may find deeper understanding, renewed trust, and revived intimacy, that is, they have a future ahead of them.

First task, though, is mourning the old, forever lost relationship. Some lines from a poem by Eloise Klein Healy expresses the way we hope this is not true, while we know it is:

> . . . Like that day,
> I was taking a shower
> with my lover and she told me
> she was sleeping with
> her ex-lover again. Wasn't
> a fire supposed to leap
> out of me, or wasn't water
> there to drown the flames,
> or wash her clean of betrayal?
> . . . Wasn't some wind going to blow
> those words away and leave us
> soapy and sweet smelling
> in that shower, just about to
> towel off, have a drink,
> cook dinner and read a little?
> Wasn't my love for her supposed to mean
> I could step into the same river
> over and over again?

The story of love and long-term relationship *is* one of hard times as much as of romance and happiness—news we keep resisting. In many years of practice, I have never seen a long-term relationship, gay or straight, that did not also have at least one long period of crisis—a really difficult struggle and a time of deep unhappiness. Many have more than one. These crises are a crucible in which the couple learns whether they are still viable, whether what they have together is worth it. They will end the relationship there or they will go on, perhaps more securely or perhaps with scar tissue, but definitely altered. It's the part of the story usually left out.

Because human relationships are difficult, and long-term intimacy especially so, we are poorly prepared for them by a popular culture that suggests love is all there is. Many couples who have faced an affair are convinced that they *should not* go on. They believe theirs is a fundamentally flawed relationship. Consider Sarah and Mickie, who came to therapy after Mickie confessed to Sarah that she had had an affair. It was a stunning disclosure. Sarah idealized their relationship: both of them were honest, sensitive, open, devoted, or so she thought. How was it possible that Mickie had deceived her so completely? Did it mean their relationship was a sham?

Surviving Betrayals

Mickie and Sarah were both very involved with their church. Sarah had even returned to graduate school to prepare as a minister. Between work and classes she did not spend much time at home. Mickie was lonely. Her only protest about Sarah's absence came as complaint that she carried too much of the responsibility for the house, the cars, and the cooking. Ultimately she decided it was a reasonable imbalance, given the demands on Sarah's time. To fill her empty hours she spent a lot of time with the women's group at the church. Sarah realized Mickie was getting close with Anna, another woman in the group, but she was mostly relieved. She felt guilty for being away so much.

After Sarah finished school it became clear that Sarah's lack of focus at home had hurt more than their division of labor. Slowly they began talking about Mickie's disappointments. Sarah noticed that Mickie no longer went to the women's group and did not see Anna any more. Mickie shrugged this off at first, then finally admitted she and Anna had had an affair that ended when Sarah finished school. Sarah was stunned. An affair seemed completely out of character for Mickie. She was furious with her and felt a painful loss of innocence. She did not think good people did things like that. Mickie's guilt and remorse, her willingness to listen to Sarah's feelings in the first weeks after the disclosure, were extremely helpful.

The meaning of the affair has been difficult for both of them: not simply that Mickie felt abandoned and Sarah felt betrayed, but that their way of dealing with things was to sweep trouble nobly aside. The hard work of recovery for this couple was to accept the tarnishing of their ideals of relationship. Emotional honesty seemed hurtful to them so they avoided it. The irony of that view is apparent, yet they still resisted the discomfort. After a long period of work together, which helped them tolerate more honesty and conflict, they became closer and more sexually intimate than they had been before the affair.

The difficult passage through infidelity is perhaps the same for all couples, even if the definition varies. There's pain, the potential for rupture, the possibility of recovery. Whatever else infidelity means to a couple, it means broken faith. It means the necessity of restoring faith in another form if they are to survive.

REFERENCES

Becker, C. *Unbroken Ties: Lesbian Ex-Lovers*. Boston: Alyson Publications, 1988.

Benkov, L. *Reinventing the Family: The Emerging Story of Lesbian and Gay Parents*. New York: Crown Publishers, 1994.

Blumstein, P. and P. Schwartz. *American Couples*. New York: Wm. Morrow, 1983.

Burch, B. *On Intimate Terms: The Psychology of Difference in Lesbian Relationships*. Chicago: University of Illinois Press, 1993.

Burch, B. *Other Women: Lesbian/Bisexual Experience and Psychoanalytic Views of Women*. New York: Columbia University Press, 1997.

Healy, E. K. "The Elements." In *The Islands Project: Poems for Sappho*. Los Angeles: Red Hen Press, 2007: 48–49.

Smith-Rosenberg, C. "The Female World of Love and Ritual: Relations ?Betweex0n Women in Nineteenth-Century America." *Signs,* 1(1), 1975: 1–30.

Spring, J. A. *After the Affair*. New York: Harper Collins, 1996.

Weston, K. *Families We Choose: Lesbians, Gays, Kinship*. New York: Columbia University Press, 1991.

Just Molly and Me, and Donor Makes Three: Lesbian Motherhood in the Age of Assisted Reproductive Technology

Diane Ehrensaft

SUMMARY. The psychological experiences of lesbian mothers, both coupled and single, are compared and contrasted with heterosexual and gay parents who use assisted reproductive technology, focusing on issues of parental desire, fertility, babies conceived from science rather than sex, presence of an outside party in conception, genetic asymmetry, social anxieties, legal protections, disclosure, and gender. The psychological meaning of the donor or surrogate as an "extra" and "missing" piece of the family, along with the interactive effects of homophobia and "reproductive technophobia" are considered. Lesbian families are recognized to be constructing a new narrative of a bio-social family as they define and live their experience.

Diane Ehrensaft, Ph.D., is the author of *Mommies, Daddies, Donors, Surrogates* (Guilford Press, 2005), her fourth book about parenting. She has a private practice in Oakland, California, and has served on the faculty of The Wright Institute, and the Psychoanalytic Institute of Northern California. She is on the editorial board of the journal *Studies in Gender and Sexuality.*

Over a century ago, in 1884, Dr. William Pancoast performed the first donor insemination in the United States on a comatose woman, who was never informed of the insemination. She and her husband were having difficulty conceiving. The doctor discovered the father was infertile as a result of gonorrhea from a past liaison. Upon the suggestion of a medical student, the doctor appealed to his students, with a contest among them for the best looking, to donate their sperm. Under the pretense of performing a gynecological procedure, Dr. Pancoast gave this mother the child she was waiting for—made by her and the first documented sperm donor. Although the father was eventually informed by Dr. Pancoast, the mother was never to know that her husband was not the genetic father of their child (Henig, 2004). Throughout the following century reproductive medicine continued to offer donor insemination to infertile heterosexual couples, this time with full disclosure to both husband and wife but often with secrecy to the outside world. Now, as the twenty-first century has rolled in, we are witnessing a sea change in the cohort of parents who have turned to donor insemination and newer forms of assisted reproductive technology, including donor eggs, surrogacy, gestational carriers, and embryo adoption, to build their families. One of the fastest growing segments of this new cohort are women who have absolutely nothing wrong with their bodies but are missing a body to have a baby with—that would be lesbian couples and lesbian single women. As Vaughn points out (2006), we are in the midst of a gayby boom: 25% of same sex couples have children, 47% of female couples, and 22% of male couples. Those in the gayby boom who have turned to assisted reproductive technology to have their children, along with their heterosexual single mother and more recently single father counterparts, have forced the world of reproductive medicine to re-examine its practices and have been responsible for ushering in more progressive, expansive family-friendly policies, such as identity release programs that allow donor offspring the opportunity to contact their donors, rather than live their lives within a genealogical void.

As all the revolutionary reproductive activity has been unfolding, we may have overlooked a critical piece of this radical transformation in family life. While the medical field has forged ahead beyond the informal practices of turkey basters and baggies of sperm, both the legal and mental health fields have chased behind, breathless in their struggles to make quick, unprecedented legal decisions and to develop psychological understanding of the experience of "Molly and me, and donor makes three" or alternatively, "Molly and me and baby makes three or four or more."

While I will make reference to some of the legal conundrums of the assisted reproductive technology lesbian family, my main intent in this discussion is to focus our attention on the psychological experiences of lesbians who came of age with the belief that motherhood would be denied them and have now discovered that with the help of assisted reproductive technology, they, too, can become mothers with children biologically related to themselves, to their partner (if they have one), or to both of them, as in egg mommy, womb mommy families.

THE BIRTH OTHER

I will be talking about women who have included a "birth other" in their family building. Let me explain. In typing up notes on surrogacy, I discovered a typo—I had typed in "birth other" when I meant "birth mother" (Ehrensaft, 2005). For months I had been struggling to find a singular word to refer to the outside party who either donates gametes or allows her womb to be used so that another individual or individuals can have a baby of their own. These outside parties would include sperm donors, egg donors, surrogates, and gestational carriers. I objected to a term that would include the word "mother" or "father," as I felt these terms should be reserved for the people who intended to have the baby, not the people who helped make the baby. Thus, far better than "birth mother," birth other seemed a fine solution, an "other," either male or female, who helps someone else have a child. So I want to pose two questions about lesbian families, "What are the psychological and social effects of having a birth other involved in building one's family, both for the mothers and for the children?" and "How are the experiences of lesbian birth other families the same and how are they different from heterosexual birth other families?" I will be specifically addressing the tensions surrounding genetic asymmetry between biological and non-biological mothers and the psychological defenses called into play in accommodating to the presence of a birth other. I would like to share what I have learned from twenty plus years of documenting my clinical work with gay and lesbian families as well as heterosexual birth other families in my roles as parent consultant, family therapist, individual therapist to both parents and children, mediator, custody evaluator, and expert witness to the court.

UNTO US A CHILD IS BORN

A Family's Narrative

David is a child from a divorced lesbian family. He was conceived with the sperm of an anonymous donor found informally through the mothers' social networks. Later, by accident, due to the seemingly zero degrees of separation in the local gay and lesbian community, this man was identified to the mothers as David's donor, but he has no relationship with the family. David has an older brother, Joshua, to whom he has no genetic ties. Joshua was conceived with the help of a known donor, Fred, a gay friend of Sylvia's, one of the mothers. Fred has stepped in to be more than a donor, but rather a father to both Joshua, his biological son, and David, to whom he has no biological relationship. By fluke, Fred is actually an acquaintance of David's donor. Sylvia is the biological mother of Joshua. Natalie is the biological mother of David. Natalie has legally adopted Joshua, but Sylvia has not adopted David, as Sylvia and Natalie's relationship began to deteriorate during Natalie's pregnancy and terminated when David was only five months old. It is daunting to explain all this, let alone expect a reader to hold all its complexity in mind. Yet David and his family live seamlessly within this gay and lesbian family in a fertile new world.

I began seeing David when he was five, when he was not having a good go of it in kindergarten. It is now eight years later and I have been invited to attend his Bar Mitzvah ceremony. On the bema to celebrate with him are his two mothers, his non-biological maternal grandmother (Sylvia's mother), his non-biological father and his non-biological grandfather, Fred's father. His biological grandparents on Natalie's side are deceased. While Fred is the only one who explicitly addresses the "alternative" nature of their family in his Bar Mitzvah blessings to David, all of his three parents independently highlight David's Jewish heritage and the family legacy he carries from his three parents' Jewish ancestors. His donor is not Jewish. David in his Bar Mitzvah speech offers a moving tribute to his grandfather, Fred's father, a holocaust survivor approaching 100 years old and still running his own small shul. I, too, am Jewish, and, as I listen to the prayers and blessings, I reflect on the strong emphasis placed on bloodlines in my religion and culture. Yet I watch David's family weave together a moving tale of Jewish family heritage that overrides biological ties and makes no mention of the "missing piece" of David's lineage—the non-Jewish bloodline of his sperm donor. Regarding David's own thoughts and feelings about his blood ties, he has over time expressed only one strong desire: to have come from Dad's (Fred's) sperm like his brother did.

The Psychological Journey of Two Women, a Birth Other, and a Baby

I share this story with you because I find it emblematic of the complicated and innovative psychological journey that unfolds when two women fall in love and decide to have children together. Sylvia and Natalie's two children were brought into the world not by an act of sexual intercourse, but by a scientific joining of egg and sperm that does not equate with a union between a mother and a father. Neither of them initially intended to have a father in their family; they conceived of themselves as a two-mother family. Fred never intended to be a father, just a friend who would help two women have a baby. Yet when Joshua was born, his feelings changed. Where other mothers in Sylvia and Natalie's situation might have felt threatened by Fred's change of heart, experiencing it as the aggressive act of an uninvited interloper, Sylvia and Natalie embraced Fred as a welcome addition to their family, as long as it was clear that they, the two mothers, were the primary parents. Unfortunately, the two mothers did not have the same easy time embracing each other. Natalie at first felt insecure and unacknowledged as Joshua's non-biological mother. When it came time for her to take a turn birthing a child, Fred was no longer interested in being a donor, so she had to look elsewhere to find a donor for David. While Natalie was pregnant, Sylvia grew resentful of Natalie's diminished interest in Joshua; at the same time, Natalie felt pangs of jealousy that Joshua would always know his donor while her unborn child never would. When David was finally born Sylvia found Natalie's "maternal preoccupation" unbearable. Soon after, they separated. Herein lie all of the stresses of genetic asymmetry, genealogical bewilderment (not having access to half the child's genetic history), maternal competition, and the resultant challenges of building a hybrid bio-social family that can tear a lesbian birth other family apart.

Yet the story is not just one of anguish but also one of growth and creativity. Let us return to David's Bar Mitzvah day. A Bar Mitzvah marks the day that a Jewish boy establishes a new identity (as a man). In David's case, his identity embraces the experience of a boy who has grown up with two mothers in two different households, one his genetic and legal mother, the other his non-biological and non-legal mother; a donor who he may never meet; a social father who is his brother's genetic father but not his; and a brother to whom he has no genetic ties and lives with only part of each week. His identity includes a narrative of origins in which he was not the product of sexual intercourse between a man and a woman but was conceived from science rather than sex, an insemination that took place in a doctor's office. Although their romantic ties were broken, both Sylvia and Natalie were still able to build a "family matrix" for David and his brother that interwove genetic and social ties, as reflected in their collective acknowledgement of David's Jewish heritage. As we now move on to explore the psychological issues outlined in the introduction, I would like us to hold in mind David's Bar Mitzah tale as we consider the following question: In defining their familial relationship to David and David's relationship to his origins, is David's family creating for him a mythical tale of family heritage that grossly denies the reality of his full genetic history, or are his two mothers liberating themselves (and us) to operate within a shifting paradigm that privileges social ties over blood ties and creates space for same-sex families to be visible and legitimized?

WE ARE THE SAME, WE ARE DIFFERENT

Lesbian families who turn to assisted reproductive technology to have babies have become strange bedfellows with heterosexual families who have turned to assisted reproductive technology as a result of primary or secondary infertility. Anyone who uses a birth other to build a family, regardless of sexual orientation, gender, or marital/partnered status, will hold in common several vital components of parenthood.

Commonalities

First comes the overarching and vibrant desire to have a child. Historically, both lesbians and infertile men and women were expected to cut their losses and come to terms with the fact that they would never have children of their own, the first group because they lacked a body to conceive with (and also were perceived, and still are among some, to be unfit to be parents); the second group because they had a broken body that could not conceive. The advances in reproductive medicine have removed that barrier and afforded anyone who has damage to their body or anyone who is missing a body with whom to conceive the opportunity to become parents to genetically related or biologically related children. Whereas all parents celebrate the birth of their children, the strength of the desire for children may be heightened and fortified for all birth other families both by the newfound opportunity and by the extra steps that need to be taken to hold that "bundle of joy" in their arms.

The second commonality of all birth other families is that each of their children will be conceived by a scientific procedure rather than a sexual union. Jody Messler Davies wrote about the erotic feelings that surface in psychotherapy: "Each of us is conceived out of the desire of two significant others" (1998: 810). If Davies is referencing the erotic desire that culminates in a sexual union, this statement is outmoded. Instead, the amended quote, taking into account alternative forms of conception, should read, "Each of us is conceived out of the desire of one or more people and possibly the assistance of one or more people who participated in our conception or gestation not out of sexual desire but out of the willingness to provide use of their uterus or to donate their gametes so that we could be born." Any parent who has used a donor, surrogate, or gestational carrier to have a child will live and breathe this expanded statement. They will hold in mind that their child will not conform to the "old-fashioned" narrative of origins and they themselves will not conform to the "old-fashioned" story of first comes love, then comes sexual intercourse, and then comes baby.

These "new-fangled" ways of having children generate a level of social anxiety or outright hostility that may need to be confronted by any person who turns to a donor, surrogate, or gestational carrier to conceive or gestate their child. I have dubbed these negative feelings "reproductive technophobia" (Ehrensaft, 2005), and have come to understand that such attitudes emanate not just from the external world but also from the internalized discomfort and dis-ease within parents themselves as they experience, either consciously or unconsciously, shame, guilt, or angst about their "alternative" means of conception.

In those households that are *two*-parent families, the two parenting partners, along with their children, may also confront the reality of genetic asymmetry. One of the parents will have a genetic link with their child; the other parent will not. Even in lesbian families where one mother donates her egg and the baby gestates in the other mother's womb, genetic asymmetry cannot be circumvented. The field of reproductive medicine speaks from both sides of its mouth when it comes to the issue of genetics. On the one hand they join with prospective parents in advocating that genetic links are so important that many dollars and medical interventions are worth the investment to have a genetically linked child of one's own. On the other hand, they assume that genetics will have no import as they collect sperm or extract eggs from the birth others who are expected to go home and live their own lives without a thought to the genetic progeny they have helped create, or as they tell the non-genetic parents to give it not a second thought that the child will not be genetically theirs. All two-parent birth other families, regardless of gender or sexual orientation, must deal with the complexity of this paradoxical "genes matter/genes don't" as they attempt a balancing act of acknowledging the legitimacy of the non-genetic parent while warding off the tugs-of-war that may ensue when one parent feels the baby more his or hers as a result of genetic ties.

Most importantly, what binds all parents together if they have turned to a donor, surrogate, or gestational carrier to have a child is that there will be by definition the presence of an outside person in their family narrative who is not a parent but who contributed gametes or womb so that they could have a child. These people are more than a vial of sperm or a dish of eggs; they are real men and women with feelings, motivations, and thoughts of their own. Regardless of whether that person is known or unknown to the family, the birth other will inevitably enter the minds of both the parents and the children in any birth other family, a reality that, as we will discuss shortly, can both enrich and complicate, enhance and intrude upon family life.

Uniqueness of Lesbian Birth Other Families

With commonalities established, I now want to highlight the uniqueness of the lesbian birth other family. Although lesbian families may find themselves sharing the waiting room at the fertility clinic or sperm bank with their heterosexual counterparts, their countenance may be one of celebration rather than anxiety or distress. That is because many of the lesbian clientele are coming to the clinic not as a second choice or last chance effort after facing the painful reality of infertility; instead, they may feel celebratory in their newfound ability to create families of their own in ways heretofore unavailable to them. There may be nothing wrong with their bodies (although lesbian women are not exempt from the vagaries and toils of infertility); they are just missing a body, or more specifically, a body's product, with which to conceive a baby. It is not that heterosexual infertile patients are not also buoyed up by the chance to transcend their bodies' malfunctioning in the arena of reproduction; it is just that those people may simultaneously be feeling the weight of mourning and loss after years of trying desperately to claim something they always thought to be their birthright—the opportunity to bear or sire a child of their own. So if you want to pick out the lesbians (or gay men) in the waiting room of a clinic, pay attention to who is smiling the most.

The exemption of many lesbian birth other families from the pain of infertility is tempered by the troubling double exposure of birth other families to both reproductive technophobia *and* homophobia. There are many in this society who do not believe that gay men and lesbians should become parents and will go to extremes to prevent them from doing so. For example, some fertility clinics refuse to offer donor conception services to gay or lesbian families, and, until recently, no federal guidelines, constitutional directives, or legal statutes existed to prevent these private agencies from banning gays and limiting their services to heterosexual married couples. If we combine those homophobic attitudes with the queasy or hostile attitudes of many toward reproductive techniques that tamper with Mother Nature, the lethal combination can range from annoying to destructive for the mothers and children who are assaulted, either subtly or frontally, with such prejudice. If left untreated, the interactive effects of homophobia and reproductive technophobia can compromise both positive identity formation in the children and mothers' confidence in their capacity to provide a safe and supportive environment for their children. Conversely, it can build resilience as parents and children come together to establish pride in their families and learn strategies to handle those who would deny them that.

In recent years more attention has been paid to cutting-edge techniques that may allow people to conceive with skin cells or other non-reproductive tissue and at its extreme, afford people the opportunity to create clones of themselves. At the present time, however, lesbian couples are the only families in existence who can combine the biology of both parents to create two same-gender biological parents: One mother can extract her eggs to be placed in the womb of the other mother for gestation, after an in-vitro fertilization with sperm from a donor. The child born will bear a biological relationship with each of her parents, one as her gestational mother, the other as her genetic mother. Ironically, as so poignantly and painfully exposed in the recent court case of E.G. and K.M. that was finally settled in the California Supreme Court (Egelko, 2005), at this moment in history the womb mother will be awarded more legal legitimacy than the egg mother, but if we take it out of a court of law into an intact lesbian family's home, the egg mother/womb mother combination becomes a transcendent strategy that allows their particular assisted reproductive technology family the opportunity to create a new kind of biological parenting partnership.

Heterosexual families are often plagued by the decision as to whether or not to disclose to their children. Historically, donor insemination was established in a veil of secrecy. Doctors afforded infertile men the opportunity to become fathers without anyone, even their own children, ever needing to know that the men were shooting blanks. This veil of secrecy continues to shroud the thinking of many reproductive specialists and their heterosexual clientele. Lesbian families, along with their gay brethren, have no choice but to explain to their children how they came to be. There is no veil to hide behind. The policy directive put forth by the American Society for Reproductive Medicine that states that it is in the best interests of a child to be informed of his or her donor conception (Ethics Committee, ASRM, 2004) is no new stance for lesbian families. This is not to say that the telling does not come with its own set of conundrums and confusions about what to say and when, and how to correct for children's misconceptions (no pun intended). Rather, the agonizing decision, "To tell or not to tell," is not one with which lesbians ever have to contend—in the context of present reproductive realities, they will have to tell their children *something* about from whence they came.

Lesbians may be free from disclosure dilemmas; but the trade-off is that they do not have the same protection from unwanted intrusion that heterosexual couples have. Presently, the legal system offers few protections to lesbian families. There are no boilerplate parenting agreements offered to prospective parents outlining the roles and legal rights of all the parties involved in creating a family. The policies at the fertility clinics are typically designed with heterosexual, not lesbian, families in mind, as when clinics ask an egg donor to sign away her parenting rights and do not take into consideration those lesbian families in which the egg donor has every intention of being a mother, along with her womb mother partner. Further, because the assisted reproductive procedures are at their most informal among lesbian partners—a turkey baster and baggie may be all that one needs—there are no legal statutes, guidelines, or monitoring to assure that the birth other will remain just that, and not come later to establish rights as a parent. In that regard, lesbian families have the least protection against the unwanted intruder in their family life: the donor who comes like Rumplestiltskin to claim their child as his own.

Here is a case in point. A lesbian couple of many years decided they wanted to have a baby. They approached a co-worker of one of the women, a gay man in a couple, and invited him to be their donor. He agreed. Without legal counsel (regretfully), they decided to put his name on the birth certificate. All the while they saw him only as a donor and intended for the non-biological mother to adopt their baby. But then some months into the child's first year, the donor put a stop to that process, claiming he was the father, the other legal parent. He went to court and demanded visitation rights. He blocked the non-biological mother's adoption. He claimed his intent was always to be this baby's father. The court, believing every child needs a father, awarded him legal parentage and visitation rights. The two mothers never intended to co-parent with this man. As far as they were concerned, their little girl already had two parents—her two mommies. They felt their life had been torn asunder by this conniving kidnapper coming to claim his child. They went on to have a second child, this time with the other mother as biological mother, and the choice of an anonymous donor who would always remain just that. A heterosexual couple would have been protected from such unwelcome intrusion by the donor, as the husband would automatically appear on the birth certificate as the other legal parent, regardless of the participation of a sperm donor in their child's conception. The lesbian family has no such assured protections.

Lesbian vs. Gay Birth Other Families

Lesbian birth mothers are unique in contrast to their heterosexual counterparts, but how about in contrast to their gay brethren, who in increasing numbers are also becoming fathers with the advent of gestational surrogacy programs? Historically, lesbians repudiated the prescribed roles of wife and mother in their revolt against cultural standards of femininity. With a move from binary gender to gender fluidity and with the availability of both adoption and assisted reproductive technology services, lesbians are now freer to claim motherhood as their own. Gay men historically repudiated monogamy and fatherhood as they sowed their wild oats as sexually active single men. That has changed. For the same reason that lesbians now embrace motherhood, gay men are increasingly claiming their rights to fatherhood. To that end, gay men have had to convince the outside world that there can be a primary parent who is *not* a woman (Friedman, 2006). In contrast, lesbian couples have had to prove that a child can have two primary mothers, not just one, and that they do not need a father. Gay two-parent families are missing a mother. Lesbian two-parent families have too many.

YOURS, OURS, OR MINE

Genetic Asymmetry

I now want to focus on the significance of genetic asymmetry in lesbian two-parent birth other families—one mother in a couple is a genetic parent whereas the other is not. Many people refer to the non-genetic mother as the "other mother." This term reveals the privilege given to the genetic mother and comes with the subtle innuendo that the non-genetic mother is not closer in, but rather further out—other, implying more psychologically distant. In fact, the outside world and lesbian couples themselves often find themselves privileging the genetic mother as more "real." Until recently this was supported by the law, with non-genetic mothers holding no parenting rights unless they formally adopted, which is still not possible in many states in the United States. Many lesbian couples can transcend this genetic asymmetry that privileges the genetic over the non-genetic mother by avoiding parental hierarchy and making a full commitment to shared and equal motherhood, irrespective of biological ties. But others are taken aback as the non-genetic mother begins to feel like a "birth nobody," the genetic mother unconsciously or subliminally privileges herself as the "primary" parent, and both feel triangulated by the presence of the birth other, the sperm donor who has created a "union" with one of the mothers, but not the other. It is a phenomenon of "Are you mine?" in dialectical tension with "Mine more than yours."

Miranda and Rachel have come to me to seek out therapy for their seven-year-old daughter, Sophie. The therapy was court-mandated, following an arduous custody battle after the two mothers split up. Miranda is Sophie's genetic mother. Sophie was conceived with sperm from a known donor. Rachel, Sophie's non-biological mother, was involved in meeting the donor and was present at the insemination. When Sophie was born, Miranda became a stay-at-home mom and Rachel, a physician, became the full-time breadwinner. Rachel never adopted Sophie. By Rachel's report, she just never got around to it and Miranda kept pushing the issue of adoption aside. According to Miranda, Miranda already knew the relationship was doomed to failure by the time Sophie was born and there was no way she was going to let Rachel adopt "her" child. When Sophie was six years old, the two women finally separated, after years of acrimonious tension. Rachel filed for parenting rights. Miranda objected. It went to court soon after the three 2005 California Supreme Court decisions came out that granted parenting rights to lesbian parents who had intended to have a child with their partner and then went on to raise that child, regardless of genetic ties to the child. On the basis of that recent legal precedent, Rachel was granted full parentage of Sophie, as she fit all the stipulated qualifications: As Miranda's long-term partner, she was involved in baby-planning and then participated in the daily care of Sophie within the same household as Miranda for six plus years. In the face of the court's ruling, Rachel was ecstatic, Miranda apoplectically chagrined.

From Miranda's point of view, Sophie now had no home, had been ripped away from the primary mother she knew and needed, and was exhibiting severe signs of depression and anxiety. As far as Rachel was concerned, Sophie was doing fine, could not be doing better—the only problem was Miranda's overwrought clinginess to Sophie. They continue to dispute the custody arrangement. Rachel would like more time, as much as Miranda has with their daughter. Miranda feels Rachel already has far more time than is in Sophie's best interests, particularly because Miranda has always been Sophie's primary caretaker and Rachel had functioned more like a traditional dad, absorbed in work and around only late evenings and weekends. As for Sophie, *her* main preoccupation is terminating the life of Miranda's new lover's son—"He's mean, I hate him, and he gets his clothes washed with mine—Yuck!" As for what Sophie wants for her custody arrangement, "the same, the same with each mom—five days, five days, five days, five days." One mother's parade is the other mother's funeral procession, as the child marches on.

Laying Claim to the Children

Miranda and Rachel's story is emblematic of the often-unanticipated tensions and conflicts women may go through as they struggle to share mothering. Blood ties may trump social bonds as the mothers find themselves vying for first place in a parent–child attachment competition with each other. In this regard, the two mothers may be no different than heterosexual couples who set out to share equally in the task of parenting and find themselves unexpectedly in a tug-of-war, with the mothers in particular feeling edgy about relinquishing their "maternal preoccupation" to the fathers of their children (Ehrensaft, 1987). The difference is that the heterosexual mothers and fathers' fight for first place may be held in check by the fact that both parents are the legal and genetic parents of the children and that laws are in place to keep them both in line if one or the other attempts to take the baby and run. Lesbian couples have no such automatic protections. Some of the contentious and painful battles between divorced lesbian mothers over custody of the children, where the legal mother bars access of the non-legal mother to their child and rewrites history to negate the non-legal mother's parenting status as parent, would most likely be routinely replicated by heterosexual divorcing parents if only the law allowed them get away with it.

The competition about "possession" and legitimacy as a mother is most saliently highlighted in divorced lesbian families, but it may also be present in intact lesbian families where both mothers are committed to acknowledging each other as mothers and to building a family together. In this regard, lesbian families share the same tensions that may surface in heterosexual families that have genetic asymmetry as a result of using a birth other to build their families. "Are you mine?" or "Are you mine more than hers?" are gnawing questions that can surface in the subtlest of ways. A newly walking baby tumbles over and cries, a non-genetic, non breast-feeding mother picks him up to comfort him. The child's genetic, breast-feeding mother then rushes over and begins rubbing their son's back. Soon she is enwrapping herself around their son and gently disengaging him from the non-genetic mother's arms as she takes him over to the rocking chair to comfort him by suckling him at her breast. The non-genetic mother stands empty-handed. We have just witnessed a subtle privileging of blood ties over love ties as the genetic mother inserts herself as the primary comforter of the child. The conscious rationale that the child needs soothing at the breast can obfuscate a deeper psychological reality: One mother implicitly feels herself to be "more" of the mother; the other has to vie for her position to be one.

Being Versus Being in Two-Mother Families

Comparing lesbian to gay families, the tensions over "mine, yours, or ours" may be more intense between two mothers than two fathers in birth other families, even though both sets of families will find themselves with genetic asymmetry and to date with few legal protections. In previous research interviewing men and women in intact families who were committed to sharing the care of their children, I found that, based on socially constructed gender socialization and perhaps the inevitable divide that women can get pregnant, birth, and breast-feed and men cannot, men *do* parenting, whereas women *are* parents (Ehrensaft, 1987). Using Winnicott's (1971) description of doing versus being, men more typically experienced parenting as a set of activities and tasks they did among other roles, particularly their work roles. Women, on the other hand, did not experience parenting as discrete acts they could do and then stop doing, but rather as a wall-to-wall experience that was at the soul of their being, no matter if they were with their children or apart from them. Although such binary gender divisions are often challenged by the developmental course and psychological experience of gay men and lesbian women, it has been my clinical experience that gender socialization may still trump sexual orientation in the gender-divided experience of being and doing. For example, in Johnny

Symons' moving film, *Beyond Conception* (2006), he follows the course of two men and a surrogate as they traverse from the choice of surrogate to the birth of their child. Notably, both fathers miss the actual birth of their child, even though the filmmakers, who had a further distance to travel, did not. We can wonder if this evidences the "doing" of parenthood by men, and we can wonder whether two mothers would have more likely made it on time for their child's birth by a surrogate. With that said, if we put two women together and make each of them mothers, the challenges of establishing parity for *both* mothers and creating space for both mothers to *be* mothers can be daunting. It would behoove lesbian couples who are building families to be apprised of this challenge in their effort to create a harmonious household in which both women can *be* mothers together. Such recognition will allow them to address the tensions generated by genetic asymmetry and by legal proscriptions that may disallow the non-genetic or non-birth mother from legal status as a parent.

"HONEY, I SHRUNK THE DONOR" PLAYS ALONGSIDE "FROM THIS BEAN A FATHER DID GROW"

Birth Other as Both Missing Piece and Extra Piece

Genetic asymmetry can link up with the presence of the "outsider," the birth other, to create a conundrum for the lesbian family. In families who use a sperm donor, that person simultaneously becomes an "extra" piece and a "missing" piece of the family. Two mothers have a baby. Their family feels complete. The donor, if perceived in any way as a father, as can happen through the reactions of the outside world or the queries or fantasies of the child him or herself ("Where's my daddy?"), may come to feel like an interloper who might come to claim his progeny. Sometimes this can actually happen, as in the much-publicized case of Young v. Steele, in which Thomas Steele, the donor to two mothers, Russo and Young, went to court to claim paternal rights to his daughter, Ry (cf., Dominus, 2004). Many mothers, to avoid the pain of the actual or fantasized man in their child's life, may deny the personhood of this "extra piece" by reducing him to a body part—there is no donor, only a vial of sperm.

Alternatively, there is the problem of lesbian couples or lesbian single mothers experiencing their family as having a "missing" part—a man who would be father, in answer to the children's or the outside world's persistent question, "So where's your daddy? Everyone has to have one" (Ehrensaft,

2000). The family narrative, "There are many different kinds of families, in our family there are two mommies (or one mommy)" offers assurance that there is no missing part and is an extremely helpful map for both the child and the outside world. Yet some families still find themselves inadvertently trying to create a "father" from whole cloth to compensate for a missing piece. Thus, Anonymous Donor #157 is transformed in both fantasy and family dialogue into "your wonderful father from whom you got your musical talent."

Both psychological strategies, "Honey, I shrunk the donor" and "From this bean a father did grow" can become a slippery slope toward "immaculate deception" fantasies. In such fantasies the reality of the child's origins is either denied or distorted, as when one lesbian mother-to-be insisted that she and her partner conceived their baby, no one else, as she was the one who brought the baggie of sperm to the insemination, kept warm under her armpit until they reached the doctor's office. Not just the mothers, but professional researchers and writers on the topic of lesbian families can engage in immaculate deception as they not only reduce the donor to a vial of sperm but ignore his existence completely in their discussion of lesbian families (cf. Tasker and Golombok, 1997, where there is not one mention made of the donor in discussing lesbian family life).

The Family Reverie

The family reverie, in which mothers and their children together share thoughts and fantasies about the donor, whether he is known or unknown, can counteract this slippery slope toward immaculate deception, allowing the thoughts and feelings about the donor to come to the light of day and providing an opportunity for him to be collectively recognized as a birth other, not a father, a man who is part of the family matrix because of his genetic ties to the child and his participation in building the family of two mothers and a child. There is a tendency among lesbian families to foreclose such fantasies once the baby is actually born, at which point the "nice" donor may be transformed in fantasy into the conniving kidnapper who must be kept at bay, lest he come to claim his rights as the missing father. If a donor begins to take on the form of "father," such transformation can be particularly threatening to the non-biological or non-legal mother. Even legal status as co-parent does not take away the threat that the "real" parent is not her, but rather the other genetic "parent," and that this intruder can provide what she cannot—a dad. Yet efforts to either sustain or resurrect such collective reveries once the child is born, rather than suppressing them, have been clinically demonstrated to strengthen rather than weaken attachments, build intimacy within the family, and protect against immaculate deception (Corbett, 2001). Finally, the family reveries serve a vital function for the child: They free the child to engage in his or her own internal imaginings that incorporate the donor as the child moves to individuate and establish his or her own positive personal identity as a birth other child.

CONCLUSION

I would like to conclude by returning to the question about David's two mothers—Are they creating mythical tales or positively reconstructing the social narrative of family in defining their family relationship? The concepts discussed in this article confirm the latter: As a gay and lesbian family, they are on the cutting edge of constructing, embracing, and pushing forward a new hybrid bio-social family, one that pertains not only to them but to any postmodern twenty-first-century family that blends social and genetic parenting. They will best do this if they can simultaneously address the tensions and challenges that accompany such family building, and hold in mind that there is no baby without the parents who plan for and care for the baby and the birth other or birth others who helped that baby come into being.

REFERENCES

Egelko, B. "Court Grants Equal Rights to Same-Sex Parents: Breaking Up Partnerships Doesn't End Parental Obligations." *San Francisco Chronicle*, August 23, 2005: A1.

Ethics Committee, American Society for Reproductive Medicine. "Informing Offspring of Their Conception by Gamete Donation." *Fertility and Sterility*, 81, 2004: 527–531.

Corbett, K. "Nontraditional Family Romance." *Psychoanalytic Quarterly,* 52, 2001: 599–624.

Davies, J. M. "Thoughts on the Nature of Desires: The Ambiguous, the Transitional, and the Poetic." Reply to Commentaries [on 'Between the disclosure and Foreclosure of Erotic Transference-Counter-Transference]. *Psychoanalytic Dialogues*, 8, 1998: 805–823.

Dominus, S. "Got a Problem with My Mothers?" *The New York Times Magazine,* October 24, 2004: 68–75, 84, 143–144.

Ehrensaft, D. *Parenting Together: Men and Women Sharing the Care of Their Children.* New York: The Free Press, 1987.

Ehrensaft, D. "Alternatives to the Stork: Fatherhood Fantasies in Donor Insemination Families." *Studies in Gender and Sexuality*, 1, 2000: 371–397.

Ehrensaft, D. *Mommies, Daddies, Donors, Surrogates: Answering Tough Questions and Building Strong Families*. New York: Guilford Press, 2005.

Friedman, C. *"First Comes Love, Then Comes Marriage, Then Comes BabyCarriage": Perspectives on Gay Parenting and Reproductive Technology*. Paper presented at a conference on Mothers and Fathers of Invention: Developing New Family Narratives, sponsored by Institute of Psychoanalytic Training and Research, Child and Adolescent Psychotherapy, October 23, 2006, New York, NY.

Henig, R.M.*Pandora's Baby: How the First Test Tube Babies Sparked the Reproductive Revolution*. Boston: Houghton Mifflin Company, 2004.

Symons, J. *Beyond Conception: Men Having Babies*. A Documentary Film, 2006.

Tasker, F. I., and S. Golombok. *Growing Up in a Lesbian Family.* New York: Guilford Press, 1997.

Vaughn, S. *Scrambled Eggs: Psychological Meanings of New Reproductive Choice for Lesbians*. Paper presented at conference on Mothers and Fathers of Invention: Developing New Family Narratives, sponsored by Institute of Psychoanalytic Training and Research, Child and Adolescent Psychotherapy, October 23, 2006, New York, NY.

Winnicott, D.W. *Playing and Reality*. London: Tavistock, 1971.

The Masculine Principle in Lesbian Families: A Jungian Understanding

Amy Weston

ABSTRACT. Using the concepts of individuation and masculine and feminine principles from Jungian psychology, the author explores the use of the masculine principle in parenting male children in families without an embodied father. The role of lesbian parents' own relationship with the masculine within themselves, features of the initiation process, and the function that team sports can play in a boy child's development are presented and examined. Lesbian parenting of sons is explored from both personal and professional perspectives.

Psychological androgyny, the balancing of masculine and feminine energies within each of us, has long held a fascination and a truth for me. Even as a child, the expansive possibilities inherent in an identity that included qualities associated with both genders seemed obvious and preferable. Thus, being a tomboy and coming out as lesbian each meant freedom to be more fully myself, albeit not without struggle.

Amy Weston, Ph.D., is a clinical psychologist in private practice, and a Jungian psychoanalyst. She is a member of the Berkeley Psychotherapy Institute and the C.G. Jung Institute of San Francisco, where she is on the teaching and supervising faculty. This article is a revision of a panel presentation on Homosexuality and the Archetype of the Father, given in June 2005 at the San Francisco Jung Institute.

Studying psychological androgyny in my dissertation and later becoming a Jungian psychoanalyst furthered my understanding. Then I became a mother of two very vigorous male beings, and theory had to become practice in brand new ways. My partner and I were faced with the challenge of how to parent our boys within a family structure that does not include an embodied father. My lived experience and my Jungian orientation led me to reframe the question to ask: How do lesbian families carry the masculine principle, in particular with regard to parenting youth? Some Jungian concepts have been central to my thinking about this question, and I will begin by describing them briefly.

INDIVIDUATION

Jung's (1951) concept of individuation offers all sexual minorities a compelling way to think about psychological development. Individuation is the realizing of one's fullest self (including a gay/lesbian self), where a person embraces their innermost uniqueness. When a person consciously attempts to understand and develop the innate potential of his or her psyche, that is individuation. According to Jung, individuation is an unavoidable part of life's course. Individuation is happening when the personality is being true to its own deeper potentialities rather than following egocentric or narcissistic tendencies, or identifying with cultural roles (Jung, 1951).

The Tension of Opposites

Jung felt that each person's life course is driven by opposites (such as light/dark, or masculine/feminine) that exist in the psyche (Jung, 1951). Usually, we are conscious of the existence in us of one side more than the other. To be our fullest self, or individuate, we have to discover and become conscious about the opposite as well. Jung said that we have to encounter our shadow—and that includes everything that we have learned to disown, both positive and negative, about our self.

When we can bring what is disowned (in the shadow) into the light of consciousness, we can claim it as part of ourselves, face whatever emotions we have repressed, and be more fully ourselves. Once we identify with the opposite of a conscious part of ourselves, we are challenged to "hold both," or live in the tension of the pair. For example, if I think of myself as a generous person, and have an experience of my greediness, the challenge is not to collapse into shame or self-denigration, but to incorporate my greediness into a self-image that also includes generosity, a more whole self-image. A more dramatic and typical clinical example might be the survivor of abuse who must find a way to integrate her own healthy aggression without denying it or feeling that she is becoming like an abuser.

Individuation and Lesbian Identity

Anyone struggling to claim, integrate, and value a sexual identity differing from the heterosexual norm will recognize that her identity is seen by the society or culture as "Other." To embrace this Otherness requires that we sacrifice our ego's wish to conform and belong, in the service of being our fullest selves. Claiming our minority identity requires reframing rejected parts of the society's shadow as positive parts of our own identity. In this sense, in coming out, lesbians are thrust upon a path to individuation.

This path immediately brings an encounter with what Jung sees as a fundamental polarity, or pair of opposites, in the psyche: the polarity of masculine and feminine principles. All the questions in coming out about gender identity, sex role, and sexuality can emerge—with attendant confusion and yet tremendous opportunity for expansion, redefinition and fluidity. This encounter has offered enormous and challenging opportunities for individuation on the personal level, and for transformation of cultural models of marriage and family on the sociocultural (collective) level.

MASCULINE AND FEMININE PRINCIPLES

Feminists, including myself, have rightly disputed categorizing personality traits as innately belonging to either men or women. If one of our developmental goals is the capacity for psychological androgyny, an integrated wholeness encompassing both? masculine and feminine, Jungians suggest that we move toward that goal when we look at what has been imaged as masculine and feminine in the human psyche as archetype, existing in myth, dreams, art, and folklore across cultures. These archetypes go beyond what is in the personal unconscious, and exist in the unconscious on cultural and collective levels. We all carry these potentialities simply by being human. Seeking out the "archaic" and "typical" aspects of the masculine and feminine can allow us to go beyond the limitations of our particular cultural sex roles.

As a Jungian analyst, whenever I work with someone's thwarted healthy grandiosity—their fears of their own aggression or authority, their inability to have dreams for themselves, or their difficulties with outer authority manifested in repeated failures at rites of passage such as licensure, the bar, or promotions—we are in the domain of the masculine principle.

Jungian analyst Gareth Hill (1992) has adapted Jung's original identification of the archetypal patterns of masculine and feminine. Masculine and feminine are seen as complementary, and Hill has created a developmental model of their relationships with each other. Building on Neumann's (1955)idea that these principles are transformative elements, Hill suggests that masculine and feminine have both static and dynamic aspects. By defining the dynamic and static masculine, it is easier to understand how we foster their development in our male and female children in gay and lesbian families. I want to describe, from my point of view as a lesbian parent, how the masculine principle appears in youth.

The Masculine Principle

The dynamic masculine is expressed in images of seeking and penetrating, in initiative and action directed toward a goal (Whitmont, 1969). In nature, Hill contends, it is expressed in mating behaviors and the strategies of the hunt. In the human arena, the classic image of the hero slaying the dragon is an expression of the archetypal dynamic masculine, with its drive to conquer and master in the service of individual interests. In movies, we have Rambo. Some would say our current unilateral, militaristic foreign policy is dominated by the dynamic masculine. Developmentally, the dragon-slaying hero carries the energies needed to differentiate from the archetypal feminine. On the human level, the exercise of dynamic masculine consciousness is the child's need to claim its own existence apart from the mothering person, whether at age two, as a teenager, or whenever else. In myths, female carriers of the dynamic masculine are familiar to lesbian audiences. Here we find the Amazon, astride a rearing horse and aiming her spear at a lion, and Artemis the woman warrior in the forest with her band of fellow female huntresses. In contemporary culture, the assertive, action-oriented aspect of any professional person, male or female, is carrying the dynamic masculine.

The static aspect of the masculine principle is expressed in hierarchical systems of order. In modern life, the images of the Supreme Court justices, including both O'Connor and Ginsberg, sitting at their elevated bench, is the essence of the static masculine. Hill describes the static masculine as

"The tendency toward organization based on rational knowledge and linear systems of meaning. It systematizes knowledge and codifies rules of order. It uses its systems and codes in the service of impersonal 'objectivity' in judging. Its central value is Logos" (Hill, 1992: 16). Here we have Zeus the great Father, and Athena, born from his head, representing reasoned behavior and merciful justice, and acting as colleague and participant in the proper conduct of worldly matters.

Mastering the Dynamic Masculine

The developmentally necessary transition—from the grandiosity of dynamic masculine striving where individual will and interests rule, to an adaptation to community, with rules and realities of the material and social world—requires sacrifice. Hill sees this transition coming about through an initiation, where new psychic development occurs through suffering experiences that challenge old ways of being. He calls this the fiery initiation. This young person is inspired to sacrifice their grandiosity because they idealize people in their environment who embody desired qualities and carry these values as examples of possible self-development. Hill (1992: 39) states that:

> These initiations are fiery both because the initiate must go through the fiery hoops of the trials set for him or her and because the fiery hot affects of frustrated individualism have to be swallowed and suffered within rather than enacted; Individual will must be given over to the will of the group.

As parents we are sometimes the masters at these initiations, and our parental part always includes carrying the benign static masculine function of soothing the natural frustrations of coming up against these limits, while at the same time enforcing them.

My Personal Relationship to the Masculine Principle

How do we carry these dimensions of development of the masculine principle to our children, in lesbian families without an embodied father? To answer this, I first asked myself how these dimensions of the masculine came to me. I resonate so strongly with ideas about a masculine and feminine principle within all of us, regardless of our gender, because I have always felt their presence within myself. The masculine was dominant in both of my parents in the value they placed on goal-directed athletic activities and academic achievements. My father was a high school teacher, and my mother was well educated in comparison to most women of her era. They were Jews from immigrant families and valued education as a source of growth and as the ticket to success. Both of my parents, but especially my mother, were also avid baseball fans, first for the underdog Brooklyn Dodgers and then the likewise NY Mets. My dad encouraged me to play competitive tennis, his sport. An early feminist, he pulled me from a co-ed summer camp and sent me to an all-girls camp because girls were not being given the same access to activities as were the boys. My performance was attended to closely, for better and worse, and they did their best to help me manage those fiery hoops of initiation, while of course always expecting me to jump through them.

My partner, while not encouraged athletically, had academics as her arena of excellence and her ticket out of the South, where girls married after high school and started having children soon after. She managed the fiery hoops of college and law school, entering into the heart of Logos in her own unique way.

So, when it came time to become parents, we each had life experience with these dimensions of the masculine principle. Growing up in a patriarchal culture with its defined sex roles, we each also had the experience of being not quite typical. This, of course, came from being lesbian. But additionally, we each had always felt different, an otherness that I believe had to do with valuing and developing a relationship with the masculine within ourselves. We knew how much we had gained by not disowning the masculine in the service of being conventionally female.

This sense of otherness helped in our decision to become parents. We knew that we knew little about how to parent, but did not feel the absence of a dad as an inadequacy. Interestingly, this feeling is borne out in research by Hand (1991). Using a measure of psychological androgyny (the Bem Sex Role Inventory), as well as interviews and observational data, she compared lesbian and heterosexual parents of two year olds, as well as lesbian non-parents. Twice as many lesbian parents were classified as "masculine" on the sex role inventory as lesbian non-parents. Interview data indicated that both the lesbian biological mother and lesbian co-parent participate in parenting in both "female" and "male" ways, which was less true of heterosexual couples. Hand theorizes that, through the process of creating a family and sharing parenting, both lesbian parents, out of necessity, develop feminine and masculine aspects of themselves, and that these maternal and paternal qualities are available to the children. When there is an absence, creative energies can develop to fill it.

Children sometimes lead their parents to what the children need for their development. Our children have led us into male worlds that have had some semblance of familiarity, but have seemed quite "other" as well. Both of my sons have a passion for team sports. They immerse themselves, year round, in packs of males doing aggressive physical activities under the auspices of mostly male coaches and lots of rules. This passion for sports is felt by players and fans alike, parents being a unique subset of fans. All the bad press about fan violence and over-identified parents are sad negative manifestations of this passion gone awry, but the gripping power of a sport for its devotees shows that something archetypal has been stirred.

RAISING SONS IN SPORTS AND IN THE ARCHETYPAL MASCULINE

What is it about the pursuit of athletic excellence that grabs us to participate and to witness? What does subsuming oneself in the team energy offer? What does the scrutiny of one's own or a star athlete's statistics, as well as their humble origins and heroic rise to success, evoke in a child? What is it about our team coming from behind, not giving up, and triumphing in the end, that delights us? I believe these all express positive dimensions of the archetypal masculine.

The origins of the Olympic Games speak to archetypal features of sports competitions as religious ritual. Corford (1962) argues that the Games came about as a s ritual celebration of the ascendance of the New Year God, displacing the old King. The homage to the gods, and the initiatory contests with a nameless hero emerging, evoke these archetypal dimensions.

Kids, Sports, and the Hero Archetype

So what of the Hero's journey? Jung himself found an equation between the hero archetype and American sports. In 1918 he wrote:

> The hero is always the embodiment of man's highest and most powerful aspiration, or of what this aspiration ought ideally to be and what he would most gladly realize. It is therefore of importance what kind of fantasy constitutes the hero-motif. In American hero fantasy the Indian's character plays a leading role. the Indian rites of initiation

can compare with. a rigorous American training. The performance of American athletes is therefore admirable. (paragraph 100)

Hero myths traditionally express a universal pattern, and there are parallels between the universal hero and a star athlete. Jung (1964) tells us that storybook heroes typically emerge from a miraculous but humble birth. Likewise, athletes that capture us often come from modest backgrounds and triumph over obscurity and poverty. Early proof of superhuman strength is another characteristic of the mythic hero. Star athletes-to-be are often noticed in high school or earlier for having special aptitude. A rapid rise to prominence is part of the storybook hero's journey. This is reminiscent of star athlete's skipping over the more usual career steps, to vault to the professional level out of high school. A fairytale hero also displays a triumphant struggle over arduous tasks, vanquishing evil in the form of dragons or monsters. The animals and archetypal mascots of today's sports teams take the place of beasts of old, athletes battling now against Lions, Vikings, and Bears to make the final winning run, throw the touchdown pass, or recoup the trophy.

Children's need to idealize and identify with heroes is realized through participation in sports. When my older son had to write an essay on someone he admires, he described Tim Duncan's poverty-stricken origins in the Dominican Republic and rise through college to the NBA, stats and all. My younger son likes to wear his baseball pants pulled to the knee, like Barry Zito, formerly of the Oakland A's. He chose #8, catcher Yogi Berra's number, for?his jersey, because he is also a catcher.

The grandiosity of personal best is nourished at this age, in the context of becoming a team player, not only a star, and by the hard work and discipline demanded at frequent practices. Rules of sportsmanship are strictly enforced, with punitive laps run and suspensions handed down for serious rule-breaking. Here are examples of fiery initiations, where submission to umpires and refs, coaches, and the actual rulebook itself, come into play.

In the years I was an assistant coach, I shared in these initiatory experiences as well. Literally wearing the coach's hat, I quickly learned the implicit masculine rules that make up the culture of the ball field. For example, I would spend all week in my work as a Jungian analyst exploring the nuances of patients' feelings. On the field, when kids would suffer physical and emotional pain, choking back or bursting into tears at disappointments in their own or others' performances, the coach is to respond with the harsh bark of "shake it off, the ball's coming to you next, get focused!" This contrast carried an "opposite" that at first shocked me. But it was literally true, everyone knew it, and therefore it was an adaptive life lesson I soon came to value, and even include in my parenting off the field. Another funny lesson: when coaching third, I had to learn to "high five" a stolen base or hit. Hugs did not cut it.

The Archetype of Play and the Archetype of the Game

To recognize the initiatory and transforming potential of sports, it helps to think of play as a sort of religious ritual revealing a "higher order." Turner (1983) talks about play as a spiritual experience when he describes the player's immersion in the game—"flow"—as the merging of action and awareness in a state of non-self-consciousness, in which a player exists in space and time outside of ordinary reality and in service to a "higher order." I asked my 13-year-old basketball player what he gets out of playing ball. He said "I get to relax, not as in laid back, but that all my worries disappear when I concentrate just on the game and what's happening." Flow.

In the archetype of the game, the struggle against a worthy opponent to seek and gain the victory and/or to accept defeat, represents a profound inner psychological experience. Walker (1980: 37), writing about the Olympic Games, states that they "were concerned with knowledge and transformation of wild masculine instinctuality into a force which can be fruitful in life, serve life, and therefore be truly humane." I think this alludes to the initiatory potential for athlete and fan alike. Odell (1994: 236) notes that "sporting events tap into both the psyche's instinctual nature and inner archetypal patterns. When these dual aspects of the psyche are set in motion, energy is released and peak experiences occur." Athletes feel it and fans witness it. Sporting events appear to be contests between individuals, or between teams of players, but in truth the real challenge is always with oneself. I think this is where the sacrifice of ego can be experienced, and a player emerges not with personal glory so much as a sense of surrender to the power of the moment and the power of the event.

A Family Example

My younger son enjoys team sports involving body contact. He plays ice hockey and is a catcher on his baseball team. One day, he was on third base trying to steal home—a potentially glorious and yet risky task. His good friend was catching, blocking the plate to receive the throw. My son, knowing full well the rule that, at his level (unlike in the Major leagues) he must slide into home, chose a tackle instead, hoping to knock the ball out of his friend's glove. Both kids go down, tears flow, and whistles blow. Kids are given ice packs and our coach gives all (except my son, who is sitting on the sidelines with his ice pack) a stern lecture on safety. He is ejected from the game but no one tells him! So he is in the on deck circle when the coach notices and tells him he is out of the game. They walk away and handle it, and the team gets an out each time his turn at bat comes up. We win anyway. That night, we parents get an e-mail telling us that the rules state he is suspended from the next game, and must appear in full uniform but sit on the bench. The code section is cited. Attempting to summon the appropriate "master of initiation," we ask the coach to deliver this news to our son. He does, and again they handle it. Michael shows up and mans the bench, cheers the team, warms up pitchers, and life goes on. It's over and he is fine. As the events unfolded, my son accepted them without question, and continues to be an important team member in everyone's eyes. We can only assume that the fiery protests we the parents frequently hear from him at *our* rules were suffered internally, because he wanted to remain a team player. Interestingly, this vignette also illustrates some breakdowns in communication that epitomize the static masculine at its most sterile.

CONCLUSION

Other activities carry these dimensions of the masculine for all of our children as well. For Jewish kids, the bar and bat Mitzvah is an obvious example. Learning the rituals, interpreting Torah oneself, and leading the service as an adult member for the first time, require many hours of surrender to present authority and ancient religious codes; and these are all initiatory and transforming experiences. My older son drew the parallel between the bar Mitzvah and his passion for sports when he used some of his bar Mitzvah gift money to donate a basketball hoop to the new synagogue building.

When parents in alternative families join these collective arenas of socialization, we are often the "different family." I value participating for our family's sake, as well as for others', when we offer the perennial challenge to stereotyping and homophobia by just showing up as who we are. When notions about gender can be expanded beyond biology, the fluidity that emerges offers great possibilities for development, both individually and collectively. There are negative dimensions to the static and dynamic masculine that are certainly present in sports—including kids' sports—such as favoritism over merit, the arbitrary exercise of authority, and sexism, never mind the celebration of individualism inherent in illegal steroid use. My focus here, however, is on access to the positive masculine that is available through sport.

REFERENCES

Corford, F. M. "The Origins of the Olympic Games." In J. E. Harrison, ed. *Epilegomena to the Study of Greek Religion and Themis*. New Hyde Park, NJ: University Books, 1962: 220–237.

Hand, S. *The Lesbian Parenting Couple*. Unpublished doctoral dissertation, Professional School of Psychology, San Francisco, CA, 1991.

Hill, G. *Masculine and Feminine: The Natural Flow of Opposites in the Psyche*. Boston: Shambala Publications, Inc., 1992.

Jung, C. G. "The Role of the Unconscious." In *Collected Works*, Volume 10. Princeton, NJ: Princeton University Press, 1918: 3–28.

Jung, C. G. "On the Psychology of the Unconscious." In *Collected Works*, Volume 7. Princeton, NJ: Princeton University Press, 1951.

Jung, C. G. *Two Essays on the Unconscious*. Princeton, NJ: Princeton University Press, 1964.

Neumann, E. *The Great Mother: An Analysis of the Archetype*. Princeton, NJ: Princeton University Press, 1955.

Odell, C. "Sports and the Archetypal Hero." In M. Stein and I. Hollowitz eds. *Psyche and Sports*. Wilmette, IL: Chiron Publications, 1994: 235–243.

Turner, V. "Liminal to Liminoid in Play, Flow and Ritual: An Essay in Comparativ Symbology." In J. Harris and R. Park, eds. *Play, Games and Sports in Cultural Contexts*. Champaign: University of Illinois Press, 1983: 160–162.

Walker, R. C. *The Athletic Motif*. Unpublished candidate thesis. C. G. Jung Institute, New York, 1980.

Whitmont, E. *The Symbolic Quest*. New York: Putnam, 1969.

Lesbian Mothering in the Context
of Intimate Partner Violence

Jennifer L. Hardesty
Ramona Faith Oswald
Lyndal Khaw
Carol Fonseca
Grace H. Chung

Jennifer L. Hardesty, Ph.D., is an Assistant Professor of Human and Community Development at the University of Illinois at Urbana-Champaign. She received her Ph.D. in Human Development/Family Studies from the University of Missouri, Columbia in 2001.

Ramona Faith Oswald is an Associate Professor of Family Studies at the University of Illinois at Urbana-Champaign. She earned her Ph.D. in Family Social Science from the University of Minnesota in 1998.

Lyndal Khaw is a doctoral student at the University of Illinois at Urbana-Champaign, where she also obtained her B.S. and M.S. degrees.

Carol A. Fonseca is currently a Ph.D. student in Counseling Psychology at the University of Illinois at Urbana-Champaign. She received her B.A. in psychology at the University of Texas, El Paso in 2005.

Grace Chung is a postdoctoral fellow at the Center for Culture and Health at UCLA. She received her Ph.D. in Human and Community Development at the University of Illinois at Urbana-Champaign.

This research was funded by a grant from the Lesbian Health Fund, a program of the Gay and Lesbian Medical Association.

SUMMARY. Twenty-four lesbian mothers (12 African American, 9 White, and 3 Latina) who had experienced physical abuse by a same-sex partner were interviewed. Three types of IPV were found: intimate terrorism, situational violence, and mutual violent control. Further, relationships between mothers/abusers, mothers/children, and abusers/children were examined. Regarding relationships with abusers, 71% of mothers reported lengthy sagas, 17% had worked it out, and 13% made a clean break from the abuser. Regarding relationships with their children, 48% of mothers hid the violence, 26% minimized it, and 26% openly communicated about the situation. Relationships between abusers and the mothers' children were found to be either co-parental (29%), playmate (21%), abusive (21%), or non-parental (21%). Correlations among relational and demographic variables were also examined.

We have 25 years of research on lesbian mothers, and none has examined intimate partner violence (IPV). It is perhaps with good reason that lesbian mothers' experiences with IPV are absent from the literature. Struggles by lesbian and gay families to gain equal rights and recognition have made academicians reluctant to draw attention to any "negative" issues (Stacey and Biblarz, 2001). The fear that opponents of lesbian and gay parenting would use such "negative" research to influence policy is very real (Stacey and Biblarz, 2001). However, the effects of IPV on lesbian mothers and their children are also very real. We contend that remaining silent compromises women and children's safety and health and may also hide the unique strengths of lesbian mothering. Therefore the purpose of our research was to explore the experience of IPV in a sample of lesbian mothers.

Existing Literature

In Renzetti's (1988) groundbreaking study, 35 out of 100 battered lesbians had lived with their own or their partner's children. Almost 30% of the lesbian mothers reported that their partner also abused the children, and 20% indicated they had been physically abused in front of their own or their partner's children. Although the growing literature on lesbian IPV addresses the rates and correlates of violence (West, 2002), Renzetti's findings constitute the extent of our knowledge about lesbian mothers who experience abuse. Given that an estimated 1/3 of all lesbian partner households include minor children (Smith and Gates, 2001), and given that

rates of IPV appear to be similar in same-sex and opposite-sex relationships (Owen and Burke, 2004; West, 2002), there is a compelling need for
further research on lesbian mothers experiencing IPV.

Heterosexual mothers' experiences with IPV are clearly documented in
the literature. Despite the violence they experience, these mothers have
been found to be nurturing and caring mothers who essentially want to
do what is best for their children (Sullivan, Nguyen, Allen, Bybee, and
Juras, 2000). They worry about their children's safety and seek to create
order in the context of disorder (Humphreys, 1995). Concern about the
impact of abuse on their children has been found to significantly predict
mothers' decisions to leave abusive partners (Ericksen and Henderson,
1998), and the direct threat of violence against mothers has been found to
compel mothers to seek refuge at a shelter with their children (Humphreys,
1995). Alternatively, children's attachment to the abuser has delayed the
process of seeking help (Zink, Elder, and Jacobson, 2003), and many
women continue to experience violence after they leave, when they share
parenting with abusive former partners (Hardesty and Ganong, 2006).

Research on the dynamics of lesbian relationships with IPV suggests little to no differences between the varieties of IPV experienced by same-sex
and heterosexual couples (Turell, 2000). Thus, the experiences of lesbian
and heterosexual mothers experiencing IPV is likely to be comparable.
However, lesbian mothers' experiences are uniquely complicated by heterosexism and homophobia that impose chronic and acute stressors to
be managed. For example, research on lesbian mothers in general indicates that daily life involves managing discrimination and prejudice while
promoting children's well being (Hare, 1994; Lott-Whitehead and Tully,
1999; Sullivan, 2001; Wright, 2001). Although lesbian mothers may be
gaining societal visibility despite prejudice, abused lesbians (mothers or
not) continue to be a hidden group for many reasons, including the fear
of being politically incorrect and facing the possibility of being ostracized
by exposing IPV among lesbians (Renzetti, 1988) and of losing custody of
their children due to their sexual orientation (Patterson, 1992; Stacey and
Biblarz, 2001).

RESEARCH QUESTIONS

Given the current gap in our knowledge, we sought to explore violence and parenting through interviews with 24 lesbian mothers. Our specific research questions include: What types of IPV do lesbian mothers

experience? What are their relationships with abusers? How does IPV influence their relationships with their children? What is the quality of relationships between children and abusers?

METHOD

Data Collection

Our recruitment efforts targeted all lesbian, gay, bisexual, transgender (LGBT) and domestic violence (DV) organizations within the state of Illinois, as well as several national DV organizations and Internet resources. Announcements included a toll-free number for potential participants to call, at which time they were given more information about the study. Interviews were scheduled with 24 women who agreed to participate and who reported being a mother while experiencing physical IPV by a female partner. Interviews were conducted at a university office, the mother's residence, or by phone, and lasted 60–90 minutes. After creating a family diagram to identify the different people in their story, participants were asked to tell the story of their relationship with their abuser, to talk about how the violence affected their children and/or their parenting, to discuss help seeking within specific community contexts, and to describe current needs and concerns. Each interview was audio-recorded and transcribed. To protect confidentiality, pseudonyms were used in the transcription process and by the research team. Participants were given $25 and a list of resources. In the case of phone interviews where payment and resources were mailed to the participant, we confirmed that the address they provided was indeed a safe place for them to receive mail.

Data Analysis

Participant recruitment and data analysis were concurrent, as is recommended by grounded theory methodologists (Charmaz, 2000; Strauss and Corbin, 1998). Our team discussed each transcript as a whole prior to labeling data with codes. After discussing 10 interviews, we developed a coding scheme that was applied to all data using NVivo software. Examples of our codes include "abuser's parenting strategies" and "separation process." Data were analyzed to identify actions, facilitating and intervening conditions, context, and outcomes (Strauss and Corbin, 1998). The emergent phenomenon and related properties were checked against the data and discussed as a team until consensus was reached regarding the trustworthiness of our results (Lincoln and Guba, 1985).

After completing our qualitative analysis, we entered our emergent category codes into SPSS as dummy variables. For example, we created a set of three dummy variables for "type of violence" that included 1 = intimate terrorism, 0 = other; 1 = situational violence, 0 = other; and 1 = mutual violent control, 0 = other. After creating our dummy variable sets for all constructs, we conducted a non-parametric correlation matrix, using Spearman's rho, to examine links between these constructs (Bazeley, 1999). We also included demographic characteristics in this analysis (e.g., 1 = professional employment, 0 = other; 1 = service employment, 0 = other; 1 = unemployed, 0 = other). Correlation results are integrated into our manuscript when significant at the .05 (*), .01 (**), or .00 (***) level. Significant correlations should be interpreted as indicators of linkage between constructs rather than statements about group differences. For example, we found a negative correlation (*rho* = −.48*) between mothers' relationships with abusers being "lengthy sagas" and mothers' reports of "situational violence." This finding indicates that mothers in these relationships were less likely to report situational violence compared to the other two types of violence that we found. This within-group trend information is useful for understanding the complexity of experience that grounded theorists seek to establish. Readers should be reminded that our small and non-representative sample prevents us from making any conclusions about group differences.

Sample

Twenty-four lesbian mothers (12 African American, 9 White, and 3 Latina) who had been physically abused by a same-sex partner were interviewed. We refer to the women that we interviewed as "mothers" and their abusive partners as "abusers." Nineteen (79%) mothers were completely out as lesbian, and 5 (21%) were at least somewhat closeted. Their median education was an associate's degree (ranging from junior high school to a B.A.). Eleven (46%) mothers were unemployed during the abusive relationship. Those that were employed at that time held either service (*n* = 8) or professional (*n* = 5) positions. Mothers with professional employment were more likely to be White (*rho* = .66***). At the time of data collection, half of the mothers (*n* = 12) were employed. Half of the unemployed mothers (*n* = 6) lost their jobs for reasons related to IPV, and this was significantly related to holding a service-level position (*rho* = .40*). The 24 mothers entered into the relationship with the abuser at an average age of 32 (*SD* = 9) years. Although three mothers birthed or adopted children during those relationships (and 2 abusers were legal co-parents), most families were stepfamilies. Mothers had a mean of 2 children (*SD* = 1), typically (83%) from previous heterosexual relationships. Oldest or only children at the time of relationship formation were a mean age of 9 years (*SD* = 7). The youngest child of mothers who had more than one child was *M* = 6 (*SD* = 7) years at the time of relationship formation. Compared to professionals, mothers with service-level jobs had been mothers for a longer period of time when the relationship started (*rho* = .51*).

Abusers were on average 36 (*SD* = 10) years old when the relationship started. Five abusers brought minor aged (under 12 years) children into the relationship.

Relationships lasted an average of 6 (*SD* = 4) years. These relationships did not start out being abusive; sometimes several years passed before the onset of violence. Seventy-five percent of mothers reported three or more incidents of physical violence. Fifteen mothers sought therapy (63%), 14 (58%) had contact with the police, and 9 (38%) received medical intervention. Ten (42%) were afraid of losing custody of their children if IPV were exposed. Custody concerns were more likely to occur when abusers were older (*rho* = .42*) and when children had been born into the relationship (*rho* = .53**). At the time of the interview, 9 mothers (38%) were still with their abusers, 8 (33%) were in new relationships, and 7 (29%) were single.

RESULTS

Results are summarized in Figure 1.

Types of Intimate Partner Violence

Using Johnson and Ferraro's (2000) typology, we categorized 17 (71%) mothers as experiencing "intimate terrorism" at the hands of their partner, 4 (17%) experiencing "situational violence," and 3 (13%) reporting "mutual violent control." We did not observe any cases of "violent resistance." Twenty-one (84%) mothers believed that substance abuse, especially on the part of abusers, was related to the onset and/or continuation of violence. One mother evocatively described her abuser as a "werewolf" when drinking.

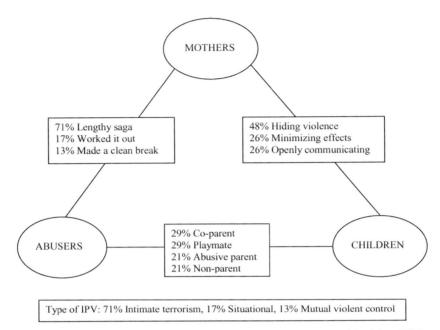

FIGURE 1. Relationship dynamics within the context of lesbian IPV

Intimate Terrorism

In intimate terrorism, violence is just one tactic among many used by the abuser to exert control over the mother. For example, Claudia said that her abuser, Leslie, destroyed her property, prevented her from having friends, and monitored her daily activities. For example, Leslie would go to work and then:

> She's calling on breaks. If I'm not here [at home] to answer the phone, you know, she will literally leave her job and come home . . . to find out what I'm doing. And I could be asleep! [Leslie would say], 'Well why are you asleep? It's the middle of the day.' What the . . . what do you mean it's the middle of the day?! So what if it's the middle of the day? I'm tired! So there goes a fight. I'm always left with the marks though.

This category did not correlate with any other construct.

Situational Violence

Situational violence occurs in the context of specific arguments and is not accompanied by attempts to control the mother. For example, Anne described what unfolded after she broke up with her partner, Carla:

> Carla called and there was something that was said that upset her in a 'I need you back,' desperation, kind of a way. . . . And so, the next thing I knew was she was at my door. . . . And I didn't, I didn't let her in. We're talking through the door . . . and you know [our son] was sleeping. And I was actually holding him at that point to keep him asleep . . . but I ended up opening the door and Carla didn't cross the threshold. She was standing outside of my door. . . . And she squirted her water bottle in my face. Like, really angrily, like she wanted to hit me, but she squirted water on my face instead and I was holding [our son], who got soaked and awakened, and I slammed the door in Carla's face, and told her to leave. [But] she wouldn't leave and she like wouldn't leave for like a half an hour.

Anne believed that the intense emotions surrounding the break up resulted in Carla lashing out on a couple of occasions immediately following separation. However, neither violence nor control was characteristic of their relationship. Overall, mothers in this category reported less frequent violence (*rho* = −.48*).

Mutual Violent Control

Mutual violent control occurs when, according to mothers' reports, both partners initiate violence in an attempt to control each other. For example, Mary described two different incidents involving IPV with her abuser, Laura: One in which Mary broke Laura's arm, the other when Laura broke Mary's ankle. Accompanied by Laura, Mary went to the emergency room for help with her ankle. When the health care providers screened her for violence, Mary told them that she:

> . . . fell off the porch, but as soon as they left the room, I said 'I'm going to tell them that you pushed me off the porch!' [Be]cause that's like my control, you know? She was like 'Stop, stop, stop it, stop it!' I'm not going to tell them. They'd come out and I wouldn't tell them.

Mothers' Relationships with Abusers

In addition to deductively coding for type of violence, we inductively observed three different relationship dynamics between mothers and abusers. Seventeen (71%) relationships were "lengthy sagas," 4 (17%) had "worked it out," and 3 (13%) made a "clean break" from the abuser.

Lengthy Sagas

In lengthy sagas, mothers became increasingly isolated as they tried hard to "make it work" (many mothers used this phrase). These mothers were less likely to have children born into the abusive relationship (*rho* = −.45*). They were also less likely to report situational violence (*rho* = −.48*). Their accounts often referenced attempts to reason with the abuser, and not realizing the futility of such efforts. Often the violence was recognized as such only after mothers had come out of their own self-described "denial" about the situation. Denial often included ignoring information or advice from friends. For example, Elizabeth was told by the abuser's own mother to "get out before she kills you" but did not act on this advice for several years. Coming out of denial typically included acknowledging that they felt "embarrassed" or "ashamed" about being abused, and realizing that the abuser was not going to change. The majority of these relationships had ended by the time of our interview, and mothers' leaving processes were typically in-and-out with high conflict before finally separating. Edna said:

> I believe I do love her. Then it's hard . . . I kept getting promises that it wasn't going to happen anymore and 'I apologize, I apologize and I was wrong,' and 'I know I hurt you' and this, that, and the other, and 'I won't do it again.' And it wasn't one time, not twice; it was maybe 3 or 4 times that this occurred. And I just got tired of the apologies because after each apology, nothing ever changed; it was always the same thing.

Working it Out

Mothers who worked it out with their abusers had abusers who were willing to change and who sought help to do so. Mothers who worked it out were more likely to report situational violence rather than terrorism or mutual violence (*rho* = .40*). Their children were more likely to have been born in the relationship (*rho* = .45*). Further, mothers in these relationships defined their abusers' behavior as exceptional in some way. For example, Francine noted that "[her abuser]'s a good person but she had a rough life and bad tendencies." Because abusers ended their violent behavior, and because mothers consciously decided to maintain contact with them, their lives continued to intersect without violence. To illustrate, after describing a painful post-separation adjustment process, Anne and Carla (her abuser) negotiated how to continue co-parenting their child. Anne explained, ". . . right now we basically see each other just once a week for Friday transfer and the Wednesday transfer happens to be at the day care. So they're going much better than they did."

Clean Break

Mothers who made a clean break were physically abused one time or for a short duration. Their relationships were shorter in length overall (*rho* = −.42*), and they were less likely to seek therapy (*rho* = −.49*). Children were either adults, living with grandparents, or in-utero. For example, Kylie, pregnant after being raped by a man, entered into a relationship with her abuser, Sharon, while pregnant. At first, Sharon had showed interest in wanting to co-parent the child but soon expressed jealousy due to her own infertility. She became increasingly violent, driving Kylie to flee to a different city just prior to her daughter's birth. She is in hiding from the abuser but otherwise has made a clean physical and emotional break from the situation.

Mothers' Relationships with Children

All mothers in our study tried to protect their children from violence. Their strategies varied in three distinct ways: 11 (48%) mothers tried to hide the violence, 6 (26%) minimized its effects on children, and 6 (26%) openly communicated with their children about the situation. One mother did not fall in any of these categories; her child resided with the maternal grandmother, and although the child visited her mother and the abuser, the child was absent when violence occurred and was not aware of why the mother ended the couple relationship.

Hiders

Hiders believed that their children did not know and should not know about the violence and that they could keep their relationships with their children separate from their relationships with their partners. Mothers hid the violence to protect their children, to avoid the possibility of losing custody, and because they were ashamed of the violence or of being in a same-sex relationship. For example, a mother of an adult son who lived in the home kept the violence secret from him because she did not want him to view her as weak.

Strategies mothers used to hide the violence included sending children to their rooms or to relatives' or friends' houses when violence erupted or, for mothers with adult children who lived elsewhere, discouraging children from visiting. According to the mothers, abusers also tried to hide the violence from children by timing the violence to coincide with children being gone or asleep and by leaving bruises in places the mother could cover with clothing. Over time, the children of two hiders eventually figured out their mothers were being abused and confronted them about the violence, after which mothers became more communicative about the situation. In both situations at least one child was an adult, and both mothers had significant health/disability issues that necessitated practical assistance from their children (e.g., an adult son helped his mother replace her wheelchair after the abuser destroyed it).

Hiders were more likely to be African American or Latina than White ($rho = -.54**$). They were less likely to be professionally employed ($rho = -.47*$).

Minimizers

Minimizers were aware that their children knew about the violence but downplayed its effects on children. Their youngest children were younger than those in other groups ($rho = -.61**$). Similar to hiders, minimizers tried to protect their children from violence by sending them to their rooms or to friends' or relatives' houses. These mothers also made active efforts to console children who cried or worried about the violence. At the same time, however, mothers told children that there was nothing to worry about and tried to preoccupy or distract children from thinking about the violence. For example, one mother with two young children explained:

> [The children] would start crying . . . really crying, yelling crying, really loud. And I would try to console them like, 'OK, just go in the room and just lay down. It's OK.' And she [the abuser] would be walking back and forth saying, 'I hate you. I hate these kids. I want you guys out.' And the kids, they were still little . . . they would start questioning like, 'Do we have to get out?'. . . And I would say 'No, no, just lay down. It's ok. Go to sleep. Don't worry about it.'

Communicators

Communicators talked openly with their children about the violence and about their worries. Similar to other mothers, communicators tried to protect their children from violence by sending them to their rooms or to someone else's house. They differed from other mothers in that, in addition to consoling the children, they acknowledged their partners' violence and the children's worries and encouraged children to talk about their feelings. These mothers were also likely to assume a mediator role between their children and the abuser. For example, the mothers would discourage abusers from saying cruel things to the children or otherwise set boundaries around arguing in front of the children. Communicators also attempted to manage their own and their children's behavior to avoid provoking violence. In this way, several mothers formed alliances with their children in which they worked together to keep their activities separate from the abuser and to avoid upsetting the abuser. As one mother recalled:

> I was always trying to smooth things over and make sure that [the children] didn't do anything that was going to upset her, to make sure that I wasn't doing anything that was going to upset her . . . I was trying to kind of usher the kids around and do things like that. So what that created too was more of a close relationship between me and them because we were hiding together. . . . So we would do things . . . in one of the kids' rooms, or I would take them upstairs and she would be downstairs. Whenever I had to go or do anything, they'd always come with me.

Several of these mothers also employed rituals after leaving the abuser to help the children grieve their attachments to the abuser and recover from the experience. For example, one mother and her children celebrated the separation by throwing the abuser's clothes away after she failed to retrieve them.

Communicators were more likely to have held a professional job during the relationship ($rho = .65$**). They were less likely to still be in the abusive relationship ($rho = -.45$*). All of the communicators were White.

Children's Relationships with Abusers

Regarding parenting, we found that 7 of the abusers (29%) were "co-parents," 7 (29%) were "playmates," 5 (21%) were "abusive parents," and 5 (21%) were "non-parents." Within these categories, there were variations in the attachments children felt toward abusers, and attachments influenced children's responses to separation when mothers ended the relationship.

Co-Parents

Co-parents were actively and positively involved in raising the mothers' children, particularly at the beginning of the relationship. In these situations, biological fathers were either uninvolved or non-existent. (Two of the mothers and abusers were legal co-parents who brought their child into the world together). For example, when asked if her abusive ex-partner played a mothering role in her children's lives, Kate responded:

> Initially she did. Initially it was almost 50–50 in terms of how much work we did. She would wash, I would fold. She would fold, I would wash. She would wash up Matthew and I would give Debbie a bath. She would do hair in the morning. Um, that's a big job (*laughs*) if she did hair with my baby. So she would do hair and I would make breakfast. It was kind of like 50–50, you know?

In these families, it was common for mothers to report that their children had a strong and positive attachment to the abuser. Co-parents did not abuse the mothers' children and took steps to hide the fact that they were violent toward the children's mother. For example, Linda explained that her abuser, Connie was ". . . always very, very good to Peter and Preston. She never threatened them. She never hurt them. She never touched them in an inappropriate way. She cared for them greatly. . . I do believe that they loved her."

When mothers ended or took a hiatus from their relationships with abusers who were co-parents, they typically enabled children to continue having a positive relationship with the abuser. When asked if her children would maintain contact with the abuser after separation, one mother said:

> . . . Yeah because she's been the [only] one in [their] lives. She's been in their lives for 7 years; it's gonna be 8, so . . . she's all they know, you know, as far as Mom being in a relationship. You know what I'm saying? So they're going to want to continue to see her; they're going to want to continue to see *her* mom. They call her mom Grandma, her dad Granddad. So they [are] gonna love to keep that relationship because like when we're together the kids go over there for weekends and stuff like that.

Playmates

Playmates had a friendly relationship with the mother's children but did not take on the disciplinary or caregiving responsibilities of childrearing. They often used money to curry favor with children. April, for example, said, ". . . they would do stuff like hang out and/or she would rent movies. And she would just basically spoil them, and I think [the kids] more so enjoyed that than anything else."

Mothers described their children's attachment to playmates as ambivalent at best and often commented that their children could "see through" the insincerity of playmates' behavior. Elizabeth described her abuser's interactions with her children:

> She would get them lavish, lavish gifts and the funny thing is they knew that. They saw right through it. And of course they're children. They liked getting stuff, but it was also the only reason they'd wanted her around was she bought them stuff.

When mothers ended or took a hiatus from their abusers, children did not seem to miss their adult playmates at all, as described in the following excerpt of Mary's narrative:

> When she was gone or when she would leave for a period of time, they weren't asking about her. . . . But she left some artwork that was hers, and I remember after we knew she was gone for sure and some time had passed, we drug the pictures outside, poured gasoline on 'em and set 'em on fire (*laughs*)! And we all had a celebration that she was gone out of our lives . . . it was very therapeutic for us to do that.

Playmates were younger than other abusers ($rho = -.48*$). Mothers spent less time in the abusive relationship ($rho = -.47*$) and were less likely to still be in the relationship ($rho = -.45*$). Mothers with playmate abusers were also less likely to have custody concerns ($rho = -.49*$).

Abusive Parents

Abusive parents either verbally or physically abused the children, manipulated the mother by using the children as leverage, or controlled the behavior of children. Emily's abuser, Rhonda, actually threatened Emily's adolescent daughter to a fight. She noted, "[Rhonda] challenged my daughter to a fight that night and I had to come between them. And that's when I made my decision to leave out of town with my daughter."

Despite the negative behavior of abusive parents, children developed attachments to them. Thus, children had a difficult time when their mothers ended the relationship. Emily, who had left after the abuser challenged her teen-aged daughter to a fight, said that leaving ". . . was hard for her [the daughter] too because she loves Rhonda a lot. And she had a hard time with her feelings."

Mothers with abusers who also abused the children were more likely to express custody concerns (*rho* = .49*). During our interviews, no mothers reported that their child(ren) were currently being abused.

Non-Parents

Non-parents were not involved in the mothers' children's lives. Most often, the children were adults or residing in a different household. For example, Brianna described her abuser as a "straight up kid-hater" who resented Brianna's grown children:

> [The kids would] like come over but she wouldn't be there. And she'd come home and they'd feel uneasy because she'd be like, you know, (*making a monster-like sound*) 'Oh they're here again.' She'd go into the room, slam the door; my kids would be like, 'OK, Mom. See ya.' And then she's like, 'Damn, why do you have to have the kids over here? I don't like kids.' You know, and then she'd go on and on. . .

According to their mothers, children were not attached to non-parents and did not show any response but relief when and if the relationship ended. Mothers with non-parent abusers were more likely to still be in the relationship at the time of the interview than were mothers in the other abuser–child relationship groups (*rho* = .45*).

DISCUSSION

Our study is the first to document and explicate IPV in the lives of lesbian mothers. Our findings show that lesbian mothers experience a range of violence types and severity, perhaps because we did not limit our sample to shelter residents (Johnson, 1995). Further, we demonstrate that, even within a given IPV type, there is variation in the dynamics between mothers, children, and abusers. This variation is partly explained by the intersectionality of sexuality with race and class, as well as by the quality of relationship between abusers and mothers' children.

Intersectionality

Intersectionality refers to the ways that personal experience is shaped by where one fits on a range of interacting social hierarchies (e.g., sexuality, gender, race, and class), and their attendant privileges or derogations (Collins, 1990; de Reus, Few, and Blume, 2005).

Existing literature on lesbian IPV suggests that gender/sexuality hierarchies may be experienced as the fear of being outed as lesbian if one discloses the abuse (National Coalition of Anti-Violence Programs, 2004). However, the mothers in our sample were largely out. They did not fear disclosure of their sexuality, and their abusers did not use the threat of outing to control them. About half did, however, fear that their children could be taken away because of the violence compounded by their sexuality. These mothers feared unwanted intrusion into their families by children's biological fathers and grandparents, as well as legal authorities. For example, two abusers had filed complaints against the mothers with their state's Department of Family and Children Services. Practitioners should be mindful that lesbian mothers experiencing IPV may be more worried about the legal insecurity of their families than their sexuality per se.

Despite this array of potential threats, custody concerns were more likely when abusers presumably had more legitimacy as family members (e.g. by being parents, albeit abusive, and not mere "playmates") and possibly more power (e.g., by being older). The practice of choosing family members is a resiliency strategy within GLBT family networks (Oswald, 2002), and differs from the heteronormative practice of basing family membership on biological and legal "givens" (Weston, 1991). Choosing family is typically, and positively, discussed as defining family to include same-sex partners. Ironically, lesbian mothers experiencing IPV may be well served by defining family boundaries in such a way that abusers are excluded. Well meaning efforts to see the same-sex couple as legitimate should be tempered with an awareness that mother-children ties may take precedence over the partnership when there is violence.

Race and class intersections were salient in the context of mother–child relationships: Mothers who hid IPV from their children were more likely to be Black or Latina than White. They were more likely to work in service occupations during the relationship. Further, mothers in service occupations were more likely to have lost their jobs for reasons related to IPV. Collins (1990) argues that African American mothers promote their children's survival by shielding them from the effects of injustice (e.g., IPV) for as long as possible. They may feel that unless children are directly threatened, there is no need to discuss the situation, as communicating about IPV would further burden their children, who are already struggling to survive in a context of economic insecurity. In light of the custody concerns mentioned earlier, they may also be socializing their children to limit disclosure of personal information when that information could be used against them by authorities (Dodson and Schmalzbauer, 2005). Conversely, mothers who openly communicated about IPV with their children were 100% White. Communicators were also more likely to have ended the abusive relationship. They were more likely to hold professional employment during the relationship, and maintain it upon separation. Thus, these mothers managed IPV without managing economic insecurity simultaneously. Open communication about IPV may be a class-based socialization practice that promotes children's success by teaching them to acknowledge when they have been wronged and pursue remedy (Lareau, 2003), and profoundly contrasts with the experience of poor Black and Latina lesbian mothers in our sample.

Given these class/race distinctions, we caution practitioners against assuming that open communication about IPV is always best. Rather, we encourage recognition of the fact that lesbian mothers and their children experiencing IPV may be equally or more concerned about economic survival than the IPV itself. That being said, we also want to acknowledge the deleterious impact of IPV on children even when mothers believe that their children are being shielded from the violence.

Abuser–Child Relationships

Abuser–child relationships appear to influence lesbian mothers' decisions regarding leaving abusive relationships. Specifically, mothers were more likely to have ended the relationship when abusers were playmates. We speculate that the abusers' unhelpful role with the children may have exacerbated the mothers' stress, thereby encouraging her to leave. Mothers were likely to remain in the relationship when abusers did not have any relationship with their children. Children in these situations were older or living elsewhere; not having children in the household may have removed one motivation to leave. Mothers who "worked it out" were more likely to be legal co-parents with their abusers and to have experienced situational violence. This suggests that they have a stake in maintaining parental roles and see that this is possible because the violence was contained, rather than pervasive, in their relationship. Practitioners should tailor their interventions and advice to address not only mother/abuser or mother/children dynamics but also those between abusers and the mothers' children.

IN CONCLUSION

Readers of this work should be mindful of several limitations. First, our sample was self-selected and thus should not be interpreted as representing all lesbian mothers faced with IPV. Further, most family situations were stepfamilies and this may have enabled the separation of parent/child and parent/abuser roles, which seemed to be protective. More research on diversely structured lesbian families is needed to clarify the barriers and opportunities associated with variations in legal and biological ties between mothers, children, and abusers.

Despite these limitations, our knowledge benefits from the fact that 24 lesbian mothers were willing to come forward with their stories of surviving IPV. Further, our combination of qualitative data with a mixed-methods analysis provided complex and detailed information that redresses a significant gap in the literature; we have brought together the previously separate literatures on same-sex IPV and on lesbian mothers. Although pleased with this academic pursuit, we want to close by emphasizing how important it is to end the silence around this issue for lesbian mothers who experience IPV. As Edna told us:

> I have to thank you ladies because talking about this since this morning has helped a great deal . . . and I was kind of teetering, you know? But like I said, talking about it now, it really helps. I want to thank you guys because I'm feeling much better; I'm feeling a lot better . . . I want to stay strong; I don't want to go back this time . . . I'm hell-bent with going forward and going on with my life and that's what I plan on doing.

REFERENCES

Bazeley, P. "The *Bricoleur* with a Computer: Piecing Together Qualitative and Quantitative data." *Qualitative Health Research* 9(2), 1999: 279–287.

Charmaz, K. "Grounded Theory: Objectivist and Constructivist Methods." In N. Denzin and V. S. Lincoln, eds. *Handbook of Qualitative Research* (2nd Ed.) Thousand Oaks, CA: Sage, 2000: 509–533.

Collins, P. H. *Black Feminist Thought: Knowledge, Consciousness, and the Politics of Empowerment.* New York: Routledge, 1990.

De Reus, L., A. L. Few, and L. B. Blume."Multicultural and Critical Race Feminisms: Theorizing Families in the Third Wave." In V. Bengston, A. C. Acock, K. R. Allen, P. Dilworth-Anderson, and D. M. Klein, eds. *Sourcebook of Family Theory and Research.* Thousand Oaks, CA: Sage, 2005: 447–468.

Dodson, L. and L. Schmalzbauer. "Poor Mothers and Habits of Hiding: Participatory Methods in Poverty Research." *Journal of Marriage and Family,* 67(4), 2005: 949–959.

Ericksen, J. R. and A. D. Henderson. "Diverging Realities: Abused Women and Their Children." In J. C. Campbell, ed. *Empowering Survivors of Abuse: Health Care for Battered Women and Their Children.* Thousand Oaks, CA: Sage, 1998: 138–155.

Hardesty, J. L. and L. H. Ganong. "A Grounded Theory Model of How Women Make Custody Decisions and Manage Co-Parenting with Abusive Former Husbands." *Journal of Social and Personal Relationships,* 23(4), 2006.

Hare, J. "Concerns and Issues Faced by Families Headed by a Lesbian Couple." *Families in Society: Journal of Contemporary Human Services,* 75(1),1994: 27–35.

Humphreys, J. "The Work of Worrying: Battered Women and Their Children." *Scholarly Inquiry for Nursing Practice: An International Journal,* 9(2), 1995: 127–145.

Johnson, M. P. "Patriarchal Terrorism and Common Couple Violence: Two Forms of Violence Against Women." *Journal of Marriage and the Family,* 57(2), 1995: 283–294.

Johnson, M. P. and K. J. Ferraro. "Research on Domestic Violence in the 1990s: Making Distinctions." *Journal of Marriage and the Family,* 62(4), 2000: 948–963.

Lareau, A. *Unequal Childhoods: Class Race and Family Life.* Berkeley: University of California Press, 2003.

Lincoln, Y. and E. Guba. *Naturalistic Inquiry.* Beverly Hills, CA: Sage, 1985.

Lott-Whitehead, L. and C. Tully. "The Family Lives of Lesbian Mothers." In J. Laird, ed., *Lesbians and Lesbian Families.* New York: Columbia University Press, 1999: 243–259.

National Coalition of Anti-Violence Programs. *LGBT Domestic Violence Report in 2003.* New York: National Coalition of Anti-Violence Programs, 2004.

Oswald, R. F. (2002). "Resiliency in the Family Networks of Lesbians and Gay Men." *Journal of Marriage and Family,* 62(2), 2002: 374–383.

Owen, S. and T. Burke. "An Exploration of Prevalence of Domestic Violence in Same-Sex Relationships." *Psychological Reports,* 95, 2004: 129–132.

Patterson, C. J. "Children of Lesbian and Gay Parents." *Child Development,* 63(5),1992: 1025–1042.

Renzetti, C. M. "Violence in Lesbian Relationships: A Preliminary Analysis of Causal Factors." *Journal of Interpersonal Violence,* 3(4), 1988: 381–399.

Smith, D. and G. Gates. *Gay and Lesbian Families in the United States: Same-Sex Unmarried Partner Households.* Washington, DC: Human Rights Campaign Fund, 2001.

Stacey, J. and T. Biblarz. "(How) Does the Sexual Orientation of Parents Matter?" *American Sociological Review,* 66(2), 2001: 159–183.

Strauss, A. and J. Corbin. *Basics of Qualitative Research: Grounded Theory Procedures and Techniques.* Newbury Park, CA: Sage, 1998.

Sullivan, C. M., H. Nguyen, N. Allen, D. Bybee, and J. Juras. "Beyond Searching for Deficits: Evidence That Physically and Emotionally Abused Women are Nurturing Parents." *Journal of Emotional Abuse,* 2(1), 2000: 51–71.

Sullivan, M. "Alma Mater: Family 'Outings' and the Making of the Modern Other-Mother." In M. Bernstein and R. Reimann, eds., *Queer Families, Queer Politics: Challenging Culture and the State.* New York: Columbia University Press, 2001: 231–253.

Turell, S. C. "A Descriptive Analysis of Same-Sex Relationship Violence for a Diverse Sample." *Journal of Family Violence,* 15(3), 2000: 281–293.

West, C. M. "Lesbian Intimate Partner Violence: Prevalence and Dynamics." *Journal of Lesbian Studies,* 6(1), 2002: 121–127.

Weston, K. *Families We Choose: Lesbians Gays and Kinship.* New York: Columbia University Press, 1991.

Wright, J. "'Aside From One Tiny Little Detail, We Are So Incredibly Normal': Perspectives of Children in Lesbian Step-Families." In M. Bernstein and R. Reimann, eds., *Queer Families, Queer Politics: Challenging Culture and the State.* New York: Columbia University Press, 2001: 272–290.

Zink, T., N. Elder, and J. Jacobson. (2003) "How Children Affect the Mother/Victim's Process in Intimate Partner Violence." *Archives of Pediatric and Adolescent Medicine,* 15(6), 2003: 587–592.

"Family" Support for Family Violence: Exploring Community Support Systems for Lesbian and Bisexual Women Who Have Experienced Abuse

Susan C. Turell
Molly M. Herrmann

ABSTRACT. "Family" is a euphemistic term that lesbian, gay, bisexual, and transgender (LGBT) people use among ourselves to designate membership in lesbian, gay, bisexual, and transgender communities. Ironically, this "family" may be the most sought, yet least successful, support for dealing with the intimate partner violence that occurs within LGBT families. This study of 11 lesbian and bisexual women's experiences seeking support revealed several tiers of unmet needs within the LGBT community. They rarely used services in the general community, although these services are often the focus of both criticism and efforts to build support systems for

Susan Turell, Ph.D., is Professor of Psychology and Coordinator of Women's Studies at University of Wisconsin–Eau Claire. She is a licensed psychologist and former director of the Rape Crisis Program of the Houston Area Women's Center. Dr. Turell is a member of the LGBT committee of the Wisconsin Coalition against Sexual Assault and Wisconsin Coalition against Domestic Violence.

Molly Herrmann, M.S., is a researcher and activist in LGBT intimate partner violence (IPV). She is on local and state LGBT IPV committees, and has provided statewide domestic violence and sexual assault training. She has over 10 years experience in HIV prevention, is a public health educator for the Wisconsin Division of Public Health, and is affiliated with Critical Mass Consulting.

Acknowledgements: Wisconsin Department of Health and Family Services, Family Support Center of the Chippewa Valley, the Chippewa Valley Lesbian, Gay, Bisexual, and Transgender Community Center.

LGBT victim/survivors. A model presents the different stages and potential sources of support.

"Family" is a euphemistic term that lesbian, gay, bisexual, and transgender (LGBT) people use among ourselves to designate membership in LGBT communities. Ironically, our "family" is minimally aware of the intimate partner violence (IPV) that occurs within our families, and minimally supportive to its victims.

Many studies have now reported the prevalence of same-sex domestic violence (Bologna, Waterman, and Dawson, 1987; Brand and Kidd, 1986; Coleman, 1990; Island and Letellier, 1991; Kelly and Warshafsky, 1987; Lie and Gentlewarrier, 1991; Lie, Shilit, Bush, Montagne, and Reyes, 1991; Lockhart, White, Causby, and Issac, 1994; Loulan, 1987; Renzetti, 1992; Turell, 2000; Waldner-Haugrud and Gratch, 1997; Waldner-Haugrud, Gratch, and Magruder, 1997; and Waterman, Dawson, and Bologna, 1989). Abuses involve emotional, physical, and sexual mistreatment, and prevalence rates are comparable to those of heterosexual relationship violence (Koss et al., 1995) for both physical and sexual abuses. Physical abuse in relationships can be conservatively estimated to happen for one in three same-sex couples (Turell, 2000). Sexual abuse occurs in at least 12% of homosexual relationships (Turell, 2000). Emotional abuse is also well documented and may be present in 80% or more of same-sex couples (Bologna et al., 1987; Lie and Gentlewarrier, 1991; Lie et al, 1991.; Lockhart et al. 1994; Turell, 2000).

Most studies of IPV strongly advocate that help be available for LGBT people in abusive relationships. This request for legal, medical, shelter, and psychological assistance is typically addressed to the general community, outside of the LGBT community. However, when LGBT people seek help from these external resources, a crucial question is just how homophobic, transphobic, or heterosexist these resources will be (Balsam, 2001). The gay and lesbian community often lacks awareness, or ignores the problem (Istar, 1996). Where are these survivors of domestic violence and/or sexual assault in same-sex relationships to turn? Although many publications call for needed intervention, few have examined this problem closely.

The purpose of the study reported here is to learn from lesbian and bisexual victim/survivors about their needs for support and services to help with IPV. These personal interviews, both group and individual, yielded a model that conceptualizes how the various supports and service needs may be related to each other.

LEVELS AND TYPES OF SUPPORT/SERVICES

Support, interventions and services for battered LGBT people may take place at the societal, community, or individual levels (Dutton, 1994; Hamberger, 1996).

Counseling

Many interventions intend to bring about intrapsychic changes, in psychopathology or self-esteem; individual, couples, and group counseling are services in this domain. Most interventions for IPV focus on the individual; some focus on the batterer, others on the victim/survivor. Both Hamberger (1996) and Coleman (1990) advocated counseling with the batterer to manage or correct pathological personality characteristics. Leeder (1994) presented a model for counseling both members of the couple, individually and together. Although controversial in the domestic violence field, Istar (1996) described a model for same-sex couples counseling for battering. Other counseling interventions include support groups and systemic approaches (Coleman, 1990; Dutton, 1994; Leeder, 1994). Across modalities, therapists' homophobia and lack of training in work with same-sex couples can create problems for victims seeking mental health assistance (Hammond, 1988).

Several studies have associated substance use and lesbian battering incidents (Coleman, 1990, 71%; Kelly and Warshafsky, 1987, 33%; Shilit, Lie and Montagne, 1990, 64%). According to Renzetti (1997), the relation between substance abuse and battering is mitigated by feelings of dependency by the batterer. Even so, the association between the two suggests that interventions should include assessment of and treatment for substance abuse. No literature to date has explored this intervention for same-sex couples.

Ethnicity may impact a victim/survivor's likelihood to seek counseling. Kanuha (1990) discussed the isolation of women of color due to racism within the lesbian community and homophobia within their ethnic community. Conflicting loyalties may result in feeling trapped in the battering relationship. Lack of training for mental health care providers regarding the impact of ethnicity decreases their effectiveness if lesbians of color do seek counseling.

Macro-System Services: Legal, Medical, Shelter

Although LGBT victim/survivors use them only minimally, macro-system services are the focus of the majority of the literature about support systems for the LGBT victim/survivor of IPV. Cultural norms, patriarchal institutions, and community values limit or enhance access to legal, medical, and shelter services. LGBT victims/survivors often name fear of homophobia as a barrier to seeking services at this macro level (Balsam, 2001).

The battered lesbian would likely face homophobic police officers, attorneys, legal advocates, and judges (Hammond, 1988). Even if these members of the judicial system are sympathetic to battered women in general, they are more likely to see lesbian battering as mutual, limiting the number of remedies available. Fear of disclosure of one's sexual orientation, and the possible negative consequences, also prevents lesbians and bisexual women from reporting to law enforcement.

Hammond (1988) expressed several of these same concerns for battered lesbians' interactions with medical personnel. She noted that the battered lesbian may face homophobia and heterosexism by emergency room staff, and that her sexual orientation may become part of her permanent medical record. Emotional and financial risks may result.

Both Hammond (1988) and Renzetti (1996) examined battered lesbians' experience when attempting to use shelters. Hammond indicated several areas of concern, including homophobia on the part of shelter staff and pressure by funders to keep lesbianism invisible. In addition, same-sex violence necessitates the creation of a more complex analysis of battering; the disequilibrium this creates for staff may result in negative treatment for battered lesbians in shelters.

Renzetti (1996) surveyed domestic violence programs in the United States about their services for battered lesbians. She found that whereas most (96%) indicated they welcomed lesbians as clients, only 10% provided services or materials specifically designed for lesbian survivors. Less than half of the staff and volunteers of these programs had received training regarding lesbian battering. These findings are consistent with Hammond's (1988) concern about lesbian invisibility in shelter services and written materials. According to Renzetti (1996), only 2% of the respondents reported that 10% or more of their clients were lesbian, which indicated that lesbians either are not using shelter services or are invisible to shelter staff.

Support Services in the LGBT Community

Support is not easy to access within LGBT communities, either. Both Leeder (1994) and Hammond (1988) noted the importance of LGBT peers for lesbian victims/survivors of domestic violence and sexual assault. Several obstacles may get in the way of receiving help from peers. Poorman (2001) observed that it is hard to name the violence in same-sex relationships, and that it may be hard for lesbians to see other lesbians (indeed, any women) as violent. Additionally, just as in heterosexual relationship violence, batterers are not often held accountable for their actions. Kaschak (2001) noted that there are unique characteristics to a lesbian community that may make recognition and naming the violence difficult. The notion of a lesbian utopia can be challenged by such recognition. Also, confidentiality, so important when telling others about one's own experience of IPV, may be difficult to maintain in close-knit communities. Nonetheless, members of all underserved populations, who experience domestic violence and/or sexual assault, describe a need for support from peers who are members of their own community (Sadusky and Obinna, 2002).

METHOD

Using information from lesbian and bisexual victim/survivors, this study sought to develop a conceptual framework to reconcile, for lesbian and bisexual women, the conflict between the need to access services, the potential for homophobia/heterosexism, the need for supportive peers, and the lack of overall support within the LGBT community. This qualitative study with lesbian and bisexual women is part of a statewide project in Wisconsin to learn more about the community support needs of underserved populations who have experienced domestic violence and/or sexual assault (DV/SA).

Participants

Nine women participated in group dialogue; two additional individual interviews resulted in a total of eleven participants. The study was open to lesbian and bisexually self-identified women who had experienced IPV by women, men or both. IPV included any type of relationship abuse. The sex of the perpetrator was not a defining variable for study inclusion, because the focus was on the services sought by self-identified lesbian and bisexual women. All were from a small city in the upper Midwest.

Procedures

Posters, e-mail announcements, and word-of-mouth were used to recruit participants through therapists, community agencies, and lesbian social venues. All women who responded were pre-screened by phone. Participants were offered individual interviews in lieu of the focus group if they preferred.

The focus group was a one-time event lasting approximately two hours, facilitated by the two researchers. As each woman arrived, she was given a demographic survey to complete. The group began with introductions, payment of a $20 stipend, some background information about the purpose, and an agreement about ground rules.

The discussion was structured by pre-developed questions to elicit participants' ideas about support and services. The researcher/facilitators expanded on these questions only to clarify their meaning. The dialogue was quite informal. Facilitators took minimal notes and audiotaped the group discussion. At the close of the group, participants were given information about how to contact the facilitators and a feedback sheet to send if they had additional thoughts following the group's close.

Instruments

A pre-screening tool was used to identify participants; to screen out partners of others in the group (especially abusive partners); and to assess how safe women felt participating in a group. Women who met the sexual orientation and abuse history criteria and who felt comfortable participating in a group were invited to participate. Every attempt was made during this prescreening to keep perpetrators out of the group.

Participants completed a demographic survey to gather information on race/ethnicity, age, sexual orientation, and education and income levels.

Two questions asked participants to place themselves, and their female partners (for those abused by women), on a continuum from very femme (feminine) to very butch (masculine), with an option to indicate that these identities did not apply to them.

The surveys were completed without names and were included to allow for an aggregate description of the participants. The researchers made no attempt to match the survey data with participants.

At the end of the focus group, participants were given a feedback form to take with them, to be completed later if they chose to do so. The form included questions about participating in a group and asked for additional information or feedback.

RESULTS

Participant Characteristics

Thirteen women responded to the recruitment efforts as potential participants. Eleven women agreed to participate. Nine of these attended the focus group, and two completed individual interviews with one of the group facilitators.

Of the eleven who completed the group or an interview, nine women identified as lesbian, one as bisexual, and one as a gay woman. Three women had been abused by men and women, two by men only, and six by women only. Two participants were currently in abusive relationships.

Nine women identified as white/non-Hispanic, one as white and Native American, and one as tri-racial; this is consistent with the racial/ethnic demographics of the area. Ages ranged from 25–54 with an average of 41.1 years. The women's individual yearly income (not including the income of a partner or family member) varied considerably from one another, with participants earning incomes from less than $15,000 per year to greater than $45,000. Education ranged from completion of high school to Master's degree, with most participants having completed some schooling after high school.

Outcry: Telling Others about the Abuse

Participants were asked about their experiences telling others about the abuse. They talked about telling various categories of people, and about the variety of reactions. Some received support from unexpected sources, such as an army chaplain and a radio talk show host. Several women had experienced abuse in a same-sex relationship while in the military. The military's "don't ask, don't tell" policy on homosexuality made it very difficult for the women to tell anyone about the abuse for fear of revealing their relationship and, consequently, coming out as lesbian or bisexual.

Most participants did tell friends and were met with mixed reactions; others had not told anyone or had told very few people. Negative reactions, and having no safe people to tell, sometimes led to staying in the relationship, going back to living with the abuser, or not recognizing a relationship as abusive until it was pointed out by someone else. Isolation was a common tool used by abusers to keep the women from reaching out.

Responses that encouraged the women to leave the abusive partner, but did not include any specific guidance or assistance with leaving the relationship, were described as not helpful.

"Family" or LGBT Community/Peer Support

Participants were asked whether support from LGBT peers would be helpful and how it would look. Participants initially had mixed reactions to the idea of a need for an LGBT peer support system. They worried that the abuse would be perceived as mutual, and felt pressure to maintain a perfect image of the relationship from within it and from the LGBT community (the idea of lesbian utopia). They recalled feeling that they would be disloyal to their partner by telling about the abuse, feeling shame and embarrassment about being abused by a woman, and fearing that some friends would side with the perpetrator. It was particularly challenging to keep participants focused on support needs from within the LGBT community; instead, participants kept directing the conversations back to frustrations with general service providers

The participants spent some time defining the concept of peers, and talking about to whom they would feel comfortable reaching out. Most participants wanted their first contact to be with a woman, preferably a lesbian or bisexual woman who was trained in domestic violence advocacy. The thought of having to educate a provider about IPV or about relationships between women was overwhelming during a time of crisis.

Their biggest concerns were twofold: anonymity within the LGBT community and avoidance of homophobia/heterosexism when they reached outside the community for help. Their concern for anonymity extended beyond the need for confidentiality. They indicated the desire to remain anonymous at the outcry, or reaching out for the first time, stage. Some participants felt reluctant to tell another lesbian or bisexual woman face-to-face, or to tell lesbian or bisexual women whom they know. The fear of knowing the person they told often was based on fear that she would be a mutual friend of the abuser. Also there was a concern that LGBT people might face further discrimination if the larger community learned of domestic violence among LGBT people.

General Community Service Providers

Participants talked about general service providers and the challenges and fears associated with accessing these providers. The primary concern was how providers would react to abuse between women. Specifically, they feared that violence between women would not be taken seriously, and feared that they would have to educate the provider on sexual orientation. Participants felt there were services for women being abused by men, but that there were not similar services, such as shelter and survivor advocacy, for lesbians. For example, when a woman calls a crisis line, she is asked "Is he in the house right now?" which assumes the perpetrator is a man.

Participants said they were only willing to access general community resources if they felt empowered first from anonymous support within the LGBT community, and/or if they could be assured that the service providers were LGBT friendly. They very strongly supported training of shelter staff, medical personnel, police officers, and mental health workers. However, from the overall tone of the dialogue, we believe it is highly unlikely that victim/survivors would access general community services unless they absolutely had no other options.

Ongoing Support: Back to "Family"

After their immediate needs for services had been met through the larger community, or after the crisis was over, that was the time that participants saw a need for peer support within the LGBT community. Confidentiality was the key concern at this stage. Initially, participants wanted to seek support only from other women. When the facilitators asked about gay men as providers of peer support, the first reaction of some participants was negative; they voiced feelings that gay men did not care much about women's concerns. Other participants felt that gay men might be a source of support. After more dialogue, participants began to consider that support might come from men; they noted that being abused by a woman shows that there is not automatic safety in a group of only women.

DISCUSSION

Participants made clear distinctions between their needs from LGBT peers and the needs they had for general service providers. They wanted peer support within the LGBT community during their initial outcry and they also wanted ongoing LGBT support systems after the crisis was over. At the same time, they realized that general service providers play a vital role in accessing services that are sometimes necessary; consequently, it was unrealistic to expect that all service providers would be LGBT.

Their biggest fear in accessing these services was a homophobic, or at the very least an uninformed response, congruent with Balsam's findings (2001). For this reason, they wanted providers to be well trained in LGBT issues that may impact a domestic violence situation. This strongly felt recommendation is consistent with the work of McLaughlin and Rozee (2001) and Vickers (1996). Homophobia, or even the threat of it, would make accessing such services unlikely. Provider training, while valued, was no guarantee that this sample of women would access general community services.

Bringing it all Together: A Conceptual Model

Based on the input of the participants, the researchers envision a diamond shaped support system based on different needs women expressed at different times in their efforts to seek support. The narrow part at the top and bottom of the diamond would symbolize the smaller LGBT community, compared to the general community; the thicker middle part would represent the society as a whole and the agencies and organizations within that.

The diamond model would reflect the needs of participants to access a smaller community of LGBT individuals at the outcry and ongoing support stages; during both of these, participants strongly preferred talking to a person who identified as LGB or T, but for slightly different reasons. In the outcry stage, this need resulted from fear of a homophobic reaction during a time when they did not have the time, energy, or desire to educate a provider about their lesbianism. In the ongoing support stage, they preferred a comfort level that they hoped could be achieved by participating in support groups with other LGBT people.

The published literature supports the conceptualized diamond model. The preference for seeking support from "family" within the LGBT community is consistent with the finding that 80% of LGBT survivors will seek help from informal sources, far more than will seek help if those sources are not available (Burke and Follingstad, 1999). Support groups led by lesbian facilitators have been successfully provided (Grant, 1999). Among battered lesbians and gay men, the sources of help most frequently sought included friends, counselors, and relatives (McClennen, Summers, and Vaughan, 2002; Merrill and Wolfe, 2000; Renzetti, 1992, 1996; Scherzer 1998; Turell, 2000), and the sources of help least utilized included police and other legal services, crisis hotlines, clergy, domestic violence agency, and shelter services (Hammond, 1988; Letellier, 1994; McClennen et al, 2002; Merrill and Wolfe; Renzetti, 1992; Sherzer, 1998; Turell, 2000).

LIMITATIONS

The most obvious limitation of this study was the small sample size. Although the composition of the group reflects that of the geographic area in which they lived, it does not represent the diversity of the lesbian and bisexual population that the model is envisioned to describe; the sample was primarily White.

Additionally, we do not know whether the same responses would be gained from listening to gay and bisexual men or transgender people. Although we have used the term LGBT, the needs of all of these populations for support related to domestic violence are not well known. These researchers plan additional focus groups with gay men and transgender people regarding the role of GBT peers and other services providers for same-sex IPV.

IMPLICATIONS

These women's voices echoed a hesitance to use general service providers for fear of homophobia, a hesitance found in other studies as well. Their input strongly affirmed a desire to do anonymous outcry with other LGBT people before seeking ongoing confidential support from others in the LGBT community.

There is much work to be done with the diamond model of service needs over time and context. A first step is to assess its accuracy for lesbian and bisexual women of color, gay and bisexual men, and transgender people, and for LGBT people living in communities that vary in size and population. It may be "one size fits all," but it is more likely that the model will serve as a place to start an exploration, with modification for specific groups of people within the LGB and T communities.

If one can assume that the model is at least somewhat accurate for various groups of LGBT victims of IPV, each tier of the model will require that different steps be taken before implementation of services and support can occur. In many communities, educational efforts are in place to increase the competency of service providers to reach LGBT individuals. As with any underserved community, this process must be well planned, persistent, and ongoing.

However, these findings and the resulting model strongly support the need to develop better awareness and understanding of IPV within LGBT communities. Focus on training of organizational and agency staff all too often takes primacy over the more difficult work within our LGBT communities. Just as these participants did, it may be easier for the LGBT community to criticize the work not being done "out there" in the general community, and far more difficult to focus on what we need to improve within our own "family" circle.

We must begin and continue consistent, ongoing awareness campaigns to develop an understanding of IPV within LGBT relationships in our communities. Our sisters and brothers who are victimized by partners need to be able to tell their families of choice and their friends in the LGBT community, and we need to hear them with a good understanding of and belief in the truths about IPV. Awareness campaigns can also help victims themselves to recognize and name what is happening, and to seek support more quickly. We also need to be prepared to offer long- term support in our communities, through more formalized settings like agencies and community centers. It's time for our LGBT "family" to focus on what is happening far too often in our families and to take initiative among ourselves to deal with this problem.

REFERENCES

Balsam, K. "Nowhere to Hide: Lesbian Battering, Homophobia, and Minority Stress." *Women and Therapy,* 23, 2001: 25–37.

Bologna, M., C. Waterman, and L. Dawson. *Violence in Gay Male and Lesbian Relationships: Implications for Practitioners and Policy Makers.* Paper presented at the Third National Conference for Family Violence Researchers, Durham, NH, 1987.

Brand, P. and A. Kidd. "Frequency of Physical Aggression in Heterosexual and Female Homosexual Dyads." *Psychological Reports,* 59, 1986: 1307–1313.

Burke, L. and D. Follingstad. "Violence in Lesbian and Gay Relationships: Theory,Prevalence, and Correlational Factors." *Clinical Psychology Review,* 19, 1999: 486–512.

Coleman, V. *Violence in Lesbian Couples: A Between Group Comparison,*1990. [CD-ROM]. Abstract from: SilverPlatter File: PsychLit: Dissertation Abstracts Item: 9109022.

Dutton, D. "Patriarchy and Wife Assault: The Ecological Fallacy." *Violence and Victims,* 9, 1994: 167–182.

Grant, J. "An Argument for Separate Services." In B. Leventhal and S. E. Lundy, eds., *Same-Sex Domestic Violence: Strategies For Change.* Thousand Oaks, CA: Sage Publications, 1999.

Hamberger, L. K. "Intervention in Gay Male Intimate Violence Requires Coordinated Efforts on Multiple Levels." *Journal of Gay and Lesbian Social Services,* 4, 1996: 83–91.

Hammond, N. "Lesbian Victims of Relationship Violence." *Women and Therapy,* 8,1988: 89–105.

Island, D. and P. Letellier. *Men Who Beat the Men Who Love Them: Battered Gay Men and Domestic Violence.* New York: Haworth Press, 1991.

Istar, A. "Couple Assessment: Identifying and Intervening in Domestic Violence in Lesbian Relationships." *Journal of Gay and Lesbian Social Services,* 4, 1996: 93–106.

Kanuha, V. "Compounding the Triple Jeopardy: Battering in Lesbian of Color Relationships." *Women and Therapy,* 9, 1990: 169–184.

Kaschak, E. "Intimate Betrayal: Domestic Violence in Lesbian Relationships." *Women and Therapy,* 23, 2001: 1–5.

Kelly, E. and L. Warshafsky. *Partner Abuse in Gay Male and Lesbian Couples.* Paper presented at the Third National Conference of Family Violence Researchers, Durham, NH, 1987.

Koss, M., L. Goodwin, A. Browne, L. Fitzgerald, G. Keita, and N. Russo. *No Safe Haven: Male Violence Against Women at Home, at Work and in the Community.* Washington, DC: American Psychological Association, 1995.

Leeder, E. *Treating Abuse in Families: A Feminist and Community Approach.* New York: Springer Publishing, 1994.

Letellier, P. "Gay and Bisexual Male Domestic Violence Victimization: Challenges to Feminist Theory and Responses to Violence." *Violence and Victims,* 9, 1994: 95–106.

Lie, G-Y. and S. Gentlewarrier. "Intimate Violence in Lesbian Relationships: Discussion of Survey Findings and Practical Implications." *Journal of Social Service Research,* 15, 1991: 41–59.

Lie, G-Y., R. Shilit, J. Bush, M. Montagne, and L. Reyes. "Lesbians in Currently Aggressive Relationships: How Frequently Do They Report Aggressive Past Relationships?" *Violence and Victims,* 6, 1991: 121–135.

Lockhart, L., B. White, V. Causby, and A. Isaac. "Letting Out the Secret: Violence in Lesbian Relationships." *Journal of Interpersonal Violence,* 9, 1994: 469–492.

Loulan, J. *Lesbian Passion: Loving Ourselves and Each Other.* San Francisco: Spinsters Books, 1987.

McClennen, J., A. Summers, and C. Vaughan. "Gay Men's Domestic Violence: Dynamics, Help Seeking Behaviors, and Correlates." *Journal of Gay & Lesbian Social Services,* 14(1), 2002: 23–49.

McLaughlin, E. and P. Rozee. "Knowledge About Heterosexual Versus Lesbian Battering Among Lesbians." *Women and Therapy,* 23, 2001: 39–58.

Merrill, G. and V. Wolfe. "Battered Gay Men: An Exploration of Abuse, Help Seeking, and Why They Stay." *Journal of Homosexuality,* 39(2), 2000: 1–30.

Poorman, P. "Forging Community Links to Address Abuse in Lesbian Relationships." *Women and Therapy,* 23, 2001: 7–24.

Renzetti, C. *Violent Betrayal: Partner Abuse in Lesbian Relationships.* Newbury Park, CA: Sage, 1992.

Renzetti, C. "The Poverty of Services for Battered Lesbians." *Journal of Gay and Lesbian Social Services,* 4, 1996: 61–68.

Renzetti, C. "Violence and Abuse Among Same-Sex Couples." In A. P. Cardarelli, ed., *Violence Between Intimate Partners: Patterns, Causes and Effects.* Needham Heights, MA: Allyn & Bacon, 1997: 70–89.

Sadusky, J. and J. Obinna. *Violence Against Women: Focus Group with Culturally Distinct and Underserved Communities.* Prepared for Wisconsin Department of Health and Family Services, Rainbow Research, Minneapolis, MN, 55408, 2002.

Scherzer, T. "Domestic Violence in Lesbian Relationships: Findings of the Lesbian Relationships Research Project." *Journal of Lesbian Studies,* 2(1), 1998: 29–47.

Shilit, R., G-Y. Lie, and M. Montagne. "Substance Use as a Correlate of Violence in Intimate Lesbian Relationships." *Journal of Homosexuality,* 19, 1990: 51–65.

Turell, S. C. "A Descriptive Analysis of Same-Sex Relationship Violence for a Diverse Sample." *Journal of Family Violence,* 15, 2000: 281–293.

Vickers, L. "The Second Closet: Domestic Violence in Lesbian and Gay Relationship." *E-Law-Murdoch University Journal of Law,* 3(4), 1996, available at: http://www.murdoch.edu/au/elaw/issues/v3n4/vickers.html.

Waldner-Haugrud, L. and L. Gratch. "Sexual Coercion in Gay/Lesbian Relationships: Descriptives and Gender Differences." *Violence and Victims,* 12, 1997: 87–98.

Waldner-Haugrud, L., L. Gratch, and B. Magruder. "Victimization and Perpetration Rates of Violence in Gay and Lesbian Relationships: Gender Issues Explored." *Violence and Victims,* 12, 1997: 173–184.

Waterman, C., L. Dawson, and M. Bologna. "Sexual Coercion in Gay Male and Lesbian Relationships: Predictors and Implications for Support Services." *Journal of Sex Research,* 26, 1989: 118–124.

Lesbians Grieving the Death of a Partner: Recommendations for Practice

Debra J. Broderick
Jean M. Birbilis
Michael F. Steger

ABSTRACT. Spousal loss is a common event that has been associated with risk of depression, anxiety, and loneliness. Practitioners working with lesbians need comprehensive clinical guidelines that integrate research about lesbian partner loss with contemporary views of grief and bereavement. Using this literature, we make recommendations for clinical practice that address the possible contributions of several factors—social support, emotional closeness, relationship satisfaction, disclosure or non-disclosure of sexual identity and the relationship, faith and/or spirituality, and

Debra Broderick received her doctorate in Counseling Psychology from the University of St. Thomas in Minneapolis, where she works in their Office of Personal Counseling and Testing. Dr. Broderick also has a private practice in St. Paul, MN. She and Michael Steger received a 2007 APF Investigator Development grant to conduct further research on this topic, based on her dissertation research.

Jean Birbilis, Ph.D., L.P., is a member of the faculty at the University of St. Thomas, where she has taught in the Graduate School of Professional Psychology for the past 17 years. She is also an independent practitioner, where she focuses on the treatment of chronic pain and illness, and on life transitions such as divorce and employment changes.

Michael Steger received his Ph.D. in Counseling and Personality Psychology from the University of Minnesota in 2005. He is currently at the Colorado State University. His research focuses on how people generate the sense that their lives are meaningful, on intimacy building in romantic relationships, and on the role of meaning in stress and coping.

meaning-making—to the grieving process and positive psychological adjustment of lesbians grieving the death of a partner.

The death of a spouse or significant romantic partner is a devastating
experience that can create intense psychological distress, shatter basic
beliefs about the world, provoke doubt about one's ability to cope, and
necessitate the reconstruction of meaning (Bauer and Bonanno, 2001;
Benight, Flores, and Tashiro, 2001; Bonanno, 2001; Bonanno and Kaltman,
2001; Parkes, 1988; Reisman, 2001; Stroebe, Hansson, Stroebe, and Schut,
2001). For women, in particular, spousal loss is often associated with
an increased risk of depression, anxiety, and loneliness (Hayslip, Allen,
and McCoy-Roberts, 2001). Indeed, Parkes (1988) theorized that spousal
loss demands "... a major revision of ... assumptions about the world
(p. 53). Yet, much of the research on spousal loss has focused on married
heterosexual couples. Its applicability to lesbians grieving the death of
a partner is simply not known (Bauer and Bonanno, 2001; Benight et
al., 2001; Bonanno, 2001; Bonanno and Kaltman, 2001; Parkes, 1988;
Reisman, 2001; Stroebe et al., 2001). Given the distinct differences in
legal status, cultural support, sexual identity development, and gender
role socialization between lesbian and heterosexual relationships, it seems
unwise to assume that accounts of spousal loss among legally married,
heterosexual women can adequately describe the grief experience among
women in lesbian relationships (Division 44/APA Committee on Lesbian,
Gay, and Bisexual Concerns Joint Task Force, 2000).

The empirical literature regarding lesbian grief is limited and provides
only a few indicators of important factors in lesbians' adjustment to the
death of a partner. Consequently, there are few clinical guidelines for
psychologists, social workers, and grief counselors that integrate current
knowledge about lesbians and their relationships with the existing research on grief and bereavement. We have created clinical recommendations for practice—based on existing knowledge of lesbian relationships,
lesbian sexual identity development, the influence of homophobia, and
contemporary perspectives of grief and bereavement—and present them
here. First we will illustrate the theoretical basis of these recommendations,
by briefly considering some of the psychological and relational issues that

are specific to lesbians and their relationships, and by discussing research about spousal loss in general.

SOCIAL SUPPORT, HOMOPHOBIA, RELATIONSHIP QUALITY, AND LOSS

Although several researchers have examined mid-life and aging issues among lesbians, (Claes and Moore, 2000; D'Augelli, Grossman, Hershberger, and O'Connell, 2000; Grossman, D'Augelli and Hershberger, 2000; Jones and Nystrom, 2002), only a few discuss bereavement (Jones and Nystrom, 2002). Studies of gay men grieving the death of a partner from AIDS (e.g., Cherney and Verhey, 1996; Folkman, Chesney, Collette, Boccellari, and Cooke, 1996; Lennon, Martin, and Dean, 1990; Simmons, 1999) may provide some insight into how bereavement might be experienced by a same-sex partner in a homophobic culture. However, gay male relationships often differ from lesbian relationships in emotional intimacy, balance of power, and gender-role socialization. In addition, the stigma of AIDS influenced the quality and level of support these men received; a significant factor that is less applicable to lesbians (Simmons, 1999).

Social Support and Homophobia

A few studies include information that may apply to women grieving the death of a lesbian partner. Doka (1987) reported that, among bereaved partners in nontraditional relationships (e.g., gay male couples, cohabitating heterosexual couples, and those in extramarital affairs), ability or inability to openly mourn their loss was related to the amount of social support offered to them. Similarly, Deevey (2000) interviewed lesbians whose partners died and concluded that the undisclosed nature of the women's relationships contributed to increased feelings of loneliness and isolation.

Jones (1985), and Bent and Magilvy (2006), found that women who received low social support following the death of a partner reported having prolonged (over two years) symptoms of grief (e.g., emotional distress and sadness) compared with bereaved women experiencing high or moderate amounts of social support. Although these studies clarify the impact of social support on the grief process of lesbians, small sample sizes and lack of cultural and/or ethnic diversity limit conclusions beyond the subject groups.

Although social support appears essential for a viable grieving process, most lesbians negotiate and manage their sexual identity development within the context of a heterosexist culture that devalues sexual minorities (Garnets, 2002). If they choose to not disclose their lesbian identity, the opportunities to receive social support will be drastically curtailed. Many lesbians bear profound interpersonal and intrapersonal losses (e.g., estrangement from family, culture, and faith communities; self-esteem, religious or spiritual certainty, and ethnic/racial identity) as a result of coming out to self, family, and community. Disclosure of sexual orientation is associated with increased social support and relationship satisfaction, but disclosure can also threaten a woman's economic security, personal safety, familial and cultural relationships, and child custody rights (Beals and Peplau, 2001; Caron and Ulin, 1997; Whitman, Cormier and Boyd, 2000).

For example, Greene (1997) suggests that, in some communities, a lesbian sexual orientation may be viewed as a rejection of one's ethnic/racial culture, and lesbians of color may face strong anti-gay and anti-lesbian sentiment in ethnic/racial communities (Parks, Hughes, and Matthews, 2004). Inclusion in one's family of origin may hinge upon keeping silent about one's sexual orientation and significant romantic relationships (Greene, 1997). These psychological and social losses may require reconstruction of both self and family identities (Li and Orleans, 2001).

Not surprisingly, threat of loss leads many lesbians to diligently manage information about themselves in public milieus (e.g., work, school, family, faith) and to constantly appraise the emotional and physical safety of even the smallest gesture of disclosure (Cass, 1979, 1984; Levine, 1997; Whitman et al., 2000). Whitman et al. (2000) argue that this helps preserve self-esteem by controlling exposure to heterosexist and homophobic reactions.

Different generations experience varying degrees of social acceptance and visibility (Parks, 1999). Older lesbians may be less likely to disclose their sexual orientation (especially in non-supportive environments), increasing the potential for low self-esteem, social isolation, and less identity synthesis (Cass, 1979, 1984; Grossman, et al., 2000; Li and Orleans, 2001; Parks, 1999).

Relationship Satisfaction: Intimacy, Equality and Autonomy

Lesbians typically value an equitable balance of power (defined as the degree of influence each partner has in the relationship), egalitarian division of labor and financial responsibility, emotional intimacy, and personal autonomy in couple relationships (Caldwell and Peplau, 1984; Eldridge and Gilbert, 1990; Haas and Stafford, 1998; Lynch and Reilly, 1985). Individual perception of relational equity has been associated with relationship satisfaction, feelings of emotional closeness, and lack of conflict in lesbian couples (Caldwell and Peplau, 1984; Eldridge and Gilbert, 1990; Lynch and Reilly, 1985). Emotional intimacy is the most important factor contributing to relationship satisfaction (Eldridge and Gilbert, 1990; Schreurs and Buunk, 1996), although lesbian partners consider an equal balance of emotional closeness and personal autonomy important to relationship satisfaction (Eldridge and Gilbert, 1990; Schreurs and Buunk, 1996).

Spousal Loss: Adjustment, Coping, and Meaning-Making

If many lesbians have already experienced interpersonal and social losses, and value especially close intimate relationships, then when they lose a partner, they may be losing a more integral and fundamental part of their identity and emotional and social world than that which is typically lost by heterosexual partners. This is important because many theories of grief and adjustment emphasize the centrality of the impact of the death on the way people understand and interpret the world around them. This is the fundamental task of meaning-making following the death of a loved one. How the bereaved make sense of the death and find benefit from the experience of loss can predict positive adjustment in spousal loss (Bauer and Bonanno, 2001; Davis and Nolen-Hoeksema, 2001). The death of a spouse/partner provokes re-evaluation of previously assumed roles, identities, values, and expectations that contribute to meaning and purpose in life (Attig, 2001; Danforth and Glass, 2000; Pargament, Magyar-Russell, and Murray-Swank, 2005; Parkes, 1988; Reisman, 2001).

Religious faith or spirituality has been shown to predict positive coping and the construction of positive meaning, by serving as an organizing principle for interpreting and making sense of the death (Davis and Nolen-Hoeksema, 2001; Golsworthy and Coyle, 1999; Niemeyer, 2000). However, many lesbians experience profound religious conflict, sometimes abandoning their faith altogether, because pervasive intolerance and negative messages about homosexuality permeate many mainstream religious institutions (Morrow, 2003; Rodriguez and Ouellette, 2000; Schuck and Liddle, 2001). Although some lesbians join gay-affirming faith communities or maintain a personal definition of spirituality, others may be left without an overarching meaning system to help cope with the devastating loss of a partner (Morrow, 2003; Rodriguez and Ouellette, 2000; Park, 2005; Schuck and Liddle, 2001).

RECOMMENDATIONS FOR PRACTICE

Grief is a normal reaction to the death of a loved one, and most individuals, including lesbian women, cope with grief without clinical intervention. Nevertheless, mental health professionals should be aware of the potential influence of particular social conditions on coping, adjustment, and meaning-making for lesbians grieving the death of a partner. The following are recommendations intended to help clinicians and others who are responding to a lesbian woman's experience of grief and loss.

Consider the Impact of Previous Losses

The death of a partner can resonate with grief from previous losses (e.g., loss of family, friends, and connection to racial/ethnic/spiritual community) that are linked to the experience of homophobia. The memory of these losses can compound or exacerbate a lesbian client's feelings of isolation, abandonment, and rejection. In addition, some families, cultures, and/or faith communities assume the partner's death means the client is no longer a lesbian, forcing her to reassert her sexual identity and thus risk additional abandonment or disconnection at a most vulnerable time.

Assess Resources for Support

A partner's death appreciably disrupts support that buffers homophobia and heterosexism, and clinicians should carefully assess the support available to the client. Disclosure of sexual orientation by a lesbian couple influences the amount of social support offered to that couple, and subsequently influences the support available to a bereaved partner. Many lesbian couples have well developed social networks comprised of lesbian, gay and/or heterosexual friends who can provide much needed support and comfort. This network is especially valuable if relationships with the families of origin are estranged or conflicted.

Consider Level and Intensity of Emotional Closeness

The centrality of the relationship to the bereaved is an important factor in determining ability to cope with the loss. As many lesbian couples cultivate significant emotional intimacy in their relationships, clinicians should assess the loss of this emotional closeness in their review of client's strengths and vulnerabilities.

Consider the Impact of Bereavement Tasks on a Client's Self-Esteem

Immediately following the death of a partner, a client may have disclosed her sexual orientation to others (family, co-workers, and health care and funeral professionals) without accurately assessing the danger or safety that may result from doing so. Thus, counseling may involve processing a client's feelings of regret, shame or embarrassment related to these disclosures, particularly if she encountered negative reactions.

Meaning Can be Constructed through Rituals and Tradition

Clinicians can assist the development of meaning by encouraging rituals and traditions that express individual preference, ethnic/racial culture, and also lesbian, gay, bisexual, transgender (LGBT) culture. An interactive approach with the client helps her engage with significant persons, groups, and communities that both acknowledge her loss and affirm transition to new roles, identities, and worldview.

Explore Religious and/or Spiritual Issues

Some clients may rely on religious or spiritual beliefs to cope with the death, because religion may provide an overarching meaning system that can unify a great range of pleasant and unpleasant events (Pargament et al. 2005). The clinician may want to become familiar with the many welcoming and inclusive faith communities available to the religiously committed or spiritual lesbian client. Other organizations may also provide meaning systems into which the grieving partner might integrate her loss. Importantly, clinicians should be aware that failure on the part of a given faith community to recognize the loss of a lesbian member's partner may arouse in that client profound feelings of anger, guilt, and shame that should be addressed in the therapeutic process.

Consider Unique Psychosocial and Legal Conditions

Most lesbian relationships are not granted legal recognition, and subsequently, surviving partners lack rights of survivorship unless specifically designated prior to the death. The deceased's family may deny or limit participation in funeral services, and contest wills or prior financial plans made by the couple. Elderly lesbians, as a consequence of losing their partner, may be required to move into nursing or assisted living facilities that are unaware or dismissive of their loss, which may increase the potential for loneliness and isolation.

CONCLUSION

Grief is a common yet unique experience, influenced by multiple variables. It is imperative that clinicians consider the specific challenges faced by lesbians grieving the death of a partner. These recommendations only begin to address the complexities of lesbian bereavement. Research that will investigate the influence of lesbian relationships, identity development, culture, spirituality, ethnicity, parenting, and aging on the grief process will provide a contextual framework to better prepare practitioners to provide collaborative and empathetic grief counseling for lesbians and their families.

REFERENCES

Attig, T. "Relearning the World: Making and Finding Meanings." In R. A. Neimeyer, ed. *Meaning Reconstruction & the Experience of Loss*. Washington, DC: American Psychological Association, 2001: 13–31.

Bauer, J. J. and G. A. Bonanno. "Continuity Amid Discontinuity: Bridging One's Past and Present in Stories of Conjugal Bereavement." *Narrative Inquiry*, 11, 2001: 123–158.

Beals, K. P. and L. A. Peplau. "Social Involvement, Disclosure of Sexual Orientation, and the Quality of Lesbian Relationships." *Psychology of Women Quarterly*, 25, 2001: 10–19.

Benight, C. C., J. Flores, and T. Tashiro. "Bereavement Coping Self-Efficacy in Cancer Widows." *Death Studies*, 25, 2001: 97–125.

Bent, K. A. and J. K. Magilvy. "When a Partner Dies: Lesbian Widows." *Issues in Mental Health Nursing*, 27, 2006: 447–459.

Bonanno, G. A. "New Directions in Bereavement Research and Theory." *American Behavioral Scientist*, 44, 2001: 718–725.

Bonanno, G. A. and S. Kaltman. "The Varieties of Grief Experience." *Clinical Psychologist*, 21, 2001: 705–734.

Caldwell, M. A. and L. A. Peplau. "The Balance of Power in Lesbian Relationships." *Sex Roles*, 10(7/8), 1984: 587–599.

Caron, S. L. and M. Ulin. "Closeting and the Quality of Lesbian Relationships." *Families in Society: The Journal of Contemporary Human Services*, 78, 1997: 413–419.

Cass, V. C. "Homosexual Identity Formation: A Theoretical Model." *Journal of Homosexuality,* 4, 1979: 219–235.

Cass, V. C. "Homosexual Identity Formation: Testing a Theoretical Model." *The Journal of Sex Research,* 20, 1984: 143–167.

Cherney, P. M. and M. P. Verhey. "Grief Among Gay Men Associated with Multiple Losses from AIDS." *Death Studies*, 20, 1996: 115–132.

Claes, J. A. and W. Moore. "Issues Confronting Lesbian and Gay Elders: The Challenge for Health and Human Services Providers." *Journal of Health and Human Services Administration*, 23(2), 2000: 181–202.

Danforth, M. M. and J. C. Glass, Jr. "Listen to My Words, Give Meaning to My Sorrow: A Study in Cognitive Constructs in Middle-Aged Bereaved Widows." *Death Studies*, 25, 2000: 513–529.

D'Augelli, A. R., A. H. Grossman, S. L. Hershberger, and T. S. O'Connell. "Aspects of Mental Health Among Older Lesbian, Gay, and Bisexual Adults." *Aging & Mental Health*, 5(2), 2000: 149–158.

Davis, C. G. and S. Nolen-Hoeksema. "Loss and Meaning. How Do People Make Sense of Loss?" *American Behavioral Scientist*, 44, 2001: 726–741.

Deevey, S. "Cultural Variation in Lesbian Bereavement Experiences in Ohio." *Journal of the Gay and Lesbian Medical Association*, 4(1), 2000: 9–17.

Division 44/ Committee on Lesbian, Gay, and Bisexual Concerns Joint Task Force. "Guidelines for Psychotherapy with Lesbians, Gay, and Bisexual Clients." *American Psychologist*, 55, 2000: 1440–1451.

Doka, K. J. "Silent Sorrow: Grief and the Loss of Significant Others." *Death Studies,* 11, 1987: 455–469.

Eldridge, N. S. and L. A. Gilbert. "Correlates of Relationship Satisfaction in Lesbian Couples." *Psychology of Women Quarterly*, 14, 1990: 43–62.

Folkman, S., M. Chesney, L. Collette, A. Boccellari, and M. Cooke. "Postbereavement Depressive Mood and its Prebereavement Predictors in HIV + and HIV– Gay Men." *Journal of Personality and Social Psychology*, 70(2), 1996: 336–348.

Garnets, L. D. "Sexual Orientations in Perspective." *Cultural Diversity and Ethnic Minority Psychology*, 8, 2002: 115–129.

Greene, B. "Ethnic Minority Lesbians and Gay Men: Mental Health and Treatment Issues." In B. Greene, ed., *Ethnic and Cultural Diversity Among Lesbians and Gay Men: Psychological Perspectives on Lesbian and Gay Issues*. Thousand Oaks, CA: Sage, 1997: 216–239.

Golsworthy, R. and A. Coyle. "Spiritual Beliefs and the Search for Meaning Among Older Adults Following Partner Loss." *Mortality*, 4(1), 1999: 21–40.

Grossman, A. H., A. R. D'Augelli, and S. L. Hershberger. "Social Support Networks of Lesbian, Gay, Bisexual Adults 60 Years of Age and Older." *Journal of Gerontology: Psychological Sciences*, 55(3), 2000: 171–179.

Haas, S. M. and L. Stafford. "An Initial Examination of Maintenance Behaviors in Gay and Lesbian Relationships." *Journal of Social and Personal Relationships*, 15, 1998: 846–855.

Hayslip, B., Jr., S. E. Allen, and L. McCoy-Roberts. "The Role of Gender in a Three-Year Longitudinal Study of Bereavement: A Test of the Experienced Competence Model." In D. Lund, (volume ed.) *Men Coping with Grief: Death, Value and Meaning Series* (volume 11). Amityville, NY: Baywood, 2001: 121–146.

Jones, L. S. "The Psychological Experience of Bereavement: Lesbian Women's Perceptions of the Response of the Social Network to the Death of a Partner." (Doctoral Dissertation, Boston University, 1985). *Dissertation Abstracts International*, 46(09), 1985: 2566.

Jones, T. C. and N. M. Nystrom. "Looking Back . . . Looking Forward: Addressing the Lives of Lesbians 55 and Older." *Journal of Women & Aging*, 14(3/4), 2002: 59–76.

Lennon, M. C., J. L. Martin, and L. Dean. "The Influence of Social Support on AIDS-Related Grief Reaction Among Gay Men." *Social Science and Medicine*, 31(4), 1990: 477–484.

Levine, H. "A Further Exploration of the Lesbian Identity Development Process and its Measurement." *Journal of Homosexuality*, 34(2), 1997: 67–78.

Li, L. and M. Orleans. "Coming out Discourses of Asian American Lesbians." *Sexuality & Culture*, 5, 2001: 57–78.

Lynch, J. M. and M. E. Reilly. "Role Relationships: Lesbian Perspectives." *Journal of Homosexuality*, 12(2), 1985: 53–69.

Morrow, D. F. "Cast into the Wilderness: The Impact of Institutionalized Religion on Lesbians." *Journal of Lesbian Studies*, 7(4), 2003: 109–123.

Niemeyer, R. A. "Searching for the Meaning of Meaning: Grief Therapy and the Process of Reconstruction." *Death Studies*, 24, 2000: 541–558.

Pargament, K. I., G. M. Magyar-Russell, and N. A. Murray-Swank. "The Sacred and the Search for Significance: Religion as a Unique Process." *Journal of Social Issues*, 61(4), 2005: 665–687.

Park, C. L. "Religion as a Meaning-Making Framework in Coping with Life Stress." *Journal of Social Issues,* 61(4), 2005: 707–729.

Parkes, C. M. (1988). "Bereavement as a Psychosocial Transition: Processes of Adaptation to Change." *Journal of Social Issues*, 44(3), 53–65.

Parks, C. A. "Lesbian Identity Development: An Examination of Differences Across Generations." *American Journal of Orthopsychiatry*, 69(3), 1999: 347–361.

Parks, C. A., T. L. Hughes, and A. K. Matthews. "Race/Ethnicity and Sexual Orientation: Intersecting Identities." *Cultural Diversity and Ethnic Minority Psychology*, 10, 2004: 241–254.

Reisman, A. S. "Death of a Spouse: Illusory Basic Assumptions and Continuation of Bonds." *Death Studies*, 25, 2001: 445–460.

Rodriguez, E. M. and S. C. Ouellette. "Gay and Lesbian Christians: Homosexual and Religious Identity Integration in the Members and Participants of a Gay-Positive Church." *Journal for the Scientific Study of Religion,* 39(3), 2000: 333–348.

Schreurs, K. M. G. and B. Buunk. "Closeness, Autonomy, Equity, and Relationship Satisfaction in Lesbian Couples." *Psychology of Women Quarterly*, 20, 1996: 577–592.

Schuck, K. D. and B. J. Liddle. "Religious Conflicts Experienced by Lesbian, Gay, and Bisexual Individuals." *Journal of Gay & Lesbian Psychotherapy*, 5(20), 2001: 63–82.

Simmons, L. "The Grief Experience of HIV-Positive Gay Men Who Lose Partners to AIDS." (Doctoral dissertation, University of Missouri, 1999). *Dissertation Abstracts International*, 60(03B)

Stroebe, M., R. O. Hansson, W. Stroebe, and H. Schut, eds. *Handbook of Bereavement Research: Consequences, Coping, and Care.* (3rd edition). Washington, DC: American Psychological Association, 2001.

Whitman, J., S. Cormier, and C. J. Boyd. "Lesbian Identity Management at Various Stages of the Coming Out Process: A Qualitative Study." *International Journal of Sexuality and Gender Studies*, 5(1), 2000: 3–18.

Feeding the Hand that Bit You: Lesbian Daughters at Mid-Life Negotiating Parental Caretaking

Susan Cayleff

SUMMARY. Like other women in our culture, lesbians find parental caretaking is a gendered expectation that often falls to them. This article explores how we negotiate competing demands and integrate our parents' needs into our lives. The daughter/parent relationship may have been strained by parental homophobia, exclusion of our partner, "splitting" between our lesbian and birth family lives, and physical distance. We may recall feelings of metaphorical and physical caretaking *not* offered to us when we came out, when lack of parental support may have brought financial abandonment and emotional upset. Inversion of the relationship into the child as parental caretaker, fraught with mixed emotions, can bring resolution of long-held resentments and pain.

Susan E. Cayleff is Professor and Director of Graduate Studies in the Department of Women's Studies at San Diego State University. She is the author of four books, one of which was nominated for the Pulitzer Prize. With her sister, she helped care for their mother who passed away in June 2006 at the age of 91. She continues to care for her father, also 91, who still lives autonomously.

The author gratefully acknowledges the research assistance provided by Angela La Grotteria and Jeannette Wooden in the preparation of this article.

115

If you are a 45–50-year-old lesbian daughter and not already caring for your elderly parents, it may become an issue that you face quite soon. Nine of ten disabled elderly are cared for by relatives and friends at home. Most (70–80%) caregiving for older people is done by their relatives (Braus, 1994), and the largest group of caregivers consists of adult daughters and daughters-in-law. In 1989, the activist feminist Older Women's League estimated that 40 million women were actively involved in caregiving (Mathur and Moschis, 1999).

The presence of an adult daughter frequently determines whether an individual will spend his or her last years in a nursing home. It is an erroneous stereotype that elders in the United States are abandoned by their family members and "warehoused" in nursing homes. Only 5% of the elderly in America are institutionalized. However, 50% of elders lacking a caregiver eventually reside in nursing homes (Huyck, 2001).

The percentage of midlife adults who are taking care of parents or relatives continues to rise as the number of elderly rises. The National Family Caregivers Association estimated that, in 2000, 50 million Americans—about one quarter of the adult population—provided care for an ill, disabled, or aged family member or friend in the previous 12 months (Ruffenach, 2003). In-home care is provided by at least 25 million Americans—one in eight adults (Bader, 2000); and women provide three-quarters of this care, contributing roughly 18 hours per week for a period of four and a half years. These in-home female caregivers are unpaid (the estimated worth of this work is $200 billion per year); half have children under age 18 living at home, and two-thirds hold paid jobs while caring for an elderly family member.

By 2030, the United States will be home to 70 million elderly adults, and by that time the fastest growing age group will be 85 years and older (Bader, 2000). By 2050, the U.S. Census Bureau estimates that the percentage of Americans 65 and over will grow to 21%. In short, female caregiving at midlife will increase exponentially in the decades to come.

GENDER AND CARETAKING

The prototypical caretaker of an elderly parent is a 46-year-old female—usually a daughter (Huyck, 2001). On average she will spend 18 years of her life caring for an elderly parent. During those years she will average 18 hours per week of caregiving (Cooper, 2002). Because women outlive men by, on average, six to eight years (depending on ethnicity), it is far more likely that the parent needing care will be one's mother.

Researchers (Himes, 1994; Horowitz 1985a, 1985b) have recognized that gender is "one of the most important variables influencing the amount and the type of care provided" (Brakman, 1994: 27). Among children who are primary caregivers, daughters outnumber sons three to one. Ethnicity also influences which adult child is expected to carry out parental care (Brakman, 1994).

Roberts (1998: 194) notes that "in many families eventually the roles reverse, the daughter becomes the one in charge of the mother if she lives long enough." Even informal communication and visits fall predominantly to adult daughters, who are the primary confidantes and caretakers not only to elderly parents, but to everyone in the family (Dowling, 1997).

WOMEN'S CAREGIVING: STRESS AND BURDEN AND/OR STRENGTH AND SATISFACTION?

The backlash against feminism includes a romanticizing of the caretaking role: "[T] here is a counter theme being promoted . . . that the rewards of caregiving are so enormous, that this is such a profoundly moving experience, that nothing else compares . . . it's . . . an indirect way of saying to women that they're better off going back to this role because of the spiritual rewards. It feeds into a backlash to return women to the home. . . " (Bader, 2000: 32).

Praver (2004) asserts that relationships between caregivers, their children, spouses, and friends can grow stronger if caregivers and the elderly use this time in their lives to undertake self-understanding and self-transformation. This is no doubt true in some cases. Yet the complexities that often surround taking care of the elderly, especially for lesbian daughters, can make this vision of improved communication and positive self-transformation frustratingly elusive.

Caretaking daughters have increased stress; relations with one's spouse and children are often negatively impacted; and depressive symptoms often arise or worsen (Anastas, Gibeau, and Larson, 1990). Caregivers experience several concerns: their own stress and depression, lack of time for personal pursuits, lack of choice in the caregiving role, health problems related to care giving, and difficulties in coping with their parents' depression. Up to 30% of the senior population experiences mild to moderate depressive symptoms, and the highest rate of suicide in the country is among those 75 years and older (Huyck, 2001; Petsche, 2003; Snyder, 2001). There is still considerable hesitation among lesbians to speak out about the burdens that elder caretaking imposes. This despite decades of feminist support for women who speak about things previously considered taboo, or the Gay Liberation Movement's encouragement of lesbians to speak out about issues that oppress them.

WOMEN CAREGIVING WOMEN: GENDER ROLE COMPLEXITIES

Gender operates in other interesting ways as well. With parents' divorce or separation or the death of one parent, a greater need arises for adult children's assistance. The result of this is crucial: "a greater level of interaction is expected between daughters and mothers than by caregivers and care recipients in other child-to-parent gender relationships" (Mathur and Moschis, 1999: 79). This is compounded by the fact that married (heterosexual) children offer ". . . less basic care to older family members compared to their unmarried counterparts" (Mathur and Moschis, 1999:. 81). In short, lesbian daughters are relied on because they are daughters, because the mother–daughter expectations are the heaviest, and because heterosexually married siblings are sometimes exonerated from such caregiving tasks.

Often, daughters view their parental caretaking as "repaying the debt" of the care they received from their parents when they were young. Yet the two types of caretaking are not analogous: parents are expected to enjoy caring for children; parents anticipate needing to provide this care to young children; and parents face a legal requirement to do so. None of this holds true for adult children of elderly parents.

Despite feminist questioning of so many aspects of women's traditional roles, there is still widespread acceptance of the idea that caretaking is the role of women. At the very least "this belief system is re-enforced in sociological, cultural and religious traditions" (Brakman, 1994: 26). In fact, daughters, be they lesbian or heterosexual, tend to believe that they are the more "natural" caregivers than males and "are especially likely to see failure to care (for an elderly parent) as a moral failure" (Brakman, 1994: 26).

LESBIAN DAUGHTERS AND THE PSYCHOLOGY OF PARENTAL CARETAKING

These cultural expectations can be compounded when the caretaking daughter is lesbian. Heterosexual daughters from intact nuclear families have been imprinted with the message that "You (the parent) loved me and *never abandoned me*." Since daughters feel more guilt than sons, the "dilemma for women is that no matter how much they do, it seems to them that it is never enough to repay their parents or to meet all the needs of the parents" (Brakman, 1994: 27). But what about lesbian daughters, who *were* abandoned by their parents—at least for a time? If the birth family eventually accepted her back, there can be a sense of gratitude. Guilt can also be increased, as the lesbian recalls "how much I've put my parents through." For lesbian daughters, the family dynamics that necessitate her caretaking, if reconciliation has been reached, can deny those wounds, demanding a dutiful and grateful daughter. This makes the concept of "gratitude," as a form of reciprocity for the life one was given by birth parents or guardians, problematic at times for lesbian daughter caretakers.

In some families, lesbians, even in long-term relationships, are still viewed as "not married" in the same culturally sanctioned way that heterosexual siblings are viewed. Thus, the lesbian daughter is implicitly, often silently, presumed to be the "most available" and best able to be primary parental caretaker. It is erroneously presumed she incurs little to no loss by leaving home to become a caretaker or to take the elderly parent into her own home. This can be extremely difficult if the parent(s) are homophobic or even mildly disapproving.

Adult children who grew up with neglectful or abusive parents feel less obligated or may not have *any* obligation to their parents (Brakman, 1994), but this "allowance" rarely includes parental homophobia, which can include rejection, economic severance, years of verbal cruelty or other factors that would justify daughters' refusal to care for parents. In an effort to reconcile, adult lesbian daughters often settle for imperfect communication and recognition from their elderly parents. Years of estrangement or contentious feuding over the daughter's lesbianism may give way to a willingness to accept a parent's grudging "tolerance" of lesbianism in old age, since the parent has become dependent on the daughter.

THE LESBIAN COUPLE AS TWO
CARETAKING DAUGHTERS

It is not uncommon that both partners' elderly parents need caretaking, and look to their daughters for this care. Adelman (2000) described the pressures of gendered caretaking demands on the lesbian couple: "Because lesbian couples are formed by two women—and because women are on the 'front lines' in caring both for the elderly and infirm as well as for the young and growing—these couples can find themselves 'sandwiched' between the needs of elders and youth as well as the demands of the workplace, with scant remaining time or energy for themselves as individuals or as a couple" (Adelman, 2000: 38).

Ironically, in a lesbian relationship, both partners, as women, were socialized to see themselves as caretakers; therefore elderly parents frequently benefit by having what one elderly mothers described as "two daughters to take care of me." In fact, the spouse of the lesbian caretaker is not a daughter, but is an adult who is sacrificing her own personal family life to accommodate the needs of her spouse's parent. The lesbian couple may engage in self-negating behaviors such as: not acting affectionately within their own home lest it unsettle the parent; not referring to one another with endearing nicknames since it implies an intimacy uncomfortable for the parent to witness; or curtailing their lesbian social lives (including limiting the friends who come into their home)—all in an attempt to offer compassionate care. This has prompted some lesbian caretaking daughters to rhetorically ask: Is my own visibility and relationship intimacy a reasonable sacrifice?

Lesbian spouses, like heterosexual daughters-in-law, may be motivated to care for sick in-laws by obligation, not attachment (Globerman, 1996). In an interview study of heterosexual daughter-in-law caretakers, Globerman (1996) found that "proper caregiving" gave them a sense of order and control in their relationships, particularly when their (male) spouses felt incapable of managing the elder's needs, chose not to manage those needs, or did not notice when needs went unmet. The wives' caregiving work released husband-sons from feeling guilt and anxiety. While the work was unpaid, it was valued because it took a strain off her male spouse, gave her power and authority and allowed the husband to be somewhat more available to her within their private relationship (Globerman, 1996). This research has potential implications for lesbians. Might a lesbian, caring for her partner's sick parent, gain a sense of order, control, and authority over the in-law relationship that was previously strained and distant? Might she earn immense gratitude from her partner for her "interference running" with the sick parent? Might caretaking one's in-laws strengthen the lesbian relationship, if a primary motive for caregiving is attachment and affection for one's spouse?

The caregiving partners also need support, relief from duties, and grief counseling. Counseling would need to focus not on the parent–caregiver relationship, but the caregiver–spouse relationship, which might be significantly affected by the caregiving role (Globerman, 1996). This raises another question: while in-law caretaking might evoke positive feelings of control and gratitude, might it also be the cause of distance between lesbian partners, as attention is given to the elder in need versus the intimate relationship shared by the two women?

MOST DAUGHTERS ARE DUTIFUL, BUT VIRTUALLY NONE ARE LESBIAN

Lesbians are all too familiar with their invisibility or misrepresentation in society. In best-selling books and articles, the "dutiful daughter" caring for her elderly parents is a recurrent theme, yet rarely does one see an acknowledgment that the dutiful one may be lesbian. Early works such as Halpern's *Helping Your Aging Parents* (1987) fail to mention or consider the unique challenges facing adult lesbian daughters. Recent writings are no different. For example, Kornblum (2004: 1) asserts "Sons, daughter and caregivers; more and more of us are in similar straits: attending to aging parents." The "us" is presumed to be heterosexual because nowhere is anyone identified as lesbian or gay. The presumption that all daughters are heterosexual is at once false and ever present. Brody's *Women in the Middle: Their Parent Care Year* (2004) devotes two chapters to "Diversity Among Caregivers." She identifies married daughters, widowed daughters, divorced and separated daughters, never-married daughters, and daughters in law. But there are no lesbian daughters in her text. Even deeply touching personal accounts of daughter–mother caretaking show rare signs of lesbian experience (Sternberg, 2002). Self-help literature written for dysfunctional or "difficult" families seeking reconciliation also ignores the perspective of lesbian and gay children at midlife (Caplan, 2000; Davis,

2002; Forward, 2002). Lebow and Kane (1999), both clinical social workers and co-founders of the Aging Network Services, offer practical suggestions for overcoming many problematic situations with elderly parents:
daily tasks, unpleasant personality traits, health obsessions, and issues of
autonomy. But nowhere is there even a passing nod that the "difficulty"
in these families may stem from homophobia, devaluing the daughter's
life because she did not marry heterosexually and/or (in some instances)
chose not to reproduce. One text (Herst,1998) does mention a daughter's
lesbianism, but names the lesbianism as the problem—not the mother's
inability to accept her daughter's orientation.

The omission of the lesbian daughters' caretaking experience in the literature is in direct contrast to the lived experiences of lesbian daughters,
many of whom have internalized the message to take care of their aging parents as part of their socialization to conform to sex-role-pecific patriarchal
beliefs (Gilbert, 2004). This assumes, perhaps erroneously, that the adult
daughter has ongoing, comfortable communication and relationships with
her kin. For some lesbians, this is not the case. They may have relocated
away from parental and kin networks in order to experience the freedom
they found impossible to garner near their birthplace. While holidays, birthdays, weddings, funerals, and coming of age rituals unite families, these
events often produce painful and divisive moments for single lesbians and
couples. Problems can involve: masquerading as roommates, not openly
declaring the nature of the relationship, or "choosing" to attend family
events individually, to avoid conflicts with hostile family members.

THE MIDLIFE LESBIAN IN CONTEXT

Today's lesbians at midlife (age 40–50) were born in the 1950s and
1960s; their parents came of age when homophobic sentiment was at a
peak, during the McCarthy Era and Cold War politics. Stonewall, the
acknowledged watershed for the Gay Liberation Movement, occurred in
1969. In 1973, the American Psychiatric Association removed homosexuality from its list of mental illnesses. Thus it is likely that parents may have
first learned of their daughter's lesbianism prior to the increased social acceptance of homosexuality. Parental acceptance also depends in large part
on one's culture of origin: Orthodox Judaism, fundamentalist Christianity
and traditional Islamic cultures have done little to adjust age-old thinking. Newly arrived immigrant populations often look to their daughters to
preserve old world ways through their sexual morality in anticipation of

heterosexual marriage. So the upbeat pronouncement that "the increasingly positive social acceptance of lesbianism assists the family, over time, to come to terms with their lesbian children" (Raphael and Meyer, 2000: 141) can seem Eurocentric and exclusionary.

As lesbian daughters juggle these mixed cultural legacies, one thing is certain: they are caring for their elderly parents and will continue to do so. Fredriksen (1999) compiled the responses of 1,466 lesbian and gay caretakers, of whom slightly less than half were lesbians. In Fredriksen's survey, 60% of the caregivers who were assisting an elderly person were lesbians providing direct care. Lesbian parental caretakers were older than the median age of 50, less educated, and 69% of the lesbian caregivers were in a relationship. These lesbian caretakers reported significantly more supportiveness from their family of origin than was reported by lesbian caregivers who were not engaged in elder care (Fredriksen, 1999). Two other notable trends emerged: 82% of the caretakers had experienced verbal, emotional physical and/or sexual harassment; and most of the caregivers were openly identified as lesbian or gay to co-workers and to medical service providers.

FAMILIES OF ORIGIN AND OF CHOICE: COMPLEXITIES AND COMPLICATIONS

In their preface to *Lesbians and Gays in Couples and Families: A Handbook for Therapists*, Laird and Green (1996: 9) note that many of us are "connected to these original families. Many of us live in families of choice as well. ... We are daughters, sons, siblings, aunts, and uncles, parents and guardians. Like everyone else, most of us have continuing, complicated relationships with our families." This constant negotiation of birth and chosen families reaches peak proportions when caretaking of elders begins.

Family Rejection in Childhood

Complications begin young. Hardin (1999) chronicles lesbian and gay youth's efforts to escape rejecting families of origin. Growing up in such a family can lead to compartmentalizing one's sexual identity; outwardly gay children develop a conformist exterior "until they are able to arrange to move to an environment that is more healthy or accepting" (Hardin, 1999: 29). Living this split life leads to trying to please others rather than caring for oneself, thinking of one's own needs as invalid, unacceptable, or the more deeply held and most damaging belief that "My secret self is shameful, unworthy, evil" (Hardin, 1999: 33).

To be healthy adults, lesbians and gays must examine and unlearn these patterns. Yet, the prospect of re-immersing one's self in the midst of the family of origin to begin caretaking may mean reassuming that cloak of invisibility, and it has ominous implications for self-esteem and the ability to care for one's own needs. For lesbians, the caretaking role can be difficult (and at times impossible) depending on their prior relationship with their mothers. "The mid-life lesbian's relationship pattern with family members may change from distant to one of involvement in the closing stages of the parents' lives, or it may not be in the best interest of the lesbian daughter to become more involved with her parents. . . [This is important not only for the daughters and their parents, but for] social service providers who need to be apprised of the issues and implications" (Adelman, 2000: 149).

Compensatory Caretaking to Win Approval

Lesbian and gay children often take on the caretaker role to excess (Hardin, 1999). One writer suggests that, motivating this excessive care-taking, there "may be an element of trying to prove she is a 'good enough' daughter or the one the parents can trust the most—a form of compensation for her own loss of status or role in the family" (Raphael and Meyer, 2000: 149). This caretaking may also be intended as compensation for the stress brought into the family of origin by revealing one's lesbianism. Paula, a midlife lesbian, said of her decision to bring her elderly father into her home with her lover of eight years, "It's the least I could do after what I put them through" (Personal correspondence, pseudonym used, quoted by permission, May 2004).

Geographical proximity increases the amount of caregiving to one's older relatives. This has interesting implications for those in the lesbian and gay communities. Many have moved away from their places of birth, finding community in large urban areas and gay-friendlier communities elsewhere. Lesbian daughters who are able to assume elder care are expected to either "take in" elderly parents or return "home" (to the parent's place of residence) to care for them during times of extreme need. In contrast, the expectation that a heterosexually married daughter would return home to care for her parents is quite rare.

Revisiting Old Wounds

Assuming the caregiving role means that one may be forced to revisit old wounds. Beth MacLeod, a social worker in San Francisco who runs a support group for gay and lesbian children of aging parents, notes, "as a gay or lesbian caregiver, oftentimes the caregiving role provides the opportunity—but perhaps more often the difficulty—of having to rework or re-face the emotional issues that your parent had with your being gay. . . . It can force you to address the issue with your siblings and in some instances even with your hometown. There's a potential for all those old wounds, old resentments, and old unmet needs to be faced again" (MacLeod, cited in Gallagher, 1998: 42). For example, JoAnn Loulan, in *Lesbian News* (1996), articulated the tensions she experienced with her elderly, frail, and terminally ill parents while they continued to fight about her lesbianism.

Fairly common misperceptions may arise with siblings as well. They may assume that, as a lesbian, you have more freedom, that your relationship is not a marriage in the same way theirs is, and that you have more usable income. These erroneous beliefs in turn prompt the belief that the lesbian daughter should take on more caretaking than a heterosexual sibling (Gallagher, 1998).

Midlife lesbians' relationships with their family of origin are significantly affected by the degree to which the daughter is out. "Closeted" lesbians, ten years after Stonewall, "reported that daughters were typically received by their families as single women who were expected to care for their aging mothers. The closeted lesbians, in turn, willingly assumed the role of caretaker" (Meyer, 1979 as cited in Adelman, 2000:. 38). Some left the home they were sharing with their lover to move in with their mothers, and justified this geographic separation from their partners because they felt their primary duty was to their mothers. Others moved the mother in with them, and moved their lover into another room, or out of the house entirely, until the mother died. Remaining closeted creates problems for the lesbian spouse of the caretaker as well: she may not be able to assist in caregiving duties, and the "[T]he very fact of being closeted may keep the lesbian daughter at both a physical as well as emotional distance" (Adelman, 2000: 149).

An interview study of the caretaking experience of nineteen midlife gay men and lesbians (Hash, 2001) revealed unique difficulties rooted in being lesbian or gay. Their interactions with formal and informal support persons were problematic and/or stressful when caring for the partner's parent, because their relationship to the parent was not legally recognized. They anticipated (and had) frequent contact with insensitive individuals. They struggled when disclosing the nature of their same-sex relationship to family, professionals, and co-workers and in reconstructing their lives following the cessation of care. Some maintained a "don't ask, don't tell" practice, while others advocated direct communication of the nature of their relationship. After care giving ended, not only did they struggle with loss and grief, but they faced the challenge of re-connecting with the gay community and, sometimes, establishing new romantic relationships (Hash, 2001).

Despite these many complications, Devine (1984) found that lesbian daughters' "Involvement in these care-giving activities actually may serve as a healing force in the relationship. . . . Family members (may) change their values regarding lesbianism in order to accept a new role for the daughter. For some parents this might not occur until old age . . . when the lesbian daughter is the one a parent turns to for caregiving or support" (Devine, 1984, cited in Raphael and Meyer, 2000: 149).

TAKING GOOD CARE OF THE LESBIAN CARETAKER

Health Needs of Lesbian Caregivers

For "intense" caregivers (those giving hands-on care more than 21 hours per week) the high-risk health problems most often noted are: depression (30–50% of caregivers are clinically depressed), chronic stress, stomach disorders, exhaustion, and anxiety (Ruffenach, 2003). Other areas of increased vulnerability include marital conflicts, cardiovascular disease, alcoholism, and other physical problems (Snyder, 2001). These problems worsen in frequency and severity for those caretakers who cannot afford to pay home-care aides to assist them (Huyck, 2001).

These symptoms sound a warning bell for lesbians engaged in caregiving. While caregivers are encouraged to seek support, utilize an adult day-care facility, ask for help with outside projects, and pursue relaxing activities with friends, a lesbian daughter who has moved from her place of birth may lack blood kin nearby and, therefore, find less assistance. In addition, the earning capabilities of two women could limit their ability to purchase additional assistance. Compared with a heterosexual or same sex male couple, who are likely to command higher (male) wages, these directives are difficult for lesbians to pursue.

The Economics of Caregiving for Lesbian Daughters

The financial costs for caregivers are substantial. Daily expenditures (for groceries, medications, car repairs, etc.) were estimated at $117/month in 1989 (Waldrop, 1989 as cited in Mathur and Moschis, 1999) and this rose to $171/month in 2003 (Mandell, 2003). The National Alliance of Caregiving estimates this cost is at $221 per month in 2004 (Kornblum, 2004).

Three-quarters of caregivers for older people also do paid work, and half of them must adjust their work lives to accommodate their care taking duties (Mandell, 2003). These adjustments include going to work late, leaving early, taking time off from work, taking a leave of absence, dropping back to part-time or taking a less demanding job, losing job benefits, turning down a promotion, choosing early retirement, or giving up work entirely (Mandell, 2003). For those classified as "intense" caregivers (21 hours per week or more), the lifelong impact has been estimated at nearly $600,000 in lost pensions, wages, and Social Security. Women are more likely than men to adjust their work schedules to perform caregiving (Mutschler, 1994; Stone and Short, 1990 as cited in Starrells Ingersoll-Dayton, Dowler and Neal, 1997).

The impact on individual women is disastrous. One study (Brody, 1985) found that 28% of caregiving daughters had quit their jobs, sacrificing employee benefits, earnings, personal satisfaction, and their future Social Security and pension payments. This results in an increase in the number of poor older women, whose own economic futures are compromised as a result. For lesbian couples in which both partners work, in-home elder care is particularly economically burdensome, given that Anglo women earn 74 cents (for Hispanic women it is 68 cents) on the dollar that men earn. These circumstances can be exacerbated for working class and working poor lesbians (Ehrenreich, 2002).

For children caring for parents and their own children simultaneously, the economic burden is even higher. This is clearly a concern among the growing percentage of lesbian and gay couples raising children.

Researchers, aware of the gendered aspects of elder care, have offered policy-based suggestions to businesses, aimed at alleviating the burdens experienced by adult women caregivers. Some companies have responded by providing resources such as scheduling flexibility, which acknowledge the "double lives" caregiving adults live. They have instituted programs that "hope to increase employee productivity and organizational commitment" (Singleton, 2000: 370). According to a survey conducted in 1995, 26% of 1,050 "major U.S. companies" increased the benefits to adult caretakers. This was up from 12% in 1990 (Scharlach and Boyd, 1989; Scharlach, Lowe, and Schneider, 1991). Despite this, the predominantly female caregiving worker "report(s) more absenteeism, more distractions at work, more physical and/or mental health problems, and loss of career advancement" (Singleton, 2000: 367). Approximately $4.8 billion is the estimated amount lost to caregiving employees (Spatler-Roth and Hartman, 1990).

In an economically helpful step, since 1993, the federal Family and Medical Leave Act (FMLA) allows for 12 weeks of unpaid leave during any 12-month period for any of these reasons: care taking a new child (birth, adoption or foster care); immediate family member with a serious health condition; and medical leave for oneself. However, this law applies only to public agencies and private employers in firms employing more than 50 employees (Mandell, 2003), and has not been increased in its eleven-year existence.

Planning for One's Own Elderly Care Needs

Lesbians are very likely to become the caretaker of their partner, and can fruitfully attempt to anticipate some of the difficulties that this will entail (Lustbader and Hooyman, 1994). As they age, if they have not raised children to look after them, their vulnerability looms large (Radina, 2003). The fantasy of living communally with other old lesbians re-emerges with regularity (Gould, 1999). Some, like Brogan (1981: 26), anticipate being economically vulnerable and isolated and ending her life in a nursing home, because she will lack a caretaking daughter. Do older lesbians, she muses, ". . . finish their lives in nursing homes, isolated and cut off from whatever lesbian community had been part of their lives? We don't even recognize who they are. I don't know how we as lesbians will work toward providing for our old ages, but we have only ourselves to count on."

Tully (1989) asked 73 midlife lesbians about their plans for old age. To maintain themselves in their communities, most said they would turn to partners, a community of friends and accepting family members. While many of their needs and concerns were similar to non-lesbians who were aging, they specifically sought health care relevant to their own lives, not to be closeted, to be in a caretaking environment where their relationships and lives were acknowledged and respected, and where their psychosocial dignity as a lesbian was upheld. The caregiving role itself has prompted midlife lesbians to become more involved in activism in the gay community, be more open about their identities, or change vocations in order to help others. In her study of lesbian caregivers, Hash found that their experiences greatly informed her subjects' awareness of the need for long-term planning for themselves, and for scripting their own decision-making processes. "In fact, some drafted advance directives to assure that professionals and family members would respect their wishes" (Hash, 2001: xi).

POLICY IMPLICATIONS

Policy, implemented through social service institutions and the workplace, needs to reflect the true magnitude and diversity of American society and its ever-growing need for elder care (Folbre and Bittman, 2004; Olson, 2001; Singleton, 2000). Without support of the larger community, women's economic vulnerability and dependency increases and the situation is morally unjust (Kittay, 1999; Brakman, 1994).

One popular policy suggestion is that family members hire "one of their own" and pay her/him to care for the elderly parent. (Anonymous, 2003) This may be viable for two-income middle class and upper middle class lesbian households. But as income levels decrease, this plan becomes unfeasible. Two ideals (at least) make this solution unlikely. First is the widespread cultural belief that caretaking of elders, particularly parents, is a "repaying of the debt" for one's own life. This, when coupled with the second ideal, the essentialist notions of women's innate nurturing abilities—and economic constraints—reinforces the likelihood that most families will not be comfortable or able to offer pay and daughters will be unlikely to accept it.

CONCLUSIONS

Lesbian daughters at midlife are actively involved in parental caregiving. The emotional, physical, and economic stressors associated with this role can exceed those encountered by their heterosexual female and male siblings. Paradoxically, caregiving can be both divisive for couples or can enhance their personal and spousal understanding. While some lesbians have configured personal solutions involving extended community assistance, or retreat from the work force, these lack viability for many. Increased governmental economic involvement and heightened sensitivity by social workers and social service agencies is needed so that the particular concerns of lesbian caretakers of elderly parents are met. For single, working class, poor working, and lesbians of color—all of whom demographically earn less than other categories of caretakers—these issues are exacerbated and can disproportionately burden them. Legal, health, and human services professional need to find ways to respond effectively to these families with the recognition and support they deserve. Research, community-based support services, and public policies are needed that sustain the strength of these families while supporting them in the various challenges they face (Fredriksen, 1999).

REFERENCES

Adelman, M., ed. *Midlife Lesbian Relationships: Friends, Lovers, Children, and Parents.* New York: Haworth, 2000.

Alford-Cooper, F. "Women as Family Caregivers: An American Social Problem." *Journal of Women & Aging*, 5,1993: 43–57.

Anastas, J., J. Gibeau, and P. Larson. "Working Families and Eldercare: A National Perspective in an Aging America." *Social Work*, 35, 1990: 405–411.

Anonymous. *Work & Family Life*, 17(9),2003: 6.

Bader, E. J. "The Personal Becomes Political: Women's Issues in Caring for the Elderly." *Lilith*, 25(1), 2000: 30–33.

Boyd, S. L. and J. Treas. "Family Care of Frail Elderly: A New Look at Women in the Middle." In J. Quadagno and D. Street, eds. *Aging For the Twenty-First Century.* New York: St. Martin's Press, 1996: 262–268.

Brakman, S. V. "Adult Daughter Caregivers." *The Hasting Report*, 24(5), 1994: 26–28.

Braus, P. "When Mom Needs Help." *American Demographics*, 16, 1994: 38–46.

Brody, E. M. "Parent Care as Normative Family Stress." *The Gerontologist*, 27, 1985: 19–28.

Brody, E. M. *Women in the Middle: Their Parent Care Year.* (2nd edition). New York: Springer, 2004.

Brogan, L. "A Year with Georgia." *Off Our Backs*, 22, 1981.

Caplan, P. *The New Don't Blame Mother: Mending the Mother-Daughter Relationship.* New York: Routledge, 2000.

Cooper, M. "The Balancing Act of Caregiving and Work." *Jewish News*, 61(43), 2002: 37.

Davis, L. *I Thought We'd Never Speak Again: The Road From Estrangement to Reconciliation.* New York: Harper Collins, 2002.

Devine, J. L. "A Systematic Inspection of Affectional Preference Orientation and the Family of Origin." *Journal of Social Work and Human Sexuality*, 2, 1984: 9–17.

Dowling, C. *Red Hot Mamas: Coming into Our Own at Fifty.* New York: Bantam, 1997.

Ehrenreich, B. *Nickel and Dimed: On (Not) Getting By in America.* New York: Henry Holt, 2002.

Folbre, N. and M. Bittman, eds. *Family Time: The Social Organization of Care.* New York: Routledge, 2004.

Forward, S. *Toxic Parents: Overcoming Their Hurtful Legacy and Reclaiming Your life.* New York: Bantam, 2002.

Fredriksen, K. I. "Family Caregiving Responsibilities Among Lesbians and Gay Men." *Social Work*, 44(2), 1999: 142–155.

Gallagher, J. "Mothering Mom." *The Advocate*, 1998: 39–45.

Gilbert, H. *Gay and Lesbian Aging: Research and Future Directions.* New York: Springer, 2004.

Globerman, J. "Motivations to Care: Daughters- and Sons-in-Law Caring for Relatives with Alzheimer's disease." *Family Relations*, 45(1), 1996: 37–45.

Gould, J. *Dutiful Daughters: Caring for our Parents as They Grow Old.* Seattle: Seal Press, 1999.

Halpern, J. *Helping Your Aging Parents.* New York: Fawcett, 1987.

Hardin, K. N. *The Gay and Lesbian Self-Esteem Book: A Guide to Loving Ourselves.* Oakland: New Harbinger, 1999.

Hash, K. "Caregiving and Post-Caregiving Experiences of Midlife and Older Gay Men and Lesbians." 2001. Retrieved October 15, 2004, from www.kmhash.tripod.com.

Herst, C. *For Mothers of Difficult Daughters: How to Enrich and Repair the Relationship in Adulthood.* New York: Villard/Random House, 1998.

Himes, C. L. "Parental Caregiving by Adult Women." *Research on Aging*, 16, 1994: 191–211.

Horowitz, A. "Family Caregiving to the Frail Elderly." In C. Eisdorfer, M. P. Lawton, and G. L. Maddox, eds. *Annual Review of Gerontology and Geriatrics.* New York: Springer,1985a: 194–246.

Horowitz, A. "Sons and Daughters as Caregivers to Older Parents: Differences in Role Performance and Consequences." *The Gerontologist*, 25(6), 1985b: 612–617.

Huyck, M. H. "Returning a Mother's Kindness." *Chicago Tribune Final Edition*, 1, 2001, May 13.

Kittay, E. F. *Love's Labor: Essay on Women, Equality, and Dependency.* New York: Routledge, 1999.

Kornblum, J. "Sons, Daughters and Caregivers; More and More of Us Are in Similar Straits: Attending to Aging Parents." *USA Today Final Edition*,1, 2004, February 17.

Laird, J. and R.-J. Green, eds. *Lesbians and Gays in Couples and Families: A Handbook for Therapists.* San Francisco: Jossey-Bass, 1996.

Lebow, G. and B. Kane. *Coping with Your Difficult Older Parent: A Guide for Stressed-Out Children.* New York: Avon, 1999.

Levine, C., S. C. Reinhard, L. F. Feinberg, S. Albert, and A. Hart. Family Caregivers on the Job: Moving Beyond ADLs and IADLs. *Generations*, 21(4), 2003/04: 17–23.

Loulan, J. "Saying Goodbye to Our Parents." *Lesbian News*, 43, 1996, April.

Lustbader, W. and N. Hooyman. *Taking Care of Aging Family Members: A Practical Guide.* New York: Free Press, 1994.

Mandell, B. R. "The Future of Caretaking." *New Politics*, 9(2), 2003: 61.

Mathur, A. and G. Moschis. "Exploring the Intergenerational Caregiver Market: A Study of Family Care Providers for the Elderly." *Journal of Marketing Theory and Practice* 7, 1999: 76–86.

Mutschler, P. H. "From Executive Suite to Production Line: How Employees in Different Occupations Manage Elder Care Responsibilities." *Research on Aging*, 16, 1994: 7–26.

Olson, L. K. "Gender and Long-Term Care: Women as Family Caregivers, Workers and Recipients." In L. K. Olson, ed. *Age Through Ethnic Lenses: Caring for the Elderly in a Multicultural Society*. Lanham, MD: Rowman & Littlefield, 2001: 230–241.

Petsche, L. M. "Caregivers—How You Can Help Them." *Our World*, 11(7), 2003, July 31: 6.

Praver, F. C. *Crossroads at Midlife: Your Aging Parents, Your Emotions, and Your Self*. Westport, CT: Praeger, 2004.

Radina, M. E. "Review of Age Through Ethnic lenses: Caring for the Elderly in a Multicultural Society." *Family Relations*, 52(3), 2003:308.

Raphael, S. and M. Meyer. "Family Support Patterns for Midlife Lesbians: Recollections of a Lesbian Couple 1971–1997." *Journal of Gay & Lesbian Social Services: Issues in Practice, Policy & research*, 11(2–3), 2000: 139–151.

Roberts, C. *We Are our Mother's Daughters*. New York: William Morrow, 1998.

Ruffenach, G. "The Ties That Bind: A Family Caring Full Time for an Aging Parents is Tested—and Inspired." *Wall Street Journal (Eastern edition)*, R4, 2003, November 10.

Scharlach, A. E. and S. L. Boyd. "Caregiving and Employment: Results of an Employee Survey." *The Gerontologist*, 29,1989: 382–387.

Scharlach, A. E., B. F. Lowe, and E. L. Schneider. *Elder Care and the Work Force*. Lexington, KY: DC Health, 1991.

Singleton, J. "Women Caring for Elderly Family Members: Shaping Non-Traditional Work and Family Initiatives." *Journal of Comparative Family Studies*, 31(3), 2000: 367–375.

Snyder, D. "Recognize Depression in Elderly and Their Caregivers: Care Giving Often Causes Emotional, Physical, Financial and Social Stress, Especially for Those Caring for Relatives." *Fairfield County Woman*, 18, 2001, November.

Spatler-Roth, R. and H. Hartman. *Unnecessary Losses: Costs to Americans of the Lack of a Family and Medical Leave*. Washington, DC: Institute for Women's Policy Research, 1990.

Starrells, M. E., B. Ingersoll-Dayton, D. Dowler, and M. B. Neal. "The Stress of Caring for a Parent: Effects of the Elder's Impairment on an Employed, Adult Child." *Journal of Marriage and the Family*, 59(4),1997: 860–872.

Sternberg, J. *Phantom Limb*. Lincoln, NE: University of Nebraska, 2002.

Tully, C. T. "Caregiving: What Do Midlife Lesbians View as Important?" *Journal of Gay & Lesbian Psychotherapy*. 1(1), 1989: 87–103.

Wolf, D. A. "Valuing Informal Elder Care." In N. Folbre and M. Bittman, eds. *Family Time: The Social Organization of Care*. New York: Routledge, 2004: 110–129.

Adult Daughters whose Mothers Come Out Later in Life: What is the Psychosocial Impact?

Kristen Davies

SUMMARY. When a family member comes out, it is a process not only for that individual lesbian but also for their entire family. Adult daughters whose mothers come out later in life have distinctive paths to navigate. This article reports findings of an interview study with six daughters who were adults when their mothers came out to them. Most daughters felt they emerged from childhood with an open mind about sexual identity, but had no idea about their mother's lesbianism until told by her. Half the participants questioned the role of women in their lives after their mother came out. Five of the six have a very close relationship, or have become closer, with their mother, since her coming out.

It is estimated that between one million and five million lesbians in the United States are mothers (Hare and Richards, 1993). As clinicians and as a community, we need to consider how the coming out process radiates

Kristen Davies received her masters in psychology/counseling at Goddard College and is currently pursuing her Ph.D. at Walden University. She does clinical work with children and families who are experiencing acute crisis.

outward from the individual lesbian, and to examine the implications of the coming out process for children, the family, and the community.

Adult daughters whose mothers came out later in life have a unique story to tell. Their experience is couched in the relationship dynamics of being mothers and daughters, of being two women, of being two adults, and of being parent and child. The mother's age as well as the age of her daughter may bring with it elements that would not exist otherwise.

Sexual identity is formed and can be reformed throughout one's life. How, if at all, does her mother's self image and sexual orientation affect the identity of the woman her daughter has become? Does a mother coming out affect her adult relationship with her daughter? To address these and related questions, interviews were conducted with six adult daughters; in addition, this research is informed by the author's standpoint as an adult daughter of a lesbian mother.

THE MOTHER/DAUGHTER DYNAMIC

Some consider the intergenerational relationship between an adult daughter and her mother an "ambivalent relationship" (Fowler, 1999) because it is the adult daughter's struggle to remain the adult child while actively living her own adult life. Some daughters have difficulty individuating from their mothers, and their struggles for independence often are linked to strong emotional conflict (Charles, Frank, and Grossman, 2001). At the same time, research suggests that many daughters want a close and mutual relationship with their mother, and that, for many, a good relationship contributes to psychological well-being. A study of 171 women ages 35–55 (Baruch and Barnett, 1983) found that adult women are psychologically better off when they have good relations with their mothers: they had higher self-esteem, felt less anxious, and less depressed than did women who were at odds with their mothers. As family therapists Walters, Carter, Papp and Silverstein (1988: 34) explain: "If the mother is the cornerstone of family life, the mother–daughter relationship is the brick and mortar that holds it together." Walters et al. note that childbirth and child rearing can create compelling emotional connection between mothers and adult daughters. Daughters want to know their mothers as real human beings (Apter, 2004). By "understanding one's mother's rough edges, regrets, and confusions it helps a daughter to negotiate her own womanhood" (Apter, 2004: 230).

THE COMING OUT PROCESS

Olson and King (1995: 38) describe the coming out process:

> [T]he model of self-identification and coming out for gays and les-
> bians [i]s like a spiral staircase with a bonfire at the bottom. The heat
> is most intense in the early stages of identification. As individuals
> successfully make each step up the ladder, the intensity of the heat
> lessens but certain fears remain... The integration of a homosexual
> self-identification may not be a linear process. It is reworked and
> reframed at each turn of the spiral.

When a family is involved in the experience of a loved one coming out,
then the family too climbs the spiral staircase.

Several authors have considered the impact of coming out on the family.
Lynch and Murray (2000) investigated the coming out decision and process
for 23 lesbian and gay custodial stepfamilies and found that, in addition
to custody worries, an equally significant concern for parents was how
children would be affected.

Beeler and DiProva (1999), studying the response of four families to
disclosure of homosexuality by a family member, found that disclosure
caused family members to second-guess the sexuality of others and made
homosexuality less exotic. Families had to work through feelings of sadness, loss, and blame; the family had to come out; and they had to develop
alternative visions of the future. Younger children had a less difficult transition than did the adolescent and adult children.

It is sometimes more difficult for gay parents to come out to an adult child
if the now-adult child has his/her own children (Corley, 1990). In addition,
some adult children, who no longer live with or near the parent, disbelieve
the disclosure. Others cut off the relationship or blame the straight parent
for causing the changed orientation (Buxton, 1994). Clinicians working
with family members will want to notice the many levels of transition for
all family members when a parent comes out.

The organization Parents, Family and Friends of Lesbians and Gays
(PFLAG, 2005) has described six stages of response when a family member
comes out: shock, denial, guilt, expressing one's feelings, decision-making,
and acceptance. Clunis and Green (2003), considering the coming out
process and family members' responses, suggest that lesbian mothers take
specific steps when coming out to their adult daughters. First, they feel
that she should sort out her feelings about being a lesbian, then have a

plan for disclosure and be prepared to answer questions. Clunis and Green cautioned that a lesbian mother should be prepared for an adult daughter to withdraw for a while, but she should stay calm about the withdrawal, because it is a common part of the process. Finally, they suggest that lesbian mothers keep communicating with their daughters, because the coming out process is ongoing. While adult daughters whose mothers "come-out" share some common experiences, it is also a very individual journey.

METHOD

The Sample

The sample included 6 women between the ages of 27 and 42 ($M = 35$ years) who responded to e-mail posts on several listservs, websites, and e-mail newsletters. Participants were accepted into this study only if their mothers had come out to them in their late adolescence or beyond. All participants self identified their ethnicity as White. Half self identified their religious affiliation as Wiccan; the other half self identified as having no religious affiliation. Two participants self identified as lesbian and four self identified as heterosexual. Participants are from Toronto, North Carolina, Mississippi, Delaware, and Vermont.

Measures

All participants were sent a postage pre-paid, pre-addressed envelope that included a consent form and a general demographic questionnaire. Variables included on the demographic questionnaire were age, race, religious affiliation, level of education, sexual orientation, children, and age when mother came out.

Recorded interviews were conducted by phone with all six participants. Every interview began with a review of the study's purpose, assurance of confidentiality, and an explanation of how the data would be handled. Each interview was no longer than an hour. The interviewer used several open-ended guiding questions, which allowed flexibility to explore the topics in depth.

Data Analysis

Once all interviews were transcribed, a critical analysis of the data was conducted. The interviews were read repeatedly and transcript segments rearranged as themes began to emerge. Consideration was given to the frequency with which similar content appeared. After my review of the transcripts, a colleague evaluated all transcribed interviews. The separate analyses were compared and reviewed for differences that arose between interpretations.

RESULTS

Five areas of concentration emerged from the interviews: perception, knowledge, relationship, sexual identity and overall process.

Perception

All six participants recalled that there was a moment in time when they became aware of same sex sexual identity. Three of the participants grew up in urban communities and three in very rural settings. The three women who grew up in an urban environment felt as if they had a wider exposure to multicultural experiences. The three women who grew up in rural surroundings said that their perception was limited because of lack of exposure to gay culture.

One participant recalled: "When I was 10 or 11 ... my mother had NOW meetings. I knew that there were women who were lesbians in those meetings, and I just knew they were, I don't know how I knew or why I knew, I just knew."

Another stated, "I was raised in a real liberal household. So, it was like never really an issue. You know, I guess when I was probably pre-teen is when I understood what it meant to be gay."

In contrast, a third explained, "I had never even thought about it. I grew up in a really small town of 5,000 people. It had never occurred to me that there were gay people, because I had never been exposed to it. [My mother] was really my first experience with knowing someone gay."

One participant became aware of gay identity paired with ridicule: "I would have to say that I was conscious of sexual identity in the 7th grade. Prior to that, I don't have any recollection. ... Kids called me gay and probably [used] the word faggot too. I remember going to the dictionary, because I wasn't sure what it meant. There was that moment that I recognized there was a thing called gay. I became aware that perhaps some of my peers could be gay."

Each participant's childhood perception of same-sex relationships was compared to their current perceptions. Five of the women maintained an open mind from childhood into adulthood. One participant maintained a negative perception from childhood into adulthood. When asked about her feeling about lesbian relationships today, she felt that she could not judge anyone, but still could not be comfortable with her mother being with another women.

Knowledge

Participants were asked whether they knew their mothers were lesbians before they were told, or in hindsight did they recognize anything that would have suggested their mother's lesbian identity. Five of the six participants stated that they had no idea that their mother was a lesbian. One participant that she was very young when she realized her mother "liked other women." However, all participants agreed that, looking back, there were signs of their mother's sexual orientation.

One participant reported, "I had an inclination before she had actually sat me down. More because people around town were talking about it, so I had heard that way."

Another said that she did not suspect that her mother was a lesbian until the day her mother told her. However, as she looked back, she recalled a more nuanced picture: "My mom and dad got divorced, and a year later she told me. In that year I was getting more of an idea. Her first partner was my 11th grade History teacher. I knew my teacher was out of the closet and when they started to hang around I was pretty sure they were together."

A third described her mother leaving the family for another women."That is when the family found out that Mom was a lesbian . . . I am not sure if my mom is really a lesbian so to speak. She is living with a woman, but they tell me all the time that they don't have sex, that it is just a companionship type of thing."

Relationship

Participants were asked about the impact of coming out on the mother–daughter relationship. Did their relationship stay the same, weaken, or perhaps grow even stronger? Three participants reported having close relationships with their mothers growing up. Those same three participants report maintaining their closeness with their mothers through their coming out process. The other three participants, who reported not having close relationships to their mothers, became closer as the daughters entered into adulthood.

Five out of six participants state they have a "very good" relationship with their mother's partner, whereas one participant stated that she "couldn't embrace anyone my mother would be involved with."

Sexual Identity

Mothers can sometimes be role models for their daughters, and daughters sometimes identify with their mothers because of being the same sex. Half of the participants questioned their sexual orientation after their mothers came out. One participant felt that she had questioned what role women played in her life, in response to her mother having come out, but stated that she had not felt any physical attraction to women.

As one participant put it: "I think, if nothing else, it made me realize that I did have choice. I wasn't limited to just being with a guy. I could, if I wanted to, be with a woman. I came out about ten years after my mom did."

On the other hand, another answered, "I never thought that perhaps I am gay too or maybe I have other choices. It never crossed my mind. I guess I always knew that I wasn't. I was heterosexual. My older sister is a lesbian. So if you were doing this interview with her she might have had a very different answer. I was aware of the possibility, but it never really crossed my mind."

A third explained that, around the time her mother came out to her, she "did some experimenting" but discovered that she was "pretty solidly into guys."

Another said that she modeled after her mother in some respects. She answered, "I questioned it not because of being attracted to women but because I always looked towards women as my support. So, I learned early on that my female friends took precedence over anything and everything. Definitely in the beginning of my marriage I put my friends before my husband. . . "

Process

Participants were asked whether they would have changed anything about the way their mother came out to them, and if so what. Half had things they would have liked to change.

One said this: "I have thought about this. It would have been easier for me to deal with this if my mother had told me sooner. . . . I asked my mother on two occasions if she was gay and on both occasions she said no. . . . The only thing I can say is, it is a process. It is like anything—what we have and what we believe to be true isn't—there is a loss in belief of what we held to be true."

Another put it this way: "I think the biggest thing is communication. I mean if communication lacks then everybody gets second hand information or you're going to come to these conclusions that are so off base that it is not going to help either one of you. I think that the key is to have an open mind."

Three participants, when asked what advice they would give to another woman in their situation, suggested finding support, whether through friends or through a professional. A third of the participants suggested keeping their mother's feelings a priority. They both offered, "If you think it is hard on you, think about how your mom feels right now. . . . It's not going to change the way your mom loves you. You can choose to react but I would just try to be happy . . . find happiness in your mother's happiness and comfort."

DISCUSSION

A mother and child bond is unlike any other bond. When life events test those bonds, families are given an opportunity to see how strong that bond can truly be. The six women who participated in this research proved, in their case, their mother child relationship could survive, even thrive, under life changing events.

The stories told about change and adjustment but, most importantly, loyalty. Each daughter felt committed to honoring her mother's sexual orientation and all that comes with that. Every daughter spoke respectfully about her mother's role in her life, then and now. There was pain, anger, and disappointment, at times along the journey. But in the end, there was always resolve.

REFERENCES

Apter, T. *You Don't Really Know Me: Why Mothers and Daughters Fight and How Both Can Win.* New York: W. W. Norton & Company, 2004.

Baruch, G. and R. C. Barnett. "Adult Daughters' Relationships With Their Mothers."*Journal of Marriage and the Family,* 45(3), 1983: 601–606.

Beeler, J. and V. DiProva. "Family Adjustment Following Disclosure of Homosexuality by a Member: Themes Discerned in Narrative Account."*Journal of Marital and Family Therapy,* 25(4), 1999: 443–459.

Buxton, A. P.*The Other Side of the Closet: The Coming-Out Crisis for Straight Spouses and Families.* Indianapolis, IN: John Wiley & Sons, Inc, 1994.

Charles, M., S. Frank, and S. Grossman. "Repetition of the Remembered Past: Patterns of Separation-Individuation in Two Generations of Mothers and Daughters." *Psychoanalytic Psychology,* 18(4), 2001: 705–728.

Clunis, D. M. and D. G. Green.*The Lesbian Parenting Book: A Guide to Creating Families and Raising Children,* 2nd ed. New York: Seal Press, 2003.

Corley, R. *The Final Closet: The Gay Parents' Guide for Coming Out to Their Children.* Miami, FL: Editech Press, 1990.

Fowler, L. K.*Family Life Month Packet, Ohio State University,* 1999. Retrieved May 18, 2005 from the World Wide Web http://www.hec.ohio.state.edul/famlife/

Hare, J. and L. Richards. "Children Raised by Lesbian Couples: Does Context of Birth Affect Father and Partner Involvement?"*Family Relations,* 42, 1993: 3–10.

Lynch, J. M. and K. Murray. "For the Love of the Children: The Coming Out Process for Lesbian and Gay Parents and Stepparents." *Journal of Homosexuality,* 39(1), 2000: 1–24.

Olson, E. D. and C. A. King. "Gay and Lesbian Self-Identification: A Response to Rotheram-Borus and Fernandez." *Suicide and Life-Threatening Behavior,* 25, 1995: 35–39.

PFLAG, (Parents, Family and Friends of Lesbians and Gays, Information retrieved May 10, 2005 from http://www.pflag.org

Walters, M., B. Carter, P. Papp, and O. Silverstein.*The Invisible Web: Gender Patterns in Family Relationships.* New York: The Guilford Press, 1988.

May–December Lesbian Relationships: Power Storms or Blue Skies?

Cindy M. Bruns

SUMMARY. What are the implications when there is considerable difference in the ages of partners in a lesbian couple? May–December lesbian relationships are those where partners are at least 10 years apart in age, and where both partners are over 30. These relationships have been either neglected or valorized in the psychological literature. Differences in socially ascribed power, women's socialization against acknowledging power, the value the lesbian community places on egalitarianism, and the interaction of other privileges, combine to impact these couples. The fluid nature of power dynamics in May–December lesbian relationships is highlighted and explored. Finally, ways that age-variant lesbian couples can navigate these power differentials in healthy ways are addressed.

Cindy M. Bruns, Ph.D., is a clinical psychologist, in practice at the Texas Woman's University Counseling Center and in private practice in Dallas, Texas. She obtained her Ph.D. in clinical psychology from the California School of Professional Psychology—San Francisco Bay Area, where her dissertation research was on complex post-traumatic stress following sexual trauma. She has also been a contributing author to the journal *Women and Therapy.*

The author thanks Carmen Cruz and Linda Louden for their insightful conversations and organizational contributions to this article. Special appreciation is due to Christianne McKee for her willingness to engage the issues discussed in this article on both theoretical and personal levels. Without her, this article would not have been possible.

Heterosexual age-variant relationships are easy targets for feminist analysis, particularly when the man in the relationship carries multiple societal privileges such as being white, older than the woman, and financially secure. Lesbian age-variant relationships, however, have rarely been examined through the same critical lens of power[1] Instead, lesbian relationships have been valorized and seen as largely immune to patriarchal socialization (Ristock, 1991, 2003), as if membership in two oppressed classes (woman and lesbian) supersedes any socially ascribed power differences within the couple.

Age differences have been ignored, assumed to be positive, or framed as encouraging healthy relationships. For example, Dunker (1987: 78) writes, "[A]ge differences aren't so important for a lesbian. . . . The older lesbian is often welcomed where younger ones gather. It's reassuring for them to know that sexual energy doesn't necessarily diminish with age." Even theorists writing about power in lesbian relationships have ignored the potential impact of age differences (e.g., Burch, 1987).

In a power analysis of May–December lesbian relationships—where there is at least a 10-year age difference between the partners (Kaslow, 1989) and both are at least 30—socially ascribed privileges associated with age can, and do, affect the couple relationship. These privileges include income/class security, experience/place in the lesbian community, life experience, and stable peer/professional group identity. Privileges associated with younger age, such as reproductive ability, and potentially greater peer acceptance/ability to be out, can also affect the couple. Women's socialization against acknowledging power, the value the lesbian community places on egalitarianism, and the interactions of other privileges (e.g., race, ethnicity, disability) add to the complexity of these potential stressors. In addition, power in May–December lesbian relationships is fluid, with different advantages being salient for the younger and older members of the couple, and with power shifts that occur when one woman enters "old age" whereas her partner enters or remains "middle aged." How can members of these age-variant couples navigate power differences in healthy ways—managing to avoid many of the "storms" and living under "blue skies" of connection and love?

VARIABLE WEATHER FORECASTED

Several kinds of issues can cloud the blue skies for these couples and each kind of issue does not exist in isolation. Rather, they interact and interrelate. In addition, societal oppression of women and lesbians introduces variability in women's coming out experience, identity development, and socioeconomic status. And aging may either bring about an increase or decrease in power, depending on experiences that have occurred across the lifespan. Even something like reproductive ability only becomes a power difference within the relationship if one or both women desire children.

Forecast: Partly Sunny or Partly Cloudy, Depending on your Perspective

"Membership has it privileges," said the old American Express commercial. But membership in which group? When considering May–December lesbian relationships, membership in each age group brings unique and overlapping privileges and oppressions.

Biology—Body Image and Reproductive Ability

Unlike the gay male community with its focus on perpetual youth, lesbian women are less likely to focus on body image, age, and maintaining the physical semblance of youth (Wagenbach, 2003). In addition, a lesbian may not feel the same pressure as heterosexual women to focus on the time-limited nature of her reproductive ability, allowing lesbians to explore a broader definition of self that is not so biologically derived. Finding encouragement in the lesbian community to question and even transcend traditional scripts concerning body image and reproduction is a privilege that can come at any age. And while there is an overall trend for women to delay childbearing (Chandra, et al., 2005), lesbian women may feel they have an even greater time window for having children because they rely on alternative conception methods that can overcome early fertility issues. A sense of flexibility and options for creating a family are also privileges not necessarily dependent upon one's age.

Yet, there is a time limit to a woman's ability to physically conceive and bear a child, and even adoption may become more difficult as a woman ages. If the older partner harbors an unfulfilled desire to conceive a child and was unable because of limited social support, underdeveloped medical technology, or discrimination by health care providers, while her younger partner retains her reproductive abilities, this power difference may emerge as grief, anger, jealousy, sadness, and resentment. On the other hand, the same feelings of grief, anger, and envy may arise if the younger woman finds herself unable physically to conceive a child while her older partner is able to do so. In this case, the power balance shifts from the (presumed) privileged younger woman to the older partner. Similarly, a lesbian who is experiencing peri-menopause or menopause may find herself buying into oppressive patriarchal scripts (Zita, 1997). Fortunately, the lesbian community can serve as a corrective, placing an emphasis on a broader identity and on the continuing contribution of women and women's wisdom across the life span.

Coming Out and Identity Consolidation

Growing older can go hand-in-hand with identity consolidation as a lesbian woman comes to know herself, grieve losses, and form a multi-faceted identity. A life structure likely has been established and perhaps even evaluated and modified during the 30s and 40s (Levinson, 1997), bringing about a sense of place and security that comes from successfully forming and integrating personal, familial, and professional identities.

When and how a lesbian woman comes out to herself and others can dramatically influence this identity consolidation process. We must discern how our sexual orientation fits with other important aspects of the life structure, such as family of origin, ethnic group, religion, work, and social circle.

At times, the younger woman in the couple may possess more privilege as she undertakes these identity development tasks; as a group, younger women come out earlier and find greater support than was available to previous generations (Grov, Bimbi, Nanín, and Parsons, 2006). Working through the stages of the coming out process often allows a woman to develop a sense of community with other lesbians and gay men, and to find community with heterosexual women and men who are accepting and supportive. These communities reinforce and support self-esteem, and also provide a buffer against experiences of prejudice and discrimination in the larger world.

However, a younger woman may find her coming out process compli-cated by simultaneous psychological separation from her family of origin, questioning of her religious faith, and a variety of other transitions—such as beginning or ending school and finding a career path. This combination can lead a younger woman to feel without roots during this time. Such a stormy period can stall the coming out process, decrease self-esteem, and create identity confusion, making the authenticity and vulnerability necessary for a healthy intimate relationship difficult.

Chronological maturation increases the likelihood that the older partner has moved through the tumultuous early stages of the coming out process, developed a sense of identity pride and honed the ability to navigate between lesbian and straight worlds (Cass, 1979). This growth can contribute to a more stable identity from which to risk intimate relationship. As a woman moves through life and successfully copes with experiences of discrimination and oppression, she may develop a "been there, done that, got the t-shirt" attitude that allows her to be less reactive and more effective at coping with future discrimination or societal backlash than her younger partner. In addition, the older partner has had more time to work through conflicts between her religious or ethnic group values and her sexual orientation, coming to a place of acceptance and understanding, while her partner is still struggling with these issues. At times, this can create a power imbalance in the age-variant relationship, as the more "adjusted" partner attempts to foreshorten her partner's struggle in these areas by "counseling" her partner or explaining away the struggle. The older partner assumes a wise counsel role in the interest of helping, but it can communicate a sense of superiority, suggesting that the struggling partner is incapable of coming to a reasonable resolution without her help.

On the other hand, this imbalance of power can lean in favor of the younger woman if her coming out process began early or was uncomplicated by experiences of internal or external homophobia. If the older partner came out in later life, has internalized homophobia or finds her community hostile to her as a lesbian, she may discover herself in a one-down position relative to her younger partner. This is especially true if the younger partner has had fewer or less extreme experiences of homophobia, judgment, and hostility, perhaps because her younger peer group, her family, and her religion have come to hold fewer prejudices against homosexuality. The younger partner may adopt the wise counsel role discussed earlier, and fail to understand her partner's fears about being out among certain people, or her struggle with self-deprecation and her questioning of the rightness of her sexual orientation.

Sexuality and Sexual Issues

For lesbian women involved in a May–December relationship, age-ist attitudes and beliefs can complicate matters. The younger or older partner, or both, may view the older partner as less sexual. One or both women may subscribe to the patriarchal narrative that attributes hyper-sexuality to younger women, especially younger lesbian women. For the older partner, coming into her own sexuality and feeling confident about her wants and desires, a younger partner's assumptions about sexual interest in later life may lead her to feel invisible and undesirable. On the other hand, the younger partner who finds she is not living into the role of being at her "sexual prime" may feel pressured by her older partner's assumptions and need for reassurance about her desirability as she ages.

These dynamics can be complicated by sex negativity and internalized homophobia that suggest to a woman that she ought not to be interested in sex in the first place, particularly lesbian sex. Depending upon a woman's upbringing, family of origin messages, prior sexual experiences with women and/or men, religious membership, ethnic group, and region of origin, either or both partners may grapple with negative feelings about sexual intimacy. At one time, the older member of the couple might have been more likely to possess these dynamics, perhaps placing her in a one-down position relative to her younger partner. However, as social mores regarding sexual activity become more permissive in many ways, while also becoming conservative in parts of the social discourse, the younger partner may not be immune to sex-negative beliefs. In addition, the extent to which either woman equates sexual interest and desire with power, even on a subconscious level, will influence the power dynamic within the couple.

Financial Issues

In Western society, sex and money are the two factors most often associated with power in the social narrative; differences in financial security and wealth can create significant power imbalances in the age-variant lesbian relationship. Barring economic disasters (such as being laid off, unemployed or chronically underemployed, or a significant health crisis), the older partner likely has had time to gain some measure of financial security, perhaps plan for retirement, and may face less economic insecurity than her younger partner. Her education is likely to be completed; additional education may further her career or facilitate a career change, but is not needed in order to enter the job market. The younger partner, who may just be establishing her career and still in the initial stages of her earning potential, may not feel she is an equal partner because she is unable to contribute equally to the financial obligations of the household.

Legal marriage, which is rarely available to lesbians, encourages a couple to view financial resources as "ours" rather than "mine" and "yours," through both social expectation and modeling. In marriage, each member of the couple is legally entitled to each other's money, reinforcing the sense of a common pool of financial resources. Although many lesbian couples blend finances and have developed a firm sense of "ours" with regard to money, thus decreasing the power differential created by earning discrepancies, many lesbian couples struggle with this. The older partner (who is earning more and therefore has more socially ascribed power) may have an easier time reaching an "ours" understanding than the younger partner.

The younger partner may be eager to develop a unified financial stance in an attempt to decrease the discomfort of income disparity. She may have the most difficulty when there is a significant earning difference. Internalized classism can bring pressure to "pass" as a member of a higher class and feelings of shame, embarrassment, and a sense of not belonging. If one member of a couple identifies as middle class or above and her partner is not in the same class, in reality or identity, a microcosm of society's class issues can be unconsciously enacted within the relationship.

While it is more likely that the older partner will experience greater earning potential, at times the reverse may be true, with the younger partner contributing more to the household income. This financial situation may arise if the younger member works in a field that compensates employees at a higher level. This power imbalance can raise feelings of anger and resentment in the older partner, who may feel less valued by society and a vague sense of something being wrong.

Retirement can also bring about a reversal of financial status within a May–December couple. The retiring partner may suddenly find herself on a fixed income and, at least in her own mind, have become a member of a different socioeconomic class. If she has been the primary wage earner, or contributed equally to the financial status of the family, this change can be disempowering and unsettling for the older partner, who may no longer be sure of her role or feel somehow dependent on her partner in a way not previously experienced.

Self-Esteem, Voice, and Relationships

The power differential in age-variant lesbian couples may include privileges that derive from differences in self-esteem—from peer and professional groups, financial security, and comfort with her overall life structure. This self-esteem can facilitate the older partner's ability to enter a couple relationship with greater surety and confidence. Unless other psychological insecurities are present, it is easier to enter a relationship when one is secure in one's self and not dependent on the intimate relationship for self-definition, as can be the case when other aspects of a woman's life structure are still in flux. Further, society often privileges the voice of the older member of a couple. In age-variant lesbian relationships, this societal privileging can empower the older partner to speak her mind more freely, consciously, or unconsciously expecting her wisdom and experience to be respected and listened to by the younger member of the couple. Likewise, the younger woman may find herself living out the social expectation and undervaluing her own experience and voice in favor of her partner's opinion.

As a couple ages together, the younger woman may come into her own voice, causing a shift in the power balance to which the couple must adjust. Over time, the older member may find herself reaching the age when society attempts to silence her voice. If one or both women buy into this societal silencing, the power dynamic will once again shift and can cause significant feelings of loss and distress for the older partner.

High Pressure Zone

Power is not one-dimensional; other forms of diversity intersect with age-related power and enhance or subtract from a woman's personal sense of power, her partner's perception of the power dynamic, and her place in society's power structure. The more layers of oppression and privilege that exist within an age-variant lesbian relationship, the more charged and pressured the power dynamics may become.

Others have written about how diversity complicates power dynamics within lesbian relationships (e.g., Burch, 1987; Greene, 1994) involving differences in race, ethnicity, or nation/region of origin; disability status; body size/shape; socioeconomic class; and religion. Each kind of diversity possesses its own socially ascribed privilege or oppression, but age and age differences may mean something different when interacting with each of these. For example, while many White and Western cultures tend to view aging as something to be avoided, that renders a person irrelevant and unable to contribute to the family or society, many other cultures hold more positive views on aging, recognizing the contributions of older members of the family and community.

For example, disability status may have one meaning for a younger woman who has lived with a disability for some time, or who has suddenly becomes disabled, whereas being disabled means something very different for an older partner whose health is declining or who experiences a sudden, catastrophic health event such as a stroke or heart attack. Both may experience grief, loss, and fear of being a burden to her partner. But when an older partner becomes disabled, the way that each woman experiences the meaning of age may determine whether she (and her partner) can rebound emotionally and discover a sense of future or whether they will become mired in negative social definitions of age and disability.

Beliefs about Aging

A woman's personal concerns about aging often include worries about changes in health and/or cognitive status, concerns about employment/income security, fears that her wisdom and experience will no longer be valued by younger members of the community, and wondering if she will remain sexually attractive. Aging can be celebrated as a new phase of life with new opportunities, or dreaded as the "beginning of the end," depending on a lesbian's narrative about aging, her experience seeing others age, her partner's reaction to her aging concerns, and the actual physical changes she experiences. Intersecting with these concerns are the younger partner's beliefs about aging in herself and her partner. An age-ist attitude in the younger partner can reinforce the older partner's negative stereotypes of aging, leading to either wholesale acceptance of stereotypes by both, or to resentment between partners as one woman experiences being treated as "old before her time" (i.e., incapable). Alternatively, a younger partner who fears aging may refuse to acknowledge and work with her partner to make adjustments to the realities that aging can bring—changes in health or physical abilities, or changes in priorities or interests that accompany a new stage of life. Similarly, the older partner may find it difficult to acknowledge that her younger partner is also aging and needs to make changes to her life structure, if to do so would mean changes in established goals and ways of relating.

Social Clock Expectations

The social clock tells us when we "should" undertake socially approved projects, and chimes out different norms for people at different ages. Parenting often highlights this social clock discrepancy for couples. A younger partner, entering a relationship with an older partner who has a child, may find herself thrust into the role of parent when she was only beginning to examine her own desires regarding childbearing and babies. This can be particularly challenging if the younger partner is not quite ready to leave behind the relatively carefree time of her 20s, assume parental responsibilities, and give up freedom and flexibility in her daily schedule and life choices. On the other hand, an older partner who has reached some resolution to not have children may find herself rethinking parenting if she enters a relationship with a younger woman who wants to include children in their family. If the couple chooses to adopt or have a child, the older partner can find herself struggling to integrate two distinct phases of life: the post-menopausal/looking toward retirement phase and the new parent phase (with its 18-year commitment).

Social clock mismatch also may occur when partners reach life structure transitions at different times. This disparity in development may bring upheaval, for the partner whose life structure is in a period of stability, or premature closure for the partner seeking transition, leading them to either feel unsettled by too much transition or "old before their time" by too much structure and routine.

In another potential timing mismatch, the younger member of the couple may find herself in the role of caregiver to her older partner at a time in her life when she was expecting to launch their children and regain some freedom and individuality. She may find herself "sandwiched" twice: first sandwiched between caring for a child and an aging parent at the same time, and then caring for a child and her partner at the same time.

Low Pressure Zone; Hidden Power

Women, lesbians, and feminists struggle with the difficult concept of power. Traditional power is identified as power over another person (patriarchal power), something all oppressed groups have experienced and associate with coercion and force, whereas women's power is seen as power-with, mutual and empowering (Kitzinger, 1992). We may want to ignore or deny power in ourselves and in our relationships, giving in to the temptation to focus on shared experiences and what we have in common, and ignoring social definitions and experiences that create power differences.

Many lesbians hold to egalitarianism as a way of understanding power within their relationships, and age-variant couples are no different. While egalitarianism properly defined does not imply the absence of power differentials (Brown, 1994), "egalitarianism = equal" is the equation writ large on lesbians' social consciousness. The result is a false "low pressure zone" for the May–December lesbian couple, where the power differences are not acknowledged, discussed, and actively addressed. However, "denied power is power run amok" (Veldhuis, 2001: 45), creating everything from vague discomfort to active distress in couples.

Rather than denying power in the hopes of creating a false sense of contentment and minimizing distress, lesbian women in age-variant relationships need to reconceptualize power differences in their relationship so that they can be addressed authentically, actively, and openly. The concept of relational power—"the ability to both produce and undergo an effect . . . the capacity both to influence others and to be influenced by others" (Loomer, 1976: 17)—more accurately captures the dynamic nature of power within May–December lesbian relationships. Relational power requires a person to be open to and include another within her world of meaning. This process becomes circular and self-sustaining as each person in a relationship, by opening themselves, simultaneously creates both the potential to be influenced and the potential to influence the other. Therefore "societal privilege does not determine relational power," but "relational power is determined by the degree to which one can actively open to the influence of others' experiences, without losing one's identity or creative freedom" and "the greater the contrast held [in the relationship], the greater the relational power" (Bruns and Trimble, 2001: 30–31).

FORECAST: CLOUDS FOLLOWED BY CLEAR SKIES

An array of issues has emerged, yet many May–December lesbian relationships survive and thrive over the long term. This section explores some concerns that age-variant couples need to work through as they create loving relationships that grow and change across the lifespan.

Potential Thunderstorms

Communication

The most important task for any intimate relationship is effective communication. Each individual must possess the ability to know, and take responsibility for, her own thoughts and feelings, needs, and desires, and must communicate these clearly and directly to her partner. In addition, each woman needs to hear and be moved by her partner—even during difficult discussions that require great contrast to be held within their relationship. Communication skills do not assure that a couple will have nothing but clear skies during their relationship. To the contrary, when a couple's communication is open and authentic, they are more likely to address difficulties rather than ignore problems in their relationship.

Differences and Relational Power

The ability to actively engage differences, and to reach compromise through mutually respectful and caring dialogue (even fighting), is vital to successful relationships. Some differences may be fleeting, easily resolved, or simple to let go. Other differences will require ongoing discussion, awareness, and working-through. Power differences within age-variant relationships are long-term dynamic issues that require visitation throughout a couple's relationship. These issues can create seemingly sudden thunderstorms (power storms) that may threaten to overwhelm a couple if they are ignored and not engaged through relational power.

How is this done? First, both partners must become aware of the privileges and oppressions each brings to their relationship. These privileges and oppressions shape each person's view of self, other, and the world, and can constrict options over the lifespan for each woman and the couple. Cultivating awareness is vital if the couple is going to be able to value and really engage around their differences. Awareness grows through education, reading, discussion with others, and ultimately through openly seeking to understand each other's experience as a woman and lesbian, through the lens of age. As part of raising our awareness, we need to commit ourselves to examining and overcoming discriminatory attitudes and beliefs that we have internalized from society and unconsciously projected on our partner, oneself, and the relationship. This work confronts internalized age-ism, homophobia, racism, able-ism, and a host of other "isms" that everyone possesses at some level.

From this place of awareness and commitment to honoring differences, a couple comes together to honestly discuss differences, rather than living out the "power-over" dynamic that society encourages, and that will erode relationships over time. Because "unity and differentiation [become] correlates rather than opposites of each other" (Johnson, 1992: 217) within relational power, a couple can view societal privilege in one member not as something that creates a hierarchy within their relationship, but as something that can be used for the overall good of the couple. Similarly, when there is a change in relative social power between individuals in the couple, such as the change in income that comes with retirement, this change can be seen relationally as an opportunity for each person to bring something new to the relationship. It is only when a couple buys into discriminatory beliefs about aging that changes in status must be experienced as loss of status, rather than as a dynamic part of life and relationship. Relational power allows the couple to grow together, embracing differences and change, adjusting their lives and relationship with the realities they encounter together.

Approaching socially ascribed power differentials within a couple relationally does not create a utopia with perpetual clear blue skies. Even when differences are honored and respected within a relationship, difficult feelings can arise. Individual losses or gains in privilege engender authentic feelings of loss, worry, guilt, envy, uncertainty, and self-doubt. Successful May–December lesbian relationships must create space for all emotions and experiences to be received as openly and non-defensively as possible, requiring high levels of emotional maturity from both women. Maintaining a sense of humor, viewing all of the issues as important but holding them lightly, can help a couple weather difficult dialogues and transitions.

Umbrellas and Sunscreen: Packing the Practical Things

Awareness, understanding, relational perspective, communication skills, and humor are vital components of the successful long-term May–December lesbian relationship. However, some practical things can assist couples to plan thoughtfully for the future, minimizing potentially stormy periods of their relationship.

Legal Documents

Same-sex couples in most states have access to legal documents that provide protection and validation of their relationship. Couples need medical and legal powers-of-attorney, wills, and disposition of remains documents, in order to care for one another in times of crisis. When couples draft living wills or directives to physicians together, they have a forum to talk through health care, end of life issues, and how they will generally handle changes in health as both individuals age or in the event of catastrophic health problems. If the couple is parenting children together, particularly in states dis-allowing same-sex second parent adoptions, authorization for consent to medical treatment of a minor is essential. Domestic partnership agreements—who provides what for the good of the relationship, covering everything from financial obligations to care of the household— also provide an opportunity for a couple to discuss their expectations of one another. Regularly revisiting these agreements ensures that the couple continues to pay attention to the ebb and flow of strengths and limitations, and adapts together for the good of each other and their relationship.

Financial Issues

Whether a couple combines financial resources into a single account or maintains separate accounts, it is essential that May–December lesbian couples view finances as a shared endeavor. Discussing income, bills, savings, and retirement plans, and spending patterns can create a sense of mutual responsibility and contribution to the financial well-being of the household. Making each other signatories on one another's accounts also can increase a sense of joint ownership and responsibility. Approaching discussions and decisions about finances from the perspective of relational power can be especially important when there are significant differences in income or debt. A relational power perspective can prevent the woman with less earning power from feeling pressured to contribute beyond her means or from viewing herself as helpless and in need of rescuing and caretaking by her more financially secure partner (who may share this view). Planning for future changes in earning such as the loss of a job, retirement, and unexpected major expenses is important preventative work that can reduce feelings of loss, fear, guilt, and resentment when a couple encounters these common life events. Such planning may include creating savings accounts, purchasing life and long-term care insurance, enrolling in a retirement account, and using other financial planning vehicles to provide a monetary cushion should the couple need one.

Long-Term Care

All couples need to discuss how they will handle long-term care when one or both experience declining health. However, this discussion is especially important in age-variant lesbian couples because it is a way of acknowledging and addressing the age-related anxieties of both women. Issues include: how the need (or desire) to move to a retirement community or assisted living would affect the younger partner, how long one partner can be cared for by the other in the couple's home, and what they expect of each other if one needs to live in an assisted or nursing-care setting. The couple needs to consider these issues, not only in relation to the older partner, but also as they may apply to the younger partner who could experience an early decline in health for reasons unrelated to her age. Knowing one another's hopes and expectations can ease difficult decision making, reduce concerns about being a burden or abandoning one's partner, and encourage a couple to work together to make their desires achievable.

Seeking Support

Being a lesbian couple with significant age difference in a patriarchal, homophobic, age-ist culture can be stressful. Couples need respite from the daily wear and tear of carrying minority status, and from direct encounters with discrimination that may block options and choices. Creating a community of support that includes other lesbian women in age-variant relationships is vital. Such a community can provide support, encouragement, and even mentoring for May–December lesbian couples. These connections allow each partner to share her experience with someone in similar circumstances, and can provide another perspective on her partner's experience. This understanding and perspective can help a couple work through an impasse by situating the problem in a larger context, making it less personal as they see they are not the first couple to struggle with a particular issue or difference.

Social support is vital to successful coping withal types of minority stress and societal discrimination. At times, however, it may not be enough. Professional counseling is another tool available to age-variant lesbian couples who find themselves struggling to work through relational issues. An affirming and educated therapist can help a couple navigate the issues, teach positive communication skills, and facilitate the resolution of personal concerns that stand in the way of healthy relating. Professional help can be especially important when underlying emotional or psychological issues are triggered for one or both women and during major life stresses or transitions.

BLUE SKIES

There is great joy in loving relationships characterized by authenticity, openness, honesty, and the ability to communicate directly—all supported by a healthy dose of humor and not taking oneself too seriously. To focus on power differentials in May–December lesbian couples does not imply that these relationships are rife with problems. To the contrary, raising these issues, making conscious what may have been operating unconsciously, reduces their power to have detrimental impact on a couple's relationship. Engaging these issues in a relational, dynamic, ongoing way, couples can weather the changes and difficulties that are part of life with greater resilience and not allow storms to overshadow their hoped-for blue skies.

NOTE

1. An important exception is the analysis of power issues and attendant challenges faced by interracial gay and lesbian couples (e.g., Greene, 1994; Poon, 2000).

REFERENCES

Brown, L.*Subversive Dialogues: Theory in Feminist Therapy.* New York: Basic Books, 1994.

Bruns, C. M. and C. Trimble. "Rising Tide: Taking Our Place as Young Feminist Psychologists."*Women & Therapy: A Feminist Quarterly,* 23(2), 2001: 19–36.

Burch, B. "Barriers to Intimacy: Conflicts Over Power, Dependency, and Nurturing in Lesbian Relationships." In The Boston Lesbian Psychologies Collective, eds.,*Lesbian Psychologies.* Urbana and Chicago: University of Illinois Press, 1987: 126–141.

Cass, V. C. "Homosexual Identity Development: A Theoretical Model."*Journal of Homosexuality,* 4(3), 1979: 219–235.

Chandra, A., G. M. Martinez, W. D. Mosher, J. C. Abma, and J. Jones. (2005). "Fertility, Family Planning, and Reproductive Health of U.S. Women: Data From the 2002 National Survey of Family Growth." In the National Center for Health Statistics, ed.,*Vital Health Statistics* 23(25), 2005. Retrieved August 7, 2006 from http://www.cdc.gov/nchs/products/pubs/pubd/series/sr23/pre-1/sr23_25.htm.

Dunker, B. "Aging Lesbians: Observations and Speculations." In The Boston Lesbian Psychologies Collective, eds.,*Lesbian Psychologies.* Urbana and Chicago: University of Illinois Press, 1987: 72–82.

Greene, B. "Lesbian Women of Color: Triple Jeopardy." In L. Comas-Diaz and B. Greene, eds.,*Women of Color: Integrating Ethnic and Gender Identities in Psychotherapy.* New York: Guilford Press, 1994: 389–427.

Grov, C., D. S. Bimbi, . J. E. Nanín, and J. T. Parsons. "Race, Ethnicity, Gender, and Generational Factors Associated with the Coming-Out Process Among Gay, Lesbian, and Bisexual Individuals." *Journal of Sex Research,* 43(2), 2006: 115–121.

Johnson, E. A.*She Who Is: The Mystery of God in Feminist Theological Development.* Cambridge, MA: Crossroad Publishing Company, 1992.

Kaslow, F. "Sexuality in May-December Marriages." In D. Kantor and B. Okun, eds.,*Intimate Environments: Sex, Intimacy, and Gender in Families.* New York: Guilford Press, 1989: 321–345.

Kitzinger, C. "Feminism, Psychology, and the Paradox of Power." In J. S. Bohan et al., eds.,*Seldom Seen, Rarely Heard: Women's Place in Psychology.* Boulder, CO: Westview Press, 1992: 423–442.

Levinson, D. J. *"Seasons of a Woman's Life."* New York: Random House, 1997.

Loomer, B. "Two Conceptions of Power."*Process Studies,* 6(1), 1976: 5–32.

Poon, M. K. L. "Inter-Racial Same-Sex Abuse: The Vulnerability of Gay Men of Asian Descent in Relationships with Caucasian Men."*Journal of Gay &Lesbian Social Services: Issues in Practice, Policy &Research,* 11(4), 2000: 39–67.

Ristock, J. L. "Beyond Ideologies: Understanding Violence in Lesbian Relationships."*Canadian Woman Studies,* 12(1), 1991: 74–79.

Ristock, J. L. "Exploring Dynamics of Abusive Lesbian Relationships: Preliminary Analysis of a Multi-Site, Qualitative Study."*American Journal of Community Psychology,* 31(3/4), 2003. Retrieved December 22, 2005 from http://proquest.umi.com/pqdweb?did = 655182551&sid = 1&Fmt = 3&clientId = 48335&RQT = 309&VName = PQD

Veldhuis, C. B. "The Trouble with Power."*Women &Therapy: A Feminist Quarterly,* 23(2), 2001: 37–56.

Wagenbach, P. "Lesbian Body Image and Eating Issues." *Journal of Psychology and Human Sexuality,* 15(4), 2003: 205–227.

Zita, J. N. "Heresy in the Female Body: The Rhetorics of Menopause." In M. Pearsall, ed., The Other Within Us: *Feminist Explorations of Women and Aging.* Boulder, CO: Westview Press, 1997: 95–112.

Women Aging Together in Community

Jane Ariel

SUMMARY. At a fiftieth birthday party 17 years ago, a group of women—lesbian, bisexual, and straight—decided to create a conscious community in which they could age together. The group, where they discuss this process and support each other, is politically and personally meaningful, and a buffer against the isolation and powerlessness many aging women experience. They meet monthly, and at weekend retreats twice a year. They have become a "family of choice," sharing holidays and celebrations and supporting each other when necessary and possible. After several years, they decided to commit for life. In the group, each feels held and seen in the complex experience of aging in today's world.

If you happened to look in the window of this house, on the first Saturday of the month, you would see six older women intently listening to a seventh. She might be talking about what happened in her life in the last month, or suggesting a topic for the group—like, what did she feel she needed to accomplish in her late sixties, or what was the nature of her sexuality these

Jane Ariel, Ph.D., is on the faculty of the Wright Institute in Berkeley, California. In addition to her private practice, she is a consultant for Visions, a national training program dedicated to developing multiculturalism. She has written on therapy with gay and lesbian families, the "chosen family," and mothering in the Jewish family. In Israel, where she lived for many years, her work focused on educational and social differences among Jewish minorities. She is a Board Member of the American Family Therapy Academy.

days. You might also see the women engaged in spontaneous conversation about how to tolerate what is going on in the world.

If you came inside and stayed for a while, you would probably sense that these women knew each other really well. You would see them laugh with the humor that comes from long years of shared history, and then, a minute later, turn to talking seriously about sensitive subjects. Tears rolling down, one woman reports about a grown child's struggle or the increasing pain in her body. Later, you might see everyone smile at stories of the satisfaction of successful leadership at work, or the completion of some creative endeavor. Finally, if you stayed for a few hours, you would experience how blessed each women feels to be part of a community dedicated to sharing the difficult and wonderful aspects of growing older.

JOINING TOGETHER

It all began nineteen years ago when six good friends, all women, were eating in a lovely, quiet French restaurant in Berkeley, California, celebrating a 51st birthday. In the midst of a lively conversation, someone said, "Let's create a group so we can support each other through menopause and aging." By this time, some of us had experienced menopause and some were on the verge. We were all aware of entering a new stage of our lives that would be challenging to our identity as women and as human beings. A group sounded like a great idea, and we decided that each of us would invite two or three people to join us the following month.

Perhaps the urge to form such a group, or a safe place to belong, came from the fact that we were already very conscious of the marginalization of women in the world (Zoelle, 2000; McCann and Kim, 2002). Some of us had been in consciousness-raising groups many years before, and knew the power of joining together to bring about change and a deeper understanding of the way social forces affect our personal and public lives, particularly in the construction of how gender is experienced. Perhaps it was that all but one of us at dinner were presently living our lives as lesbians and knew how important it would be to have the support of an intentional collectivity (Herdt and Devries, 2004; Weakes, Heaphy and Donovan, 2001). The idea of how the intertwined toxicity of homophobia and sexism had affected our lives was familiar to all of us, even though it influenced each of our lives differently.

At that moment, none of us was focused on her identity or on any conscious theoretical formulation. The spontaneous suggestion came more from our desire to create a heart-opening place where we would be consistently recognized, heard, and held as we entered into the later part of our life. If asked, we probably would have said that this personal experience would also be a political act that would counter the fragmentation that characterizes today's harried, violent world—an experience that can increase precipitously with age and its potential isolation and sense of disempowerment (Rosenthal, 1990; Wheeler, 1997).

BEGINNINGS, AND OUR DEMOGRAPHICS

Sixteen people attended the first meeting, where we began the process of figuring out how we should proceed. There were a number of questions. Would there be some criteria for belonging? What would our agenda be? Could people come and go or would the group be limited to a certain number who committed to come?

At the beginning there had been no explicit discussion about the composition of the group, although it turned out that everybody invited was white and educated. In the first group of sixteen, the majority continued to be lesbians. There were different religious backgrounds and spiritual practices, including a number of Jews, Buddhists and unaffiliated people. There was a range of class origins and present financial situations, so that some group members had family money, some earned good salaries, and some had very few material resources. Several women were published writers, some therapists, some artists, and some educators.

THE AGENDA: WEAVING THE TAPESTRIES OF OUR LIVES

Not exactly knowing how to proceed, we decided we would start with "check-ins," describing how we were and what had happened in our lives between meetings. These took much of our four-hour meeting. Then, we added broader topics, which we chose a month ahead.

After three or four meetings, nine women decided to become a closed group that would meet monthly. Given the many differences among us, we decided that we had to come to know each other better in order to create a meeting structure and an intention that would be meaningful and relevant to the group as a whole. To do this, we decided that each woman in turn would talk about the decades of her life, one at a time. It was an incredible exercise, which took a few years to complete. We were touched by the power of each decade, and often we could sense how important what happened at different points was in shaping each woman's life. Two of us, for example, had children at a very young age (seventeen and nineteen), and another had been expelled shamefully from college for initiating a relationship with another woman.

This foundation provided the kind of experience together that led to a rich intimacy (Black and Greenberg, 2002), like weaving a multi-colored tapestry with the decades of our lives. This more complex appreciation of each other yielded a greater sense of security and trust, allowing us to take more risks and be more vulnerable with each other. A year into our existence, for example, one woman's brother was diagnosed with terminal brain cancer. Our meeting was scheduled on the weekend of his exploratory surgery. She arrived extremely upset, because the surgery had revealed the inoperable nature of the spreading tumor. She came to the group to find comfort and share her grief. We began to feel how important we were becoming in each other's lives.

WAYS TO DEEPEN

Sometimes, in our monthly meetings, we felt that we did not have enough time to explore complex topics. We decided to add a retreat twice a year, where we could be together for a weekend without the usual pressures of daily life. At one of our first retreats when we rented a house with a hot tub at Sea Ranch, some three hours away from the Bay Area, we discovered that many of us loved to sing. After a rousing rendition of a popular song from the sixties, we decided that we would call ourselves the Wandering Menstruals. We quipped that the "wandering" part referred to the nature of menopause—its course was often uncharted, and we were all in different parts of it. We were quite pleased with ourselves, and the name has stuck, even though now it's entirely irrelevant. For short, we call ourselves the Mennies, even though we have long since stopped bleeding.

It is during our retreats that we deepen our experience together—whether in intimate, personal conversations, raucous laughter and dancing, or serious consideration of the process of aging or the state of the world. Our conversations find their way into moving and uncharted territory. Lingering around the dinner table, we talk about everything—sex, activism, children, the past, the present—savoring the opportunity to connect without time constraints. Some of us are very forthcoming, while others listen or are more private.

We have structured our more formal, timed meetings. We take turns facilitating, and address topics that we have chosen and recorded in our group book. This book keeps us on track in case we forget what we decided. Lately we laugh a lot about how our failing memories afford us the possibility of endlessly amusing each other with the same stories. After short check-ins, we turn to our chosen topics. Are we the people we wanted to be? What has become of our dreams? How do we relate to spirituality? How has the way we construct meaning changed over the years? One time we talked about how we wanted to die. We have talked about how being privileged affected our lives, and about our beliefs, our politics and our feelings of belonging and exclusion. One time we talked about exactly how much money we each had, almost a forbidden topic in our society.

IMAGES OF HISTORY, IMAGES OF CHANGE

We have taken pictures throughout the years, and preserve these images of our history in an album we have collated. The ending of each retreat is ritualized by the ticking of the camera's timer as one of us, with everybody shouting to hurry, runs to join the group photo before the camera flashes. Then we get into our cars to head in our different directions, carpooling when we can. Besides the memories that come when we look at the album, we are always astounded by how much we have aged. We see the gray and white hair, the changing bodies with the accumulated gravity of living for nineteen more years.

Earlier in our history, two of us were dying their hair. As staunch feminists, some felt this gave too much credence to patriarchal values. It became clear, though, how important it was to the two women to maintain their sense of feminine appeal, particularly in public settings where they often appeared. The group understood and respected that decision, and, over time, both women decided to let their hair return to its natural gray. Out of this experience came a deeper discussion of what it means to exist in the world without the power of the sex appeal that had accompanied some of us as younger women. Talking about losing it, painful as it was, made it easier to bear and integrate into our changing sense of self. Interestingly, one of the women who had not liked her body when she was younger felt more attractive as an older woman.

All our bodies were sagging, so we decided to have "sagging contests." Laughing together, we were not alone, nor did we have to accept society's view of how women were supposed to be. We each felt so accepted by the group that we could be exactly as we were without pretenses. Some said that this was the only place where they did not prepare what they were going to say. They trusted (Weakes et al., 2001).

In a more practical realm, we have also researched issues concerning aging, such as what the most effective supplements are, whether to take HRT (hormone replacement therapy), how to deal with drying vaginal walls, what is the best long-term health care, or how to make sure each of us has a living will.

TENSIONS

With the development of any intentional gathering of people, tensions arise over time. Of course there are the minor conflicts over differences in personality, such as our style of arguing or how we keep a kitchen clean, but most have been quite easily resolved. Others have required careful ongoing attention.

Feelings of Exclusion

A more substantive issue has concerned close friendships within the group. Because of these friendships, some women see each other more between meetings. Over the years, some feelings of exclusion have arisen, particularly when social events did not include everybody or when certain topics or experiences brought small sub-groupings together. The need to belong is always a tender subject, and it was with some hesitation that one or the other of us brought up our sensitivities about it. Being able to tolerate these tensions and talk about them, however, was necessary to keep the group current and emotionally alive.

Different Needs

Some tensions have to do with having different needs. For example, some of us have been single and some in long-term relationships during the life of the Mennies. The group has functioned for the single women as their closest family, whereas others belong to a committed family or couple that fulfills that role. There is an unspoken understanding about loyalty to partners and children: they hold the highest priority. Although there has been some sensitivity about this, it has mostly been expressed as longings that some of us had at various times for the availability of closeness to children or an intimate partner.

It is important to say that two people have left the group, one earlier and one recently. These departures, although very different in nature, shook the group in its core. In the early days of our group, one woman was asked to leave because of her prolonged period of absence, and our recognition that her goals for the group differed from the goals of the rest of us. Her departure was particularly difficult because we had not yet been together long enough to have a clear decision-making process. As women, we tend to be caretakers and would prefer harmony to conflict. The second person left much later, because she felt that membership in the group was conflicting with other stronger desires. When she announced this final decision at a retreat, the group was grief-stricken. We gathered by the sea, having few words as we listened to the sound of the waves together. Our chosen family was inevitably changed.

STAYING TOGETHER

Perhaps in response to this, at a subsequent retreat, we asked ourselves what had allowed the seven of us to stay together. High on our list was our like-minded political consciousness, which was strongly feminist. Many of us had been activists for progressive and radical causes as younger women, and some continued to be so.

We also agreed that it was important that nobody dominated the conversations and that we all were interested in a wide range of subjects, certainly those related to aging and conscious living. We noted that each of us had the capacity to listen and not overwhelm the others too often with our personal difficulties or needs. We thought this was related to a growing psychological maturity, supported by our membership in the group.

We included on our list the ability to confront each other when something does not feel right. It is never easy to do and often provokes anxiety, which we have learned to tolerate. Nobody withdraws or requires extensive caretaking during these exchanges. At the same time we are clear this is not a therapy group, nor do we allow ourselves to get bogged down in too much process. Sometimes we have to let go of what we do not agree about. At the same time, we share the capacity for self-reflection, which encourages honest and collaborative communication. However, this does not prevent us from hurting each other sometimes, from a lack of sensitivity or a conflicting perception.

Desire for a Supportive Community

Another important aspect of coming and staying together was the mutual desire to create a supportive community. We resemble the "family of choice" known well in the gay and lesbian community (Weston, 1991)—a loosely knit group of friends, colleagues, past lovers, and sometimes nuclear family members that queer people create as a trustworthy "kinship" network which can insulate them from a hostile, homophobic world. Powerful kinship networks like the family of choice have existed all over the world, and have been the sustaining force within which an individual, family, or group molds its identity and garners life-giving support, particularly in oppressive cultures (Schweizer and White, 1998). The Wandering Menstruals have created such a network as older women, hopefully providing a model of conscious community that could benefit people of all ages.

ACTS OF SUPPORT

As the Mennies' cohesiveness developed, there were many ways we supported each other, through illness, in success, and in celebration. This support extended to significant others as well, whom we called our "in-laws." If someone had a book signing, we were there. We prepared food for birthdays and marriages. We helped each other move. We mourned the death of loved ones. We were present if a relationship was faltering or breaking up. There was a couple in the group which broke up after a number of years, and the Mennies gathered around each of them. We learned from this experience, incidentally, that it was not a wise thing to bring a couple into a group like this. They know each other better than others, and their capacity to use the group for support can be compromised. Even so, both are still full participants today.

Three women have had cancer, one who could not work during a very difficult period of recovery. Besides helping her with hospital visits, household chores, and organization of a healing team in the wider community, the Wandering Menstruals decided that limited financial support was essential. By this time, we had established a fund; everybody contributes monthly. Because there are large differences in financial resources, we each give an amount according to our ability. Then, when money is needed, it can be distributed. In this case, individuals contributed specifically to the woman who was sick, but the group fund was also available. This fund is also used for the more extensive trip the group takes every five years to celebrate its existence. There has been a trip to Mexico, to Canada, and to Mississippi. The fund allows everybody to go; it is magical to be sitting at dinner and not have to pay the bill.

A LIFE COMMITMENT

After this experience of a life-threatening cancer, at a retreat the group again discussed the nature of our relationship to each other. It was clear that our need for support at many levels was growing as we aged. After a long and thoughtful discussion, we decided to commit for life. This meant that we would be there for each other and our significant others until we died. Our hearts were full of gratitude as we sat closely together.

Today our youngest is sixty-seven and our oldest seventy-two. We dance a little less, although we love to laugh. We still work hard, but we tire sooner than we used to. We know that we are more vulnerable to illness and accidents, and we are aware of our mortality and more interested in the spiritual as we come closer to facing death. Some of us are single and some of us are in long-term relationships. We all have grown children and some have grandchildren who grace our hearts with joy. We are either working less than we ever have, or are retired. This allows us more time for political activism or for the development of creative pursuits. As we wend our way further into old age, we remember gratefully that we are part of a very important community, a chosen family, that helps us remain vibrant, visible and conscious.

REFERENCES

Black, J. and D. Greenberg. *Women and Friendship.* Gretna, LA: Wellness Institute, Inc., 2002.

Herdt, D. and B. DeVries. *Gay and Lesbian Aging: Research and Future Directions.* New York: Springer Publishing Company, 2004.

McCann, C. and S. Kim. *Feminist Theory Reader.* New York: Routledge, 2002.

Rosenthal, E., ed. *Women, Aging, and Ageism.* New York: Haworth, 1990.

Schweizer, T. and D. White, eds. *Kinship Networks and Exchange.* Cambridge, England: Cambridge University Press, 1998.

Weakes, J, B. Heaphy, and C. Donovan. *Same Sex Intimacies: Families of Choice and Other Life Experiments.* New York: Routledge, 2001.

Weston, C. *Families We Choose: Lesbians, Gays, Kinship.* New York: Columbia University Press, 1991.

Wheeler, H. *Women and Aging*: A*Guide to the Literature.* Boulder, CO: Lynne Rienner Publishers, 1997.

Zoelle, D. *Globalizing Concern for Women's Human Rights:The Failure of the American Model.* New York: St. Martin's Press, 2000.

We Are Family: I Got All My Sisters with Me!

Mary Kay Hunyady

SUMMARY. This article introduces the reader to an unusual family of choice: a 10-year-old Internet listserv for a "family" of lesbian nuns. The purpose of this listserv, and reasons for belonging to it, are described, including as context the unique psychosocial situation of lesbian nuns. The author includes such "family dynamics" as personality differences, the presence of a famous family member, inclusion/exclusion, stability/change, and dealing with differences. Issues of privacy, danger from outside the "family," and being stigmatized are acknowledged. The author comments on the unique qualities of a "cyber-family" and compares the listserv with other kinds of families.

I am not a mother (although, at one point, the women in my religious order were called by the title of "mother," as in, Mother Hunyady, for example). I have not given birth to any children (although some in my religious order have). I have no adopted children and I do not co-parent

Mary Kay Hunyady, RSCJ, Psy.D., is a licensed psychologist in private practice, and also does in-service work with other religious who are in leadership in their congregations. Mary Kay is interested in the intersection of psychology, social justice, and spirituality/spiritual practice. Her background includes political and community organizing, and teaching religion and theology in high schools. She is a member of the San Francisco Psychotherapy Research Group. Mary Kay has been a Roman Catholic nun (a Religious of the Sacred Heart) for 30 years.

any children, although I was on a childcare team earlier in my life. So, the family that I write about is family because we choose to be, and because we fit into a certain category of persons. In these ways, my form of lesbian family is not different from other lesbian families: we are a family of choice (Weston, 1991).

A quick run-through of the 19 definitions of the word "family" in Dictionary.com shows that connection by blood is by far the most often cited commonality across the definitions. Still, there is one option: the group of people who are not typically blood related and who share similarities, such as attitudes, experiences, beliefs, or goals. Such is my Internet family of lesbian sisters, or LESTERS.

We all search for those who are like us (Slater, 1988). I am no different. In 1997, about two months after I had started back to graduate school, I was told about a place on the Internet where I would find others like me. I had read, in an occasional publication that I receive written for and by lesbian nuns, that a new listserv had begun for Roman Catholic nuns who self-identify as lesbian. With joy, I subscribed. I recall being excited to come home, to see what the conversation on the list was that day. Since then, conversations have shifted, people have come and gone, and several of us do not find the same need for the list as we once did, while others find a great need. Essentially, the listserv is a place of welcome, connection, support, challenge, discussion (which sometimes becomes shouting), resource exchange, brain-storming.

Listservs are postmodern phenomena. They allow for quick communication among those who self-select into them. They can be a means of community, or just a way to pass along information that others need. As an Internet phenomenon, people are able to communicate with others whom they do not know but with whom they feel a kinship. Someone in Thailand, for example, could be connected to others like her in the United States, Canada, Peru, and Australia. These are compelling reasons for beginning a listserv, and in the case of this family of lesbian nuns, the listserv meets these needs and more.

CATHOLIC AND LESBIAN: WELCOMING THE WARY

The very fact of being lesbian and Roman Catholic is controversial. Although there is debate among Roman Catholic theologians about the nature of homosexuality and the behavior of homosexuals, the "official" position of the institutional Roman Catholic Church states that "tradition has always declared that 'homosexual acts are *intrinsically disordered*' . . . . The number of men and women who have deep-seated homosexual tendencies is not negligible. They do not choose their homosexual *condition*; for most of them it is a *trial*" (italics mine. Episcopate of the Roman Catholic Church, 1994: 626, paragraph 2358). For many of us who are Roman Catholic nuns and lesbians, our coming out was complicated by a double dose of internalized homophobia—cultural and religious—that we have had to conquer.

The LESTERS family is there to welcome the newcomer to the list and to her sexual orientation. When someone first joins the list, it's typically because she has recently come out to herself, or because she is thinking of entering religious life and already knows that she is lesbian. Some new listerv members take pseudonyms at first, because they are frightened to trust the list—much the same way that a foster child, or a child adopted at an older age, might feel as she enters her new family. There is an adaptive element of distrust in both the newbie to the list and the foster child in her new family. The list will have to prove its trustworthiness to the new member.

When someone joins the list and introduces herself, she usually receives several responses of welcome that speak to what she wrote about herself. The new member often responds to this welcoming, writing to express gratitude for it, and sometimes, then, to give her real name or to ask a question that shows she has begun to trust her sisters on the list. Others initially "talk" only with the list owner, Fran Fasolka, IHM. Like a mother, she oversees and administers, and she comments when the list is quiet and exhorts us to conversation. Sometimes, Fran will raise a question for discussion when things get a little too quiet. She's a group animator—a role she chooses, by virtue of the fact that it is her list.

DEALING WITH DIFFERENCES AMONG FAMILY MEMBERS

Much like other families, where members have conscious and unconscious expectations for family life, LESTERS members, too, have expectations about how the list should work.

The Sounds of Silence

Silence over the Internet is different from silence in the person sitting in front of me, whom I can see and understand that she is crying, or laughing, or contemplating, or engaged in some other behavior that communicates something to me. Silence over the Internet gets interpreted. In the case of this group, it's usually interpreted negatively. The nun who posts something personal and who receives no response to it, typically will post something like: "Was it something I said?" or "Why is no one responding to what I just said?"

Three months ago, we had a heated conversation about an unstated "rule" that everyone should participate verbally. Those members who rarely do (so-called "lurkers"), felt the term "lurker" is pejorative and suggested an alternative name. The difference between introverted and extroverted personality types describes some of the difference between "lurkers" and more vocal members. There are some in this family who read a post, hit reply, and type away, much the same way an extroverted talker might participate in a conversation. There are others who read a post, want to think about it and then post something, much the same way an introverted conversationalist might participate in a discussion. "Lurkers" hoped to dispel the negative interpretations for their behavior, offering other explanations for why they don't post much: "I don't have time"; "I wish I had said [what was just posted] first"; "I don't know what more to say"; "I'm intimidated"; "By the time I get my thoughts together, the list has moved on to something else."

Perhaps when Web cams are perfected and integrated with software that maintains listservs, we will be able to see one another as we communicate. Presently, I see a semi-blank page on a computer screen when I sit to interact with the group, perhaps not unlike the "blank screen" offered by some psychotherapists, onto which the patient projects her worldview. One's psychology comes into play, as it does no matter what the form of communication.

Inclusion/Exclusion

Occasionally, listserv members meet one another—at an event for lesbian nuns, or when one of the members is visiting a city and lets the listserv know that, or when a member is taking vows and some listserv members attend her ceremony. These events make the connections among us more real, but they can also have a deleterious effect because when some listserv members share real-time experiences, it can lead to others feeling left out. For example, there is an annual gathering for lesbian nuns; when those who attend it return home, the conversation on the list is focused on the events at that gathering. Over time, I am less and less interested in attending the gathering. It seems similar to a family event that includes some members and not others—a gathering for those in one generation and not another, for example, or an event that takes place in a geographic location that allows some to attend and not others.

It becomes complex to raise the issue of being in the "in group" or the "out group," because that feels like a difficult discussion to have over the Internet. For me, that's where the group falls short. I will choose not to participate in a conversation if the listserv venue seems inappropriate for it. I imagine that there are others like me. Another aspect of the inclusion/exclusion question emerged for our family in a conversation about an upcoming meeting of lesbian nuns and women in leadership of religious orders. The meeting was to be about homophobia in religious orders, and how to move us forward in dealing with this homophobia and heterosexism. Some want to be "inclusive" about the upcoming meeting; they advocate that lesbian women who are contemplating entering a religious order have a place at the table, that those women have a vested interest much the same way someone marrying into a family would have an interest in the workings of the potential in-law family. Others feel that inviting women to the meeting who have not yet entered religious orders will make it difficult to focus on creating an agenda for change, which requires experience and capacity to take action from within. This controversy, in a listserv that is inherently a family of outsiders, raised difficult and painful questions about excluding those who are even further outside because they are not yet members of an order.

Stability and Change

I am part of a local group of lesbian nuns, most of whom are part of the LESTERS listserv. When this local group talks about the conversation on the listserv, we sometimes note that it's predictable that so-and-so said thus-and-such because that's her role; she always does that. It can go unnoticed, then, when someone is changing her thinking or manner of response, because she's been typecast as the "intellectual," or the "know-it-all" or the "wise woman." I remember being surprised when one listserv member was away from the list for quite some time, and when she came back to it, it didn't seem that she was the same person. Her responses were no longer predictable. What happens in a family when someone goes through this kind of change? It is often difficult for the family to recognize and absorb it. Family therapists talk about a family having its own homeostatic baseline, and when someone in the family makes a shift, the homeostasis of the family becomes disrupted. Until the change is integrated, the group is a little "off balance." So, too, in the listserv. When someone changes—either a personality shift, or change in status (e.g., leaving religious life)—it takes time for the group balance to be regained. For example, there's usually a lot of conversation around someone leaving religious life. Then, as the group processes it, the listserv goes back to its intermittent conversations.

A Famous Family Member

We have a "movie star" of sorts on the list. One of the women who was included in the ground-breaking 1985 book, *Lesbian Nuns Breaking Silence* (Curb and Manahan, 1985), joined the listserv about seven years ago. I recalled buying that book almost as soon as it reached bookstores. I read it under the cover of night, so to speak. I was impressed with the handful of nuns who identified as lesbian and were still in their religious orders. Now, on the LESTERS listserv, appeared the name of one who had stayed, and I knew her from the book. She was a lesbian nun foremother. I remember feeling a little star-struck when she first posted. I recognized her name from the book, and I immediately responded to her post. I felt a little embarrassed at my reaction. Just as with a blood family with a famous person in its ranks, so the listserv members have to deal with this woman's fame. Similarly, there are some who have played key roles in lesbian nun retreats or gatherings. An element of heroine worship can take place on the list, but on the whole there's not a lot of space for hotdogging.

When Debates Get Too Intense

Within the group, debates—sometime bordering on fights—occur. In the course of my nine years as a member of the listserv, I have seen many issues raised, some of which cut so close to the bone that conversation can shut down. I recall posting something myself, and the response I received from one member led me to close myself down to further dialogue in that venue, at that time, on that issue. At the time, I told myself that it did not really matter, that I knew that what I had posted was an accurate interpretation of something. The person who posted the quick response may not have even known that her post had had that effect on me. In this way we end up pigeon-holing others in the family. This does happen.

DEEP DISCUSSIONS/DEEP ISSUES

Can intimate issues be discussed by the whole group? Not so much anymore. I recall when I first joined the list, we had conversations that were deep and personal. People talked with the whole list about struggles with sexuality issues, with sexual desire, with sexual attraction, and other personal experiences. In recent years, intimate conversations happen more directly and privately; if someone writes an intimate posting, members will respond to the poster alone.

Protecting Our Privacy

This is due in part to worries about who might be on the listserv. There are some measures in place that help to ensure that a subscriber really is a Roman Catholic nun who identifies as lesbian. Still, this is a list on the Internet, and it's possible that the list's security could be breached. Given the institutional Catholic church's position on lesbianism, and given the times in which we live—where the institution recently linked pedophilia with homosexuality, and people fear that the witch hunt of homosexual priests will be extended to lesbian nuns—it's not only understandable, it's possibly even wise to tread carefully with postings that have personal content. It's much easier to have general conversations about the institution's position on homosexuality than to have conversation about sexual desire, for example, in this public forum.

Each Community Rejects Those with Multiple Identities

An issue that surfaces periodically is that in lesbian circles, it is sometimes difficult to come out as a nun. We have the experience of being ghettoized in the lesbian community. I suppose it's difficult for some to understand why a lesbian would choose to remain part of a sexist homophobic institution. For me, the answer is somewhat simple, and it's much like the answer I give when I am asked by my sisters in Nicaragua or Korea what it's like to be a U.S. citizen. With the latter question, I say that I was born into this country. There are lots of ways that I identify with the aspired-to values of the United States, and I am committed to saying "no" when I disagree with policies that the U.S. government lives out—in Iraq, for example. As with my civic citizenship, so, too, with my religion. I was born into Catholicism, and it's a religion and spirituality that is in my bones. I will not let that be taken from me, and I will stand up and say "no" when I am able. I think that most of the women in the LESTERS' family have a similar take on life as a Roman Catholic nun.

This is one issue on which we do share struggles openly on the list. When the Vatican makes an inane pronouncement on homosexuality, the family jumps on it. It's good to be part of a group with diverse coping strategies, because when one person is down, another is not, and can share an insight that helps others to reflect on the issue.

CONCLUSION

On the whole, it's a wonderful venture that Fran began in 1997. She occasionally posted the number of subscribers, and we could see it growing from 35 to 51 to 74 to.... Knowing how many were part of the family increased the sense of connection and lessened one's sense of isolation. The sense of family burgeoned, and people appreciated their cyberspace connection.

I believe that the listserv is a vital form of family. For those who post often, it is a place to listen and to be heard, to discover oneself in the act of "talking" to interested and understanding others. For the "lurkers," while they might not write often, following the discussions brings a sense of connection, new knowledge, and a stimulus to their own thinking. Those of us who have little connection to the lesbian community at large, or who have no peers in their own religious orders, can dispel our sense of isolation by belonging to this listserv. The rest of us can carry with us the sense that there is a place where it's understood that you are a nun and that you are lesbian.

REFERENCES

Curb, R. and N. Manahan. *Lesbian Nuns: Breaking the Silence.* Tallahassee, FL: Naiad Press, 1985.

Episcopate of the Roman Catholic Church. *Catechism of the Catholic Church.* New York: Image, Doubleday, 1994.

Slater, B. "Essential Issues in Working with Lesbian and Gay Male Youths [Electronic version]." *Professional Psychology: Research and Practice,* 19(2), 1988: 226–235.

Weston, K. *Families We Choose.* New York: Columbia University Press, 1991.

Choosing Family: Meaning and Membership in the Lesbian Family of Choice

Valory Mitchell

SUMMARY. This conceptual/theoretical article uses the psychodynamic Self Psychology model for the development of a vital, harmonious, and cohesive self to describe and understand the psychological importance of family for lesbian women. How can a healthy lesbian self be developed, nurtured, and maintained in an oppressive sexist and homophobic world? Family relationships are shown to fulfill the three fundamental psychological functions that sustain the lesbian self. In the absence of genetic and/or legal criteria, the basis on which someone is considered "family" is explored.

The image of the lesbian woman as ultimately lonely and alone is a big gun in the arsenal of heterosexism/homophobia. This image feeds on universal fears of isolation and abandonment (Bowlby, 1988). For lesbians (and other queer people) it is also fueled by the threat of being disowned

Valory Mitchell received her Ph.D. from the University of California, Berkeley. She has been on the faculty at the California School of Professional Psychology for 17 years. She has been a visiting research psychologist at the Institute for Personality and Social Research at UC Berkeley, and a scholar at the Rockway Institute, a research and policy institute focusing on LGBT issues. She has a psychotherapy practice in Berkeley.

or kept at a distance by one's "blood" relatives, once one has come out. In actuality however, lesbians have often managed enduring relationships with their kin despite the turmoil and tension of rejection and disapproval (Laird, 1996). In addition, as the pioneering psychiatrist Evelyn Hooker (1965) pointed out more than 25 years before Weston (1991) identified our "families of choice," lesbian and gay people often have unusually depthful and lasting friendships that ensure a lifetime of closeness and connection.

Family has great importance to many lesbians. And yet, we have not defined, explained, explored *why* this is so. Perhaps we have yielded to our own "don't ask, don't tell" policy. Fearing that if we truly put the centrality of our families on the "radar screen" they might be attacked or demeaned, we have kept to a safety in silence. But times have changed. Just as the groundswell builds toward legal same-sex marriage across the continents, so we increasingly expect that our families will be visible, legitimated, respected, and welcomed. Perhaps now it *is* safe to explore the ways that families are psychologically essential to many of us, not only as individual people, but also as lesbian women. Because we do not rely on the law or genetics to designate family membership, we may want to try to name the criteria we use to choose our families of choice. Who, in our interpersonal worlds, is (or is not) considered "family," and why?

I will suggest that, while family is essential for human psychological development generally, it has special psychological significance for lesbians (and other queer and marginalized people). This view is rooted in the understandings of Self Psychology, which incorporate the depth of the psychodynamic orientation (Kahn, 1985) while being thoroughly compatible with feminism and feminist therapy (Brems, 1991; Gardiner, 1987; Mitchell, 1989). Like the Stone Center theories of women's development (Hartling, Rosen, Walker and Jordan, 2004; Miller, 1991), Self Psychology posits that humans live in relationship like fish live in water; the relational milieu is our psychological environment all our lives. All young people develop a psychological self by gradually internalizing functions that are first performed by significant others, often others in the family. As adults, even though we are able to perform these functions for ourselves, we continue to be nourished by the infusion of these self-functions in our important adult (family) relationships.

All people develop a psychological self; but, in addition, I believe that each major facet of our identity is represented by a self—so that we have a self that is based in our ethnic/cultural identity, our class identity, our gender identity, and, certainly, our lesbian identity. What is necessary to nurture a lesbian identity, a lesbian self? How can a healthy lesbian self be developed and sustained in a sexist and homophobic world?

THE DEVELOPMENT OF THE SELF: A CONCEPTUAL OVERVIEW

What are the components of a self? Kohut (1984), the founder of Self Psychology, envisioned a self-structure where personal values/ideals and personal ambitions/goals are united by an arc of individual talents/skills through which the self manifests a program of action. Along with having values comes the capacity to modulate our feelings, to comfort and soothe ourselves in difficult times; along with goals comes self-esteem and the capacity to invest in oneself; along with the development of talents and skills that have meaning in our society comes the recognition of ourselves as members of the human community. To develop in these ways, the self must become able to take on three sustaining functions—mirroring, idealizing, and twinship—that are first (and always, to some extent) performed by important others.

Similarly, the lesbian self includes ideals and values about what it means (and should mean) to be a lesbian; hopes, ambitions, and goals for oneself as a lesbian; and talents and skills that we, as lesbians, make visible in our plans and actions. A lesbian self develops, and retains its coherence and vitality, in the same way as the more general psychological self—by internalizing self-functions that are initially performed by others in one's family or close interpersonal world. Just like the general psychological self, the lesbian self integrates these three functions as the basic parameters of a dynamic structure.

What are the mirroring, idealizing, and twinship functions, and how do they work to make the self?

Mirroring

The mirroring function begins as the capacity for delight—the "gleam in the mother's eye"—that expresses basic joy in her child's very existence. This function is called mirroring because the child can see delight reflected back at her. Over time, the child's significant others also express pride and delight in her accomplishments—her first words, first steps, the scribbled crayon drawings displayed on refrigerator doors. Later still, they are proud of "larger" achievements. Internalizing this function provides the self with a sense of fundamental self-worth, self-confidence, and self-esteem. Just as others' pride and delight begins with her existence and extends to her accomplishments, so, too, the individual's investment in the worth of the self evolves into a capacity to identify, and enduringly invest a sense of worth in, her personal ambitions, hopes and goals, and in achievements that may result from their pursuit.

Mirroring Needs of the Lesbian Self

In a society that is negative toward lesbian, gay, bisexual, and transgender (LGBT) people, there is often no one to delight in the "new-born," or newly discovered, lesbian self. Coming out may be a frightening process, rather than a celebration, precisely because we are uncertain whether our current "family" will bring their capacity for mirroring—for being welcoming, or even for accepting—to our coming out news. Without the positive recognition of mirroring, shame, or even attempts to abandon the lesbian self, can take hold, and there is no room, psychologically, for the growth of hopes about who one can become as a healthy, vital lesbian woman.

I have come to believe that we create our "families," in part, to address this (potential) deficiency in our interpersonal worlds. Our families must, include mirroring others who greet the coming out and the continuing visibility of our lesbian self with ongoing interest, curiosity about who we are, perhaps even a sense of delight and pride as our lives unfold over time. This atmosphere prompts us to explore and explain our inner life—what it means for us to be a lesbian, how that fits with other aspects of our identity, our interests, attitudes and views, our successes and even our failings.

This ongoing experience of mirroring is internalized as a realistic sense of worth as a lesbian woman. This now-internal atmosphere of acceptance allows us to avoid both the crippling anxiety, doubt and self-preoccupation that befall some, and the compensatory inflated self-regard that befalls others. The internalization of mirroring also allows us to invest in our own goals and ambitions as a lesbian, infusing our lives with an enduring vitality that comes from our own sense of accomplishment and pride.

Idealizing

Self Psychology speculates that, if a child can depend on her caregivers, she will also idealize the caregivers' "wonderfulness"—their ability to do so many things that the infant cannot, to hold a much larger perspective than the young child. As a result of these qualities, the idealized adults become a comforting and soothing presence for the child. As she grows up, adults and their former wondrousness become more ordinary human qualities, even within the reach of the growing young person. During this time, she internalizes the idealizing function and becomes increasingly able, herself, to take perspective, to comfort and soothe herself, and thus to regulate her affect. With the idealizing function comes the ability to idealize—to invest in ideals, acquire values, and to value one's own values. Self psychologists point out that we feel comforted by our values and ideals, and are soothed when our actions express and bring us close to them.

The Idealizing Needs of the Lesbian Self

Because most lesbians have heterosexual parents and siblings, we have to look beyond our "blood" kin to find lesbian models and mentors, people who hold the "big picture" on lesbian lives. When we find them—these people with their knowledge and experience—we feel a calmness and access to a sense of perspective, in the face of our troubles and confusion. We discover that we needn't be isolated when difficulties arise; it is such a comfort to know that you are not alone, that your "family" is there with the right questions, the good and informed advice. Through ongoing contact with admired others, we also discern our own values and ideals as lesbian women—what we can, and hopefully will, become—and are drawn to express these values in our daily lives.

Twinship

The last of the three central self-functions posited by Self Psychology, twinship is the recognition of being like others, a part of the human community. Caregivers provide this to their children in their expectations of common ground: we teach our children to talk like us, to eat like us, to do the things we do. As she stands beside us, brushing her teeth while we brush ours, mowing the lawn with two small and two big hands holding the mower, plunking out "Chopsticks" as we sit together on the piano bench, the growing self of the child develops her talents and acquires life skills in the context of relationship with others like herself.

The Twinship Needs of the Lesbian Self

I believe that the most profound psychological violation of LGBT people has occurred in the withholding of twinship. Being lesbian renders us different than (most of) our parents and siblings, as well as many of our friends, fellow students, colleagues, co-workers, parents of our children's friends, neighbors. Sometimes, in their eyes, being lesbian renders us not truly part of the human community. Even today, being an LGBT person is enough to keep us out of some religions, occupations, and groups; it defines us as criminals in many nations; it bars couples and parents from the security of thousands of civil rights. Where the twinship function emphasizes likeness and membership in a shared community, rejection by homophobic individuals and institutions enforces the opposite message.

In the face of this dehumanization, we seek and invite into our families people who will offer us the ongoing experience of human likeness, of twinship—the recognition that they too, are lesbians (or "queer") and so are like us in this important way, or if not, that our difference is not so different, really. In twinship with lesbian and heterosexual family members, with kin by "blood" or by choice, we "stand side by side," working together on shared tasks and toward shared goals. By so doing, the individual lesbian recognizes her talents and skills; we also recognize ourselves as contributing members of the lesbian community, as well as contributing members of other communities with which we identify, and beyond that to the human community.

The Self-Functions and the Structure of the Self

According to Self Psychology, these three functions—mirroring, idealizing, and twinship—form the central structure of the dynamic self. In a well-functioning self, we are pushed by our ambitions, and drawn toward our ideals. We integrate them by using our talents and skills in a program of action. Manifesting these, we experience the self as vital, harmonious and coherent (Kohut and Wolf, 1978).

While people, regardless of sexual orientation, have similar psychological needs, heterosexual people are privileged by a society that makes these functions readily available to them. Our society abounds with mirroring bestowed on heterosexual ambitions; heterosexual models and mentors are widely visible in the culture at large; and the experience of heterosexual twinship is offered in many popular stories, rituals, and songs. That these sociocultural experiences have (until very recently) been entirely outside the reach of LGBT people, is the embodiment of lived oppression and marginality. I believe that when we look historically, we recognize these needs have been met for lesbian women only by creating and maintaining a "family of choice"—a set of inter-connected, ongoing relationships chosen for their capacity to manifest the self functions. This is how we know that we are among family.

THE LIFELONG PROCESS OF COMING OUT

The process of coming out involves several steps (Cass, 1984), first toward exploration and discovery of an aspect of one's identity, and later toward decisions about whether (and when, how and to whom) to disclose that identity, and how one feels about doing so. The fear, or the belief, that a lesbian identity is—unacceptable, unhappy, immoral, difficult, painful, repugnant, inferior, humiliating, or illegitimate—renders the process of self-exploration and self-disclosure fraught with fear, anxiety, shame, and self-criticism.

To undertake the difficult, painful and frightening process of exploring the attitudes and beliefs about our lesbian identity that have led us to be stigmatized, marginalized, even despised (by ourselves or by others) is delicate work. Discovering and "unpacking" internalized homophobic beliefs requires a capacity to tolerate unwanted aspects of oneself. Exposing these attitudes may feel embarrassing, even shameful; fears of disapproving judgment, rejection or exclusion may loom. These issues often involve the struggle between our own gay-affirmative beliefs and the damage done by the homophobic/heterocentric attitudes and behavior of others, fears and threats stemming from those attitudes, or self-hatred and self-limitation induced by internalized homophobia/heterocentrism. The self-functions are required for this work; they create the interpersonal climate in which it can be done.

The Mirroring Function and Coming Out

To mirror the lesbian self is to be fundamentally gay-affirmative. Just as the gleam in the mother's eye reflects her pleasure at her child's very existence, the mirroring function, in relation to coming out, is about being pleased that we (*including* the lesbian aspect of us) exist. The mirroring family member approaches our coming out with a positive valence. This does not mean that they champion any particular outcome or endorse an identity about which we have serious questions or doubts; rather, they are motivated by a fundamental interest and pleasure in who we are. Mirroring brings a sense that being a lesbian can work. Just as mirroring evolves from delight to pride, gay-affirmative mirroring requires Gay Pride; the lesbian self is a welcome, valued, normal, acceptable aspect of who we are. With that pride, we establish and maintain an interpersonal (and internal) basis for self-esteem and self-worth in regard to our lesbian identity.

The Idealizing Function and Coming Out

The idealizing function comforts us in our process of coming out by putting our experience in a larger context. Brown (1994: 25), writing on feminist therapy, describes this process as cultural resistance:

> Resistance means refusal to merge with dominant cultural norms and to attend to one's own voice and integrity. . . . This influence of the dominant can be named, undermined, resisted and subverted. . . . [A]wareness and transformation mean teaching of resistance, learning the ways in which each of us is damaged by our witting or unwitting participation in dominant norms or by the ways in which such norms have been thrust upon us.

Some (perhaps many) members of our families of choice are people with whom we have a shared history. As a result, they are uniquely able to join us in reaching for the "big picture" perspective when we want to consider the impact of our past on our present. Because we are so familiar with each other over time, people who we consider family know the messages we have internalized, and can help us name and undermine those influences, counter oppressive messages, and neutralize society's condemnation. This ready access to a "big picture" perspective is a central component of the idealizing self-function.

The Twinship Function and Coming Out

For many, the initial experience that begins the coming out process is a recognition of "being different." From this early point, and throughout life, the twinship function buffers the sense of difference with a complementary sense of having things in common, of "speaking the same language." In twinship relationships, lesbian women and their kin recognize shared interests/qualities/values, and their shared humanity (Mitchell, 1996). At the deepest level, it is twinship that is conveyed in the concept of family; family members are related, they are travelers in the same convoy. Twinship is an experience of genuine, deep, and pervasive commonality—not a politically correct advocacy, or an exaggerated and repetitive recitation of "acceptance." This bond of shared understanding allows us to bear witness to one another's pain and fear, and to also witness and celebrate the vitality and exuberance of claiming oneself and finding an authentic voice. These are the hallmark experiences of the coming out process.

Homophobia/Heterocentrism after Initial Self-Disclosure

Coming out culminates, for many lesbian women, in positive self-regard and a comfortable, welcoming social network. For others, self-disclosure may be too dangerous; or important individuals, communities or institutions may fail to accept us or our relationships. Then, too, the struggle with internalized homophobia/heterocentrism may continue or recur throughout life, affecting self-esteem, couple satisfaction, or access to some of life's options, such as parenthood. In these situations of chronic or recurrent distress, a family member's ability to affirm our lesbian self (through the mirroring function), to soothe the shamed or rejected lesbian self (through the idealizing function), and to stand side-by-side as a companion in life (through the twinship function), may be essential to us for many years.

Becoming and Being Family: The Establishment of "Families of Choice"

Heterosexual couples and families are constrained and guided by many "givens"—expectations, marriage contracts, and visible models. In contrast, LGBT couples and families do not have these givens, and so have both the freedom and the need to define their commitment, boundaries, and expectations of one another (Green and Mitchell, 2002).

Weston (1991) found that lesbians and gay men are more psychologically open to broadening the concept of family to include non-biological relations (thus, "families of choice"). Like other forms of kinship, it can provide a powerful source of support. The notion of family involves a fundamental joining together and mutual commitment (often lasting a lifetime), an investment in the doings of family members, a pleasure in each other's company, a willingness to provide comfort at times of trouble, and an honest perspective. In short, family is of a set of relationships that can be counted on to perform the self-functions. I believe that we consider particular people to be part of our families when we know we can rely on them to perform these self-functions, and when we, perform these functions for them in return.

The Self-Functions and Family Building

We need to feel safe to examine our assumptions about friendship and family roles, if we are to do our family building outside societal norms. If lesbians are to feel confident in expanding non-kin relationships in these ways, we will need the mirroring function to put energy in the ambition to build our "family of choice," and the capacity to be proud of it and maintain it. To be specific, we need to believe that our couple relationships can be fulfilling and can last, that our children can grow into healthy, effective adults, that our extended kinship network can reliably reach us with the relationship experiences that address our psychological needs. We will also need access to the calming "big picture" perspective of the idealizing function as we walk the many steps in the direction of our valued goal of family building, and as we step back from our inner circle in order to contact community resources that can move us toward a more collective experience.

LGBT Families Challenge Homophobic Stereotypes

The anthropologist Kath Weston (1991: 203), writing 16 years ago, realized the critical importance of visible LGBT families in countering the depersonalizing homophobia and stereotypy that oppress us. From a self-psychological perspective, we would say that she was writing about the crucial role of twinship, not only for those within lesbian families, but reaching beyond our families to dismantle bigotry and dehumanization in the larger society. She wrote:

> To view gay identity as a species difference is to regard gay people as beings so separate, so different in kind, that many heterosexuals believe they do not know and have never met a lesbian or gay man. To make such an assertion with certitude implies a belief that the difference gay identity makes is so significant it should be immediately detectable. Stereotyping that reduces gay men and lesbians to sexual beings only reinforces this perception of utter otherness. . . . (A) discourse on gay families that encompasses non-erotic as well as erotic ties invites heterosexuals to abandon the standpoint of the voyeur in favor of searching for areas of shared experience that join the straight self to the lesbian or gay other.

THE SPEED OF CHANGE AND THE "GAY GENERATION GAP"

So much has changed, and so rapidly. The larger culture is beginning to offer some self-functions that nurture the lesbian self. For example, mainstream music and film stars are openly gay and bisexual; same-sex love stories are box office hits. Watching music videos and reading *People* magazine, youth who are coming out today are unlikely to believe, as was common in past cohorts, that they do not know of another LGBT person. Along with visibility has come the expectation of validity; lesbian women increasingly expect to enjoy access to everything from high school proms to nursing homes. Bisexual, intersex, and transgender people, long marginalized even within the gay and lesbian communities, are speaking out for visibility, validation, and access as well. With their inclusion has come a new awakening of interest and involvement in viewing sexuality and gender expression on continua (rather than as dichotomous), and a new sexual minority, the genderqueer, has emerged in some LGBT communities.

While for many lesbians the world feels much the same as it did half a century ago, for many others it is a new world. The profundity and pervasiveness of these changes have led to a "gay generation gap." The Institute for Gay and Lesbian Strategic Studies, in a report (2005, paragraph 3) on this phenomenon, concludes that "(LGBT) people from different age cohorts have very different beliefs and experiences that reflect the rapid change over time in the treatment of LGBT people in families, in the workplace, in schools, and in communities," and so they "must overcome communication challenges when working together across generations." For example, some (but not all) older lesbians may be less likely to view gender on a continuum (as many intersex and transgender people now do), or to feel that sexual orientation can be healthy as well as fluid (as many bisexual people now do). Younger lesbians may value physical over psychological expressions of gender, or distance themselves from an articulated feminism.

In our families, however, we have often found kinship that spans the generations, the different worldviews (and different worlds) that have been the context for each age cohort. We can situate ourselves by comparing and contrasting ourselves with kin of other generations. Members of younger generations can get a sense of living history from those who precede us, and members of older generations can get a sense of what we have accomplished from those coming after, who take for granted the gains we have struggled for. Many of us hold a cultural vision that telescopes back and forth between the closeted and fearful 1950s and a place in the sun in 2010.

IN CONCLUSION

Feminist researchers and therapists (Hare-Mustin, 1994; Rampage, 2002) and postmodern theorists and researchers (Freedman and Combs,

1996; Gergen, 1985) have urged us to recognize that we are all products of our intersecting demographics—age, class, sex, ethnicity/culture, race, nationality, geographical region, bodily ability, sexual orientation, and location in historical time—so that we can take these sweeping and often unconscious socialization influences into account and be more conscious about who we are.

By putting language to the needs of the lesbian self, and recognizing the role that important relationships play in addressing those needs, we can guide our choices as we choose family. With this language, as we build and express these family connections, we can recognize more readily the ways that we want to look to family for psychological sustenance. We can understand the basis for membership in a chosen family, and recognize our kin-of-choice. We can describe "family" and see its role in countering prejudice and marginalization. The family also makes it more possible for us to situate ourselves in the array of identity dimensions that make us who we are. Family relationships are the core of this endeavor, because it is through the experience of relationship that both the lesbian family of choice and the lesbian self are formed, nurtured and sustained.

REFERENCES

Bowlby, J. *A Secure Base*. London: Routledge, 1988.

Brems, C. "Self Psychology and Feminism: An Integration and Expansion." *The American Journal of Psychoanalysis*,] 51, 1991: 145–160.

Brown, L. *Subversive Dialogues: Theory in Feminist Therapy*. New York: Basic Books, 1994.

Cass, V. "Homosexual Identity Formation: Testing a Theoretical Model." *Journal of Sex Research*, 20, 1984: 143–167.

Freedman, J. and G. Combs. *Narrative Therapy: The Social Construction of Preferred Realities*. New York: Norton, 1996.

Gardiner, J. K. "Self Psychology as Feminist Theory." *Signs: Journal of Women in Culture and Society,* 12, 1987: 761–780.

Gergen, K. "The Social Constructionist Movement in Modern Psychology." *American Psychologist*, 40, 1985: 266–275.

Green, R.-J. and V. Mitchell. "Gay and Lesbian Couples in Therapy: Homophobia, Relational Ambiguity, and Social Support." In A. S. Gurman and N. S. Jacobson, eds., *Clinical Handbook of Couple Therapy, 3rd edition*. New York: The Guilford Press, 2002: 548–588.

Hare-Mustin, R. "Discourses in the Mirrored Room: A Postmodern Analysis of Therapy." *Family Process*, 33, 1994: 19–35.

Hartling, L. M., A. Rosen, M. Walker, and J. Jordan. "Shame and Humiliation." In J. V. Jordan, M. Walker, and L. M. Hartling, eds., *The Complexity of Connection: Writings from the Stone Center's Jean Baker Miller Training Institute.* New York: The Guilford Press, 2004: 179–198.

Hooker, E. "Male Homosexuals and Their Worlds." In J. Marmor, ed., *Sexual Inversion: The Multiple Roots of Homosexuality.* New York: Basic Books, 1965: 83–107.

Institute for Gay and Lesbian Strategic Studies. "New Report Outlines Ways the LGBT Community Can Overcome the 'Gay Generation Gap.'" 2005. Retrieved December 22, 2005 from http://www.div44@listserve.APA.org

Kahn, E. "Heinz Kohut and Carl Rogers: A Timely Comparison." *American Psychologist,* 40, 1985: 893–904.

Kohut, H. *How Does Analysis Cure?* Chicago: University of Chicago Press, 1984.

Kohut, H. and E. Wolf. "The Disorders of the Self and Their Treatment — An Outline." *International Journal of Psychoanalysis,* 59, 1978: 413–425.

Laird, J. (1996). "Invisible Ties: Lesbians and Their Families of Origin." In J. Laird and R.-J. Green, eds., *Lesbians and Gays in Couples and Families.* San Francisco: Jossey-Bass, 1996: 89–122.

Miller, J. B. "What Do We Mean by Relationships?" In J. Jordan, ed. *Women's Growth in Connection.* New York: Guilford Press, 1991: 120–129.

Mitchell, V. "Using Kohut's Self Psychology in Work with Lesbian Couples." *Women and Therapy,* 8, 1989: 157–166.

Mitchell, V. "Two Moms: The Contribution of the Planned Lesbian Family to the Deconstruction of Gendered Parenting." In J. Laird and R.-J. Green, eds., *Lesbianss and Gays in Couples and Families.* San Francisco: Jossey-Bass, 1996: 343–357.

Rampage, C. "Working with Gender in Couple Therapy." In A. S. Gurman and N. S. Jacobson, eds., *Clinical Handbook of Couple Therapy, 3rd edition.* New York: The Guilford Press, 2002: 533–545.

Weston, K. *Families We Choose: Lesbians, Gays, Kinship.* New York: Columbia University, 1991.

INDEX